# COLLEGE PLANNING

*using*

## Dual Enrollment

# College Planning Using Dual Enrollment

*Optimizing High School For College Admission & Financial Aid*

By

Kathe Lee

LEEWAY USA

DALLAS, TEXAS

# College Planning Using Dual Enrollment

Optimizing High School for College Admission

& Financial Aid



www.kathelee.com

Published by LeeWay USA

Dallas, Texas



*I have tried to recreate events, locales, and conversations from my memories of them. In order to maintain their anonymity in some instances I have changed the names of individuals and places. I may also have changed some identifying characteristics and details such as physical properties, occupations, and places of residence.*

Cover Design & Photo by: TeamKathe

Author's Photo by Nicholas Glover
NickGloverPhotography.com
Makeup by Rosie Moreno

ISBN: 978-0-9975734-5-9

**To John**

Who gave me the freedom to become Me.

**To Jake Lee**

For twenty-eight years you have made me happy just to wake up in the morning. Thank you for teaching me the most important lesson I may ever learn…being perfect is so much less important than being happy!

**To Jordan Lee**

The best daughter any woman could possibly hope to have. Your insight, forthrightness, and personal strength inspire me constantly to do better. You single-handedly make me hopeful for the future of our world. No Pressure ☺

# TABLE of CONTENTS

## SECTION THREE - What To Take & Why



## SECTION FOUR - Common Pitfalls & Fixes



## SECTION FIVE - Getting In & Getting Money

# ACKNOWLEDGMENTS

I am eternally grateful to my sister-friend, Rebecca Edge, who motivated, cajoled, prodded, advised, and even now continues to love me despite my all too human failings. Her focused and vigilant notations forced me to grow as a writer. This book would not exist without her expert feedback and editing. She read every word and then read them again, and again, and yet again. Her patience and faithful friendship are true blessings in my life that I value and give thanks for daily.

This book has been the culmination of many years of working with students one-on-one and gathering feedback from a myriad of experts and specialists in the fields of education, psychology, and neuroscience. To my many clients, assistants, and fellow researchers, thank you for your insights and wisdom. It is only through my experiences with you that I have been able to develop as a strategist.

Specifically, a very hearty thank you to Bonnie Hueston of Richland College. You rock! Your working friendship has been a treasure. To Diane Mannion of North Central Texas College, I wish all college personnel cared as much as you do. To Dr. Michelle MacAlpine, PhD (Braintraining.com), your brilliance is only outweighed by your generosity. Gratitudes to Michelle Graefen, Chloe' Simmons, Celia Kinville, Stephanie Briscoe, David & Leanne Beardsley, Sheila & Ashley Waters, and Kim

Brown for reading and discussing early drafts and providing me with your careful thoughts on topics wide and far.

My very sincere appreciation to my newest assistant, Carla Rowe, who was a last minute life saver with a real knack for the stringent rules of grammar and a very sharp eye.

And finally, a tremendous thanks to my many students and their families. A special thank you to Eliot Paek, Gabrielle Campbell, and Luke Dahlstrom. Your marvelous artistic submissions, intended for the cover of this book, were uniquely inspired.

Each of my students has taught me something that I have been able to use again and again, usually to the benefit of yet another student. I can't wait to see where each one of you ends up in life. You are the future. Make it count.

*"Do not train a child to learn*

*by force or harshness; but direct them to it*

*by what amuses their minds,*

*so that you may be better able to*

*discover with accuracy the*

*peculiar bent of the genius of each."*

~Plato

# GETTING EDUCATED

## An Introduction

*Kids go to school to get an education. And, getting an education is important. So much so that the U.S. allocates more than 600 billion dollars per year and millions of man hours per day to the task of educating our children. Why make such a massive investment? What's the pay off?*

*In elementary school, the goals are pretty clear. We want our children to learn to read fluently. We want them to be able to write well enough to communicate effectively, preferably using proper grammar and a smidgen of style. We would like for them to acquire a basic understanding of key scientific principals, as well as appreciate the history of their species. And of course, we want our kids to achieve a modicum of mathematical competency. Nothing difficult, just mastery of the number tables, basic geometry, and fluent manipulation of numbers by the end of sixth grade.*

*Seems reasonable enough and arguably worth $600,000,000,000 every twelve months or roughly $12,000 per child per year.*

*In middle school, we understandably expect a good deal more. We anticipate seeing notable advancements in all the core areas that were initiated in elementary, plus we hope to see each student demonstrate an aptitude towards some creative endeavor or athletic ability. Music, sports, art, dance are all seen as worthy goals. By this point, we also have firm expectations that students will have developed proper social interactions and appropriate personal behaviors. Again, the bar is not an unrealistic one.*

*As they enter the homestretch of high school, the educational focus quickly shifts away from foundational knowledge and social skills to take aim at college readiness. This goal is automatically doled out to every student regardless of how well they have managed to meet expectations up to this point.*

*The ultimate hope is that every one of the approximately four million children who start first grade every year will progressively learn a set of skills that will allow him or her to go on to college, graduate, enter the workforce, and become a financially stable and productive adult. A contributing member of society. This is the purpose of going to school today. But it didn't start out that way.*

*An organized effort to educate the masses has been in place for nearly 200 years. From the beginning, education had obvious and powerful implications for the future of American society. Even as early as 1647, the General Court of the Massachusetts Bay Colony ruled that all towns of a certain size must provide a school to teach the only two subjects that were deemed important at the time, Bible and Latin. Of course, immigrants to the New World did not always hang around these east coast towns of a certain size.*

*As colonists expanded ever outward in their search for personal freedom, education was often lacking and never standardized. But as the numbers swelled and local governments grew, an effort to control what, when, and how children were taught, took on increasing urgency.*

*By the early 1800s, in both big cities and small towns, elementary schools, akin to what we have today, were teaching children to read and write in order to foster communication. This was thought to be a basic necessity as people from diverse factions came together to form unified societies. If the general population could not read or write, then how would the government be able to disseminate information? By 1852, schooling was compulsory and by 1870 it was free, at least through the elementary years.*

*In response to massive growth in commerce and an intense demand for a somewhat educated work force, education expanded beyond just elementary school for those students who had the time and aptitude for advanced learning or vocational training. Still, middle school was as far as structured learning went for most kids, despite colonial colleges and Harvard University, which had existed since the mid 1860s. Only a few wealthy families were privileged enough to have access to an advanced education, but things were quickly changing.*

*By the start of the twentieth century, there was a collective push towards higher education for the growing number of children who seemed capable of, and interested in, expanding their intellectual boundaries. In only a few decades, large numbers of pupils were attending high schools and earning a diploma. And why not, the alternative at that time was eighteen hour days on the family farm or in a sooty factory.*

*As families moved away from farms and into cities, college attendance continued to increase. Employers needed some way of vetting potential candidates and a college degree was the perfect device. But college was expensive, in terms of both time and money. The average teenager was still more likely to end up in a warehouse, workroom, mill, or mine than in a college classroom. Then came foreign wars and a change in priorities. Following our heady success fending off aggressors in the Second World War, the G.I. Bill gave thousands of veterans money for college.*

*This shift in priorities at the national level was a game changer. For the first time in history, the average student was expected to complete eight years of primary education and four more years of higher level learning. For the quickly expanding middle class, high school graduation was an automatic conduit to university enrollment where a rapt pupil could earn a professional degree in two to four years and enter the workforce with assurances of life long financial stability. Still, less than eight percent of the populace achieved a college degree. While high schools seemed to do an excellent job of preparing students for college success, and tuition was increasingly affordable, many students chose a less academic path to their intended career. On the job training was still highly valued by employers and society.*

*Of course, not every student needed a college degree. For decades, internships, apprenticeships, and one-on-one mentoring were hugely successful in producing the large numbers of mechanics, plumbers, electricians, and repair techs that our hypersonic growth demanded. Few people graduated from college because few people really needed a college degree. As long as they worked hard and did it well, they were considered successful and received some degree of financial reward. Careers in hardware sales, HVAC, sewing, welding, horticulture, engine repair, and food services were respected by a society that desperately needed them. My! How things have changed.*

*Today, when a young man wants to be a chef, we don't float him a few thousand dollars in seed money to live off of while he learns his trade under the tutelage of a master. We send him off to a university for a four year business degree with the advice that he will need to know how to run a business if he is going to be a chef. We apparently prefer he take on tens of thousands of dollars in debt to go to college instead of going to work. And odds are he will not graduate. According to ACT Inc's National Report, 60% of high school graduates fall short of college readiness. This syncs up with statistics from the U.S. Department of Education that states only 31.4% of high school freshman are still in college after their sophomore year.* [1]

*That is not even the worst news. Turns out that even students who manage to graduate are sometimes unable to parlay their hard won and increasingly expensive degrees into a job or career. The oft heard, "What on earth are you going to do with a degree in Psychology?" quickly comes to mind in my own case. It's a fact, college is no longer a sure path to success! How did we get to this point? To answer this question we would have to backtrack.*

*After the depression, the low college graduation rate was not a problem. Anyone who could fix a toilet, weld a steel beam, or balance a ledger was able to find steady lifetime employment. Vocational schools were the rage and continued to dominate until the late '60's when cultural shifts sponsored the idea that anybody could do anything if just given the chance. Nearly overnight, a college degree became the de facto proof that you were someone.*

*Employers certainly prefer applicants who demonstrate the brain power and discipline to complete a college degree. More and more, corporate hiring is contingent upon college success, even to the point that potential employers are requiring submission of a college transcript as part of the hiring process. And of course, parents are nearly universally in favor of college attendance and graduation. Even students have come to think of college admissions as a right of passage with nearly 80% of all high school seniors heading off to a college or university after graduating.* [1]

*But college is not for every student! And it is certainly not the only path to a viable career or financial stability as proven by such diverse success stories as Steve Jobs, Ted Turner, Bill Gates, Walt Disney, and perennial favorite, Oprah. Of course, these are only the extreme cases. There are many everyday successes as well.*

*That being said, logic still seems to dictate that if a student can go to college and graduate, without undue financial or emotional hardship, then they should. Whether that degree is a PhD from Harvard, a surgical technologist certification from Dallas County Junior College, or an electrician's license from the Nascar Technical Institute, there appears to be tangible value in continuing to educate beyond high school.*

*We know this to be true, yet we are faced each day with an alternate reality. A reality that is very hard to face until someone we know becomes part of the statistic. In a nutshell, the* ***average*** *high school graduate does not make it through college. The* ***average*** *college graduate does not end up a financially stable and productive adult. Even worse, the* ***average*** *college student ends up with disturbing amounts of debt regardless of whether or not he manages to actually graduate and get a job. Obviously, there is a major conflict between the belief that a college education has merit and the reality that the system is not working. The big question is, "Why?" This is, literally, a six hundred billion dollar question. But good luck finding two "experts" who agree on the answer.*

*Experts do agree on a few things. They all recognize that the problem starts early. Those K-6th graders that we have such high hopes for are not learning to read, write, and numerically cogitate before leaving primary school. And things don't suddenly get better in middle school. By the end of 10th grade, the average student reads at or below an eighth grade level.*[2] *Grammar, spelling, and formal writing skills are often in need of remediation. And math mastery tests show that only 26% are at grade level.*[2]

*The numbers are irrefutable. By the time high school graduation rolls around, 13% are in special education classes.*[3] *Twenty-four percent are on medication for learning related issues.*[4] *Over ten percent are suicidal.*[5] *Seventeen percent are regularly using drugs or alcohol.*[6] *And nearly 25% have dropped out or are failing all together.*[7] *Of the 75% who manage to graduate high school, only one in four is demonstrably ready for college success.*[8] *These facts are hardly a secret.*

*The harsh reality is that a dozen plus years of modern schooling are not producing provable learning. The massive amounts of work that our children are asked to produce day in and day out, are not resulting in a functional education. Kids are doing a lot of schooling but not very much learning. If this fact is frustrating to you, the concerned adult, imagine how demoralizing it is to the student who is actually doing all the work! They deserve better. They deserve success.*

*Success is not something that just happens. It is the result of planning, hard work, and commitment. Our kids are working hard but they do not have a good plan. This causes their commitment to waiver. By the time they start college, many are at an emotional and academic deficit which too often leads to failure. This should not be happening, especially when we know how to avoid it.*

*In order to help students make the most of the amazing educational opportunities in this country, it is critical that we have a clear dialogue about appropriate educational goals and proven ways to achieve those goals. This book is a step down that path.*

*Appropriate educational goals in the 21st century are not that different than in the past. We still want to see our happy, healthy children grow into emotionally well balanced, productive, and financially stable adults. We still recognize that a foundational education in the core subjects of reading comprehension, paragraph writing, critical thinking, and math fluency is necessary for that to happen. With apprenticeship having gone the way of the dinosaur to a great degree, college or vocational training, along with internships, is still the best way to prepare for a career. But one thing has changed. Societal expectation. We no longer value young men and women just because they work hard and learn a trade. We value a college degree, even when it cost too much and gives little in return. We need to value real success.*

*To help our students succeed, we need to realign schooling with learning. Ideally, this should occur from the ground up. But that will take a consensus of educators and politicians, spurred by united parental pressure. This is not likely to happen in the immediate future, but fortunately that is not my challenge. My aim is to offer solutions that the parent, teacher, counselor, or student can use right now to increase learning, while still meeting the legal and societal rules of schooling. My objective is successful educational outcomes. That means increased graduation rates, decreased college debt, and better long term job security. Personal happiness would be a plus :)*

*This book is a step-by-step guide to what anyone can do right now to optimize high school for college and career success. This book is about custom-schooling using an underutilized but rapidly growing resource called dual enrollment.*

*Using dual credit combined with a customized high school plan, I am seeing struggling students get motivated, finish high school, get into top colleges, and receive maximum non-loan financial aid, thus avoiding student debt, which is at an all time high.*[9]

*Even better, they are graduating! And best of all, they have ownership of their future and feel empowered to take on life. I call that successful schooling. You could also call it successful parenting since the goal of any good parent is to turn out a happy, independent, and financially stable adult.*

*There are many ways to do school: public, private, charter, co-op, online, collegiate, or at home. Where you do school is not really the issue. It is how you do school that matters. This book will guide you through the steps of optimizing any high school program for college admissions and financial aid using a set of principles called LeeWay©. The goals of education have not changed, but how we get to those goals needs to change if we are to produce the next generation of American scholars. That change is literally at hand.*

*Happy Learning,*

**Kathe Lee**

*Researcher*
*Strategist*
*Mom*

# A NEW WAY TO SCHOOL

## The LeeWay Philosophy

# 1☞

# CUSTOM SCHOOLING

## *Kathe Lee Style*

My husband and I homeschooled our own children from birth through the first two years of college. Our methods were not exactly typical.

Many homeschoolers simply replicate the public school model at home. This makes sense if your goal is to avoid exposing your children to certain teachings or influences you prefer to avoid. This was not our goal. We simply knew from my research that the average graduate from a public or private school was bored, stressed out, and ill prepared for college, career, or even a successful life. We wanted something better for our son and daughter, and we both agreed that I was in a unique position to provide it. Were we right? Well, the proof, as people say in the part of the country where I come from, is definitely in the pudding.

When our oldest was born, I began researching how the brain learned, the role of education on mental health and adult behaviors, and the rights of parents to facilitate their own children's education. In short order, my husband and I decided that we wanted to create a customized educational experience for both of our children using the extremely family friendly homeschooling laws in our home state of Texas. In a very impromptu manner, that is exactly what we did.

For elementary school, we started with phonics, handwriting, spelling, grammar, and exploration through artistic and scientific concepts. Telling time, measuring the ingredients in pancake batter, and counting bugs in the backyard, made up the bulk of our mathematics curriculum. English was lots of read-a-louds on the sofa, while science was one big messy experiment, usually over the stove. Completely haphazard, but very Montessori in retrospect. As they grew, it became obvious that each of our children had different interests and that they learned different subjects in different ways and at different rates, and even to differing degrees. So, as their teacher, I personalized the material and schedule to fit each of their needs and interests.

Using a Charlotte Mason "follow the child" approach, we raised butterflies from larvae, mucked out local horse stalls, started a raised-bed garden in the backyard, baked bread and churned butter, went to the library incessantly, the arboretum weekly, and occasionally sat down at the table to work with some math manipulatives or to practice handwriting techniques on lined paper. We narrated far-fetched stories over dinner that later became real books with handmade bindings and custom art work, which was often little more than crayon derived stick-people. Every tiny accomplishment seemed a gigantic feather in their respective caps.

While driving from horseback lessons to soccer practice we listened to books on tape, called out spelling words, and memorized math and phonic flashcards. My kids learned time by osmosis, science from Bill Nye, politics from adult conversations, and social skills through constant interactions with others. On top of volunteering, we went outside the home for sports, robotics, knitting, sewing, science fair, immersive foreign language, computer repair, cooking, acting, singing, dancing, drawing -- you name it. If one of the kids showed an interest in something, we did it. We did not buy or use a formal curriculum or workbook. We were not concerned with accreditation. We did not care about completing an official program. We were just looking for exposure to meaningful experiences -- true learning! Everything we did was treated as something to do just for fun and was often done with a neighborhood elder, nearby homeschool family, or private tutor.

We never completed a full year of any traditional school subject. It was not necessary. They learned history through art, community service through clubs and volunteerism, math through shopping, cooking, and workshop construction, and grammar through reading great literature as a family. We watched minimal TV, avoided video games, and rarely took in a movie until they were much older. Yet, they were rarely resistant, bored, overwhelmed, argumentative, or ill behaved. They were engaged, motivated, and actively involved in their own learning. Frankly, the process was more stressful to me than to them; but in the end, the constant spark I was able to witness in my children was the motivation that I needed to continue.

When our son reached high school age, we had both kids take their first ever test, the College Board's Accuplacer exam. This was a way for me to compare them to their peers and start to understand what would be needed in order to get them ready for college. Given our approach to schooling, I expected gaps. Somewhat surprisingly, their scores outpaced their peers by several grade levels. Even math, a clear weak area for us, was above average. I do not know if this was something I should credit to my teaching methodology or a frightening indictment of the public system that set such a low bar to begin with. I do know that my kids' excellent critical thinking skills and mastery of core concepts allowed them to shine even without formal learning in certain subjects.

*It never dawned on me that our kids, who had never completed a "real" school class in their life, would score better than the vast majority of their peers in all areas of a standardized test.*

*But they did!*

Because of their amazing scores, Gay Ricks, a counselor at the college testing center suggested a free "pre-college" program called dual credit. Our oldest was turning fifteen and realizing the value of free, transferable college credits, we jumped right in.

The first hurdle was a transcript. Given the eclectic curriculum we had used, I was not even sure what grades my kids were in much less what subjects they had "officially" completed. Then I learned that their excellent test scores could place them out of tenth grade, so I simply made a traditional transcript that listed what the state required, since we had easily done it all and then some, and our test scores proved it. I turned the transcript in to the local dual enrollment (DE) officer and my son started his first class. A few months later, he had an 'A' in his first college course, something he continued to do semester after semester.

Things were not always hunky dory. Just like at most public schools, the atmosphere left a lot to be desired. Cursing was commonplace among students and staff. There were professors who bored students to the point of distraction, were disorganized, or even ill tempered. Picking the right teachers was a learning process but an obvious priority. I had to become skilled at how to drop a class when things went south, which occasionally happened. And there was always the issue of running my guys back and forth to classes at odd hours of the day. It was not always easy, but it all became surprisingly manageable as time passed. By semester three, I was an old hat.

The most challenging issue we ran into was that for the first time our son's classes were not tailor-made to fit his needs and interests. This was due to the fact that dual credit students, to a certain degree, were and are required to follow a prescribed order and choice of classes that the experts consider to be best. Just like public schools, dual credit programs follow the standard sequence of courses regardless of what a student is interested in or ready to learn. This may sound nitpicky, but brain-based learning would argue otherwise.

*Students learn best when they are engaged and motivated by the topic or long term goals of a class or subject.*

In dual enrollment, my son was suddenly faced with just taking what ever class was allowed at that moment. This was in direct opposition to my preferred model of custom homeschooling, which had produced such successful outcomes up to that point.

Initially, like most parents, I just followed the rules as I understood them and let the college pick my son's classes. But things changed when my daughter started dual credit. Although she had passed the same placement test as my son, and with equally flying colors, I felt that at 13 years of age, she was a bit young to be enrolled in college classes. Instead she and I sat in on the DE classes her brother was enrolled in. This was not brilliance on my part, but rather an attempt to minimize driving back and forth to my son's classes. The payoff was unexpected so worthy of an explanation.

Sitting in on her brother's college classes kept my daughter interested in school and learning without the burden of homework, tests, or pressure to perform. It was also a boon for me since I did not have to teach! Ironically, she went ahead and started college early the next year and proved that she was one of those people who thrives on homework, tests, and pressure to perform. After dual enrollment she went on to graduate from a "top 100" university as the number one student in her program. With her natural childhood love of learning still intact, she was a tour de force as a student and continues to be so now as an employee. My son, though not in love with college, was a top student throughout dual enrollment. Even today he loves to learn and will work incredibly hard to build a car engine from the ground up or design a new battery pack for his phone. This is the power of customized learning.

Fortunately, both of my kids ended up being so adaptable and motivated that they were able to take almost any dual credit class, with any teacher, and make an 'A'. But many of my public and private school friends were not so fortunate. Their children initially appeared to be thriving in school but when test time rolled around, their scores were well below par. In some cases it happened only in certain subjects. No one stopped to ask why smart kids, and otherwise good students, were struggling with tests or why they struggled only in certain classes. That was when I realized that even at the highest levels of schooling, it was important to work towards a student's strengths, especially when that student was dealing with learning differences or lack of mastery from early academic gaps.

By this point, I had become an educational specialist. I knew what my friends' children needed in order to succeed, but the default state degree plan for high schoolers (list of required classes) stood in my way. So I began to research and get informed about the options for bypassing this problematic document. It was at this time that I discovered a little known nugget of information that would change everything.

It turns out that enlightened parents have choices. In states with flexible alternative school laws, like Texas, a parent can control not only what their students take at home, but also what they take in dual enrollment (DE) simply by filing their own degree plan. Once I became aware of this fact, I created my own tailor-made degree plan and filed it with my children's dual credit officer. I politely requested that it be used in lieu of the state's default degree plan. It worked. My kids were free to take classes in any order that worked for them, and they were not limited to courses on the standard degree plan. My friends, in the know, quickly followed suit as did many of my early clients. As you might imagine, this did not go over well at the local DE office, at least not initially. Fortunately, all of the kids I counseled made remarkable progress. From perfect 4.0 GPAs to accelerated schedules, every single student was notable.

In time, the local college administrators came to see that indeed students did better when they were guided to take certain classes at a certain time in a certain order and with certain teachers. In the case of my clients, they did markedly better even in the face of learning differences or socioeconomic struggles.

After six years and more than three hundred students of every caliber, not a single one had dropped out of high school. They each had graduated with honors college credits, thanks to dual enrollment and my proprietary degree plan. Most of them had gone on to college and easily gained admittance plus had earned significant merit based aid. My students were avoiding debt and they were graduating. That was a big deal!

My degree plan became so popular that a college admissions officer nicknamed it the LeeWay Distinguished Degree Plan©. "LeeWay" was an obvious play on both my name and the fact that my strategy allowed students the leeway or freedom to do things in a way that worked for them. One by one, every LeeWay student graduated from high school using a custom dual enrollment strategy and went on to top universities with unparalleled merit aid. In most cases, they finished their college degrees without debt and with honors on their record!

The success of the LeeWay Distinguished Degree Plan, or LeeWay DDP for short, was such that my office began to get calls from local school districts and charter schools asking us to duplicate our success with their own students. We were happy to oblige. Through meetings with board members, teachers, and counselors, we were able to share what we had learned with a number of private schools in the area, a hand-full of charter organizations, and numerous homeschool co-ops. We showed them how to build high school to college strategies that would allow students to meet the maximum state requirements for graduation without undue stress or damage to the GPA that is inherent in a typical high school curriculum, especially at more exclusive private and university-model schools.

These groups often tailored my strategy to fit their bylaws or circumstances but they never changed the LeeWay Distinguished Degree Plan. When they were unclear how to proceed, my answer was always simple. When allowed, throw away the default state degree plan, let go of your university model goals that have been proven not to work, and customize to meet each individual student's needs to the greatest extent possible.

*Customizing a student's degree plan*
*is the secret to getting into a*
*great college and graduating*
*with minimum debt.*
*It is also the secret to producing engaged,*
*well-adjusted, and motivated students.*

Every day, families across the country either call or email my office with infinite variations of one emphatic request: "*Please help my son/daughter achieve his/her academic goals.*" This is a complex request with a very simple solution. Either on your own or with specialized help, your student needs customization using dual enrollment. When time allows, this is a service I provide one-on-one.

When possible, I meet personally with the mother, father, and student to assess where the student is academically and determine an appropriate educational goal. I gather the components of the student's high school resume, including a solid baseline test and personality assessment, from which I build a customized strategy that is intended to move the student through high school with optimal success and minimal stress. I lay out a step-by-step blueprint for the family to follow as they go back to their own educational environ, be it pubic, private, charter, collegiate, or home.

If all goes well, students spend 8th through 11th grades following our blueprint as they build an optimal high school record. They see us again before their senior year to start the momentous process of college admissions and financial aid. But life is never static. Over the course of four years, changes often occur that require adjustments to the game plan. We never view these adjustments as setbacks. It is actually a very positive thing to have access to new information and be able to make corrective revisions to the plan. Such corrections dramatically increase the odds of success. And success is the name of the game!

Custom schooling Kathe Lee style was what worked for me and what has now worked for my many clients around the world. Not everyone will need custom schooling, but when the time comes, it is great to know how to put this resource to work for your student.

# 2☞

# HOW THE BRAIN LEARNS

## *Versus How We School*

March 2, 6:27 am

SUBJECT: HELP!!!!!!!!

Good morning, Kathe. I'm sorry this will be your first email of the day. Grant was up all night in a flood of tears. He is exhausted from the constant pressure. I'm sick and tired of giving him meds just to get a good night's sleep or make it thru the day. Yesterday his counselor said he needs four more AP classes next year and he is freaking out. She said his senior year is critical for college admissions and if we stop now then all of this was for nothing. He's already doing 5-6 hours of homework every night on top of all day in the classroom. Do we need all the AP? Isn't 4.2 enough? I don't think we even care if he gets a college scholarship at this point! His self-esteem is zero and he is a nervous wreck. I'm not even sure he will survive another four years at this rate. He wants to quit. What are our options?

Sorry to dump this on you first thing in the morning. I wish I had never heard of university-model!

Brenda

Sent from my iPhone

I am an academic specialist. For more than a decade I have lectured to, written for, and provided private advising to colleges, high schools, and individual families. To help my students achieve optimal educational outcomes, I continually analyze the latest neuropsychological research. This allows me to stay up to date on how the brain learns and retains information, the effects of brain chemistry on learning, and treatments for various disorders related to the learning environment.

I am also an educational strategist. I have helped hundreds upon hundreds of families find the most efficient and effective academic route for their student. I create custom paths for each student that I advise focusing on emotional well being, academic mastery, and getting through college without going broke, an increasingly difficult task.

Before I was an educational professional, I was a homeschool mom. I custom-schooled my own children from birth through early college and both have attained an accredited high school diploma that is equivalent to any public school degree. Both completed two full years of college courses before graduating. Both played sports, joined clubs and went to prom. Both attended well-known universities and received scholarships for varying achievements. They are well-traveled, well-liked, and well-behaved. Though still young, both are socially appropriate, independent, mainstreamed adults with rich, active lives and promising careers.

My husband and I would love to claim the glory for turning two wonderfully well adjusted and motivated young people out into the world, but in reality the only thing we did differently was to customize their education, and thus their social interactions throughout their formative years. Simple yet powerful alternative school laws allowed us to utilize a wide assortment of homeschool classes, online programs, tutors, and inclusive educational cooperatives to customize our son and daughter's education in a way that honored and nurtured their interests and strengths while addressing their shortcomings through personalized instruction or therapeutic tutoring. It also allowed Mom and Dad to be the primary social models for two very impressionable minds, an objective that should never be underestimated. We may live in a brave new world technologically but when it comes to raising kids, traditional values will always be important.

Custom homeschooling allowed me to give each of my children what they needed academically exactly when they needed it. It allowed them to follow their passions and interests thus avoiding burnout and keeping the love of learning alive. It provided a network of socially appropriate children in which my son and daughter could form lifelong friendships. And it provided both of them with a free college education. For all of these reasons, I am a big believer that every child deserves an educational route architected by a strategist with experience in creating positive academic outcomes.

To clarify, homeschooling, as I define it, is not necessarily schooling at home but rather parent directed education that includes an optimal use of resources to customize each student's learning for maximum success.

That being said, custom schooling was hard. I was not able to work outside the home for over a decade. It was expensive, since on top of paying taxes to the local school district for services we could not use, we had to purchase all equipment, materials, books, outside courses, tutors, testing, and specialized assistance for learning issues. Without qualified advisers, I had to become my own professional guidance counselor. Eventually, I went back to school to extend my own learning. I shared this knowledge with my friends who were often at a loss as to how to pick curriculum, locate outside classes, and determine when their child had a learning problem or what to do about it if he did.

Through working with my public, private, and homeschool friends I came to some realizations about what works and what does not. Homeschooling does not work for everyone. Public school is not bad for everyone. Behavioral setbacks are often as much an educational issue as a parenting problem. Discipline is learned early on or not at all. Learning differences come in all shapes and sizes. Not all students learn the same way or at the same rate. And the list goes on and on. The point is that raising children involves making choices and facing problems, many of which will be directly related to the child's educational environment. How we deal with those problems will determine who the child is as an adult.

I will confess that while I have a lot of experience in this area and no shortage of positive client feedback from years of working with students one-on-one, I do not always know the answer to every problem. But I always know how to find a solution. Just as importantly, I know what absolutely will not work. This is critical since the window of opportunity for educating our kids is rapidly closing from the day they are born. We know that genetics combined with early experiences creates a unique information highway, or neural network, in each child's brain. This happens in the first few months of life and is not under our direct control as parents. To develop fully, this neural network need input and feedback.

For this reason, babies and young children need input, data to program their eagerly accepting brains. Everything a child experiences in the first few months of life (and even in the womb), influences how future information will be processed by way of the neuro-highway their brain builds during these critical early months. The internal learning process a child develops in the first year of life will solidify well before school ever starts. By first grade, problems already exist.

If we want to change a students neuro-wiring during their school years, we have to spot problems early and work to "rewire" the brain's processing pathways before it is hardwired, which appears to take place around the tweeny years. Equally problematic, experiences create neuro-habits, which influences behaviors. In association with inborn personality, neuro-habits directly contribute to attitude. If not addressed by middle school, such behaviors & attitudes will stick around forever, only becoming more ingrained over time.

**Learning differences are a set of behaviors**. We give them names like ADD (lack of focus), hyperactivity (blurting out answers without thinking or jumping around), dysgraphia (sloppy handwriting), dyslexia (poor reading), laziness, bad attitude, etc; but, they are really just neuro-habits that have developed in concert with the brain's early physiological and neurological development. In many cases there appear to be other notable processes involved but the jury is still out on the how and why of it all. The point is that learning differences are, at their core hardwired. Fortunately, the brain has some plasticity, especially at very early ages.

If we are going to ensure optimal educational outcomes in high school or college, children will need to be screened as early as possible and given targeted, individualized, and intense corrective therapy before being sent off to school. Then we need to stick with a brain-based approach to education throughout the school years. What a student studies, when he studies it, how long he studies it, and to some degree even who teaches it, is much less important than how it is taught. Thanks to the nascent field of neuroscience and fMRI studies we know more about how the brain learns, retains, and uses information than at any other time in history.

We know that vocabulary is developed through functional use. If we want our children to have a great functional vocabulary as an adult, then we must read to them incessantly through the first ten to twelve years of life. We know that school based reading assignments do NOT produce a comparable vocabulary to free reading done for fun or consistent use of books on tape. Meaning that assigned reading has limited value. We know that spelling is related to a spatial ability in the visual cortex. No amount of drills will "fix" a bad speller. You either have the ability to visualize words or you do not. We know that some brains are wired for numbers and some are not. Some brains process words fluidly and some do not. Spatial reasoning comes naturally for some and not for others. These abilities are innate and highly individualized. Having or not having them is neither good or bad. It just represents differences in processing that make us each unique and potentially amazing!

Our processing abilities remain relatively constant despite schooling or IQ, but they are heavily affected by our emotional state. The emotional state is heavily influenced by where one is, what is happening, and how much stress one perceives. For many students, school is stressful. It may be intellectually difficult, time consuming, behaviorally demanding, or downright boring. When this happens, optimal learning fails to take place and poor behaviors begin to develop.

If we want the brain to assimilate new information well, aka learn, the brain must not be in a stressed state while that new information is being inputted! The information must be taught in a way that the student can understand. It must be inputted quickly. And it must absolutely never be boring! In essence, the school curriculum and teaching methodology used must honor the five basic rules of brain-based learning.

## Rules Of Brain-Based Learning

1. *Learning requires engagement.*
2. *Learning requires active feedback.*
3. *Learning requires interaction.*
4. *Learning requires a happy brain.*
5. *Progress requires mastery.*

**LEARNING REQUIRES ENGAGEMENT**. The brain must be attuned to any incoming information in order to encode it and store it properly. If the student is not engaged in the information being taught, the brain is not attending and optimal retention will not take place. Short term and working memory will still function so the student will appear to have "got it", but when the material is brought up in a few days or weeks, it is often as if it was never learned.

This occurs because the information was not encoded and stored correctly due to the brain's inattention to the incoming information. This makes retrieval a hit and miss process and produces spotty learning. When learning is not optimal, there is no mastery and tests scores are lower than quiz scores. If the information has been accurately encoded and properly stored, end of term exam scores should not be lower than short term scores like quizzes. **Proof of mastery is a consistent 75-90% score on comprehensive assessments.** Lower is always a problem.

Attempting to teach without engagement is highly inefficient and requires that lessons be taught over and over which is the definition of emotional torture. The official name for this ever-increasing phenomenon is called "*spinning your wheels*".

**LEARNING REQUIRES FEEDBACK.** The brain of a child is analogous to a computer before all the add-ons. It has a basic operating system but needs a custom software installation in order to function best. The young brain loves ALL information and actively seeks it at ALL times, often to the annoyance of parents and teachers. But before we judge the persistent question-asker too harshly, recognize that incoming information is how the brain programs itself for life success. It is only from feedback that the brain is able to fine-tune its programming . . . a little thing called learning! Remember, you don't know what you don't know until someone points it out. In brain-based learning, a student should never work alone, since there can be no feedback in isolation. This is why homework usually ends up being nothing but busy work. Busy work is boring. Boring negates learning!

**LEARNING REQUIRES INTERACTIONS.** Well before modern science, educators recognized one truth. Kids learn better in groups. Research has now proven what we have always intuitively known. The human need to socially connect with others is as basic as our need for food or water. We literally can not survive without connecting to other human beings, and we cannot learn without interacting with others. Kids learn best when they work in very small, verbally and physically interactive groups. Ideally, the same group of kids on a very regular basis. Sixty years of research on how the brain learns and retains information gave us the well-known "Learning Pyramid" on the next page. Study after study shows that humans retain 10% of what they read or hear,

50% of what they do, and 90% of what they teach others. Let this one marinate folks.

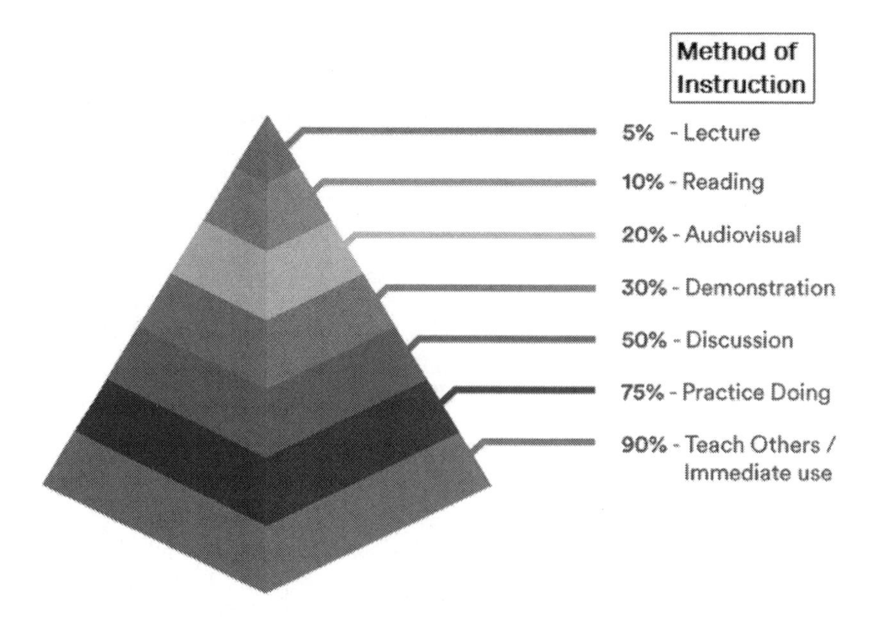


**LEARNING REQUIRES A HAPPY BRAIN.** The brain is controlled through chemistry. A healthy brain is teeming with serotonin and dopamine, while a stressed brain is flooded with cortisol. Cortisol blocks memory production in the hippocampus. Learning requires forming new memories. So learning requires a happy brain. To feel happy at school, students must feel connected to what they are learning and the people they are learning with. The teacher matters. The other students matter. The learner's state of mind matters but happiness is not always within our control. **Happiness is a chemical state not an attitude**. Happiness can not be commanded into being. Students need to be given clear rationales for what they are being asked to do. Otherwise, their brain will work against even the best learning goals. If you want a brain to study years of incremental math, then you better give it a compelling and honest reason for doing so. Otherwise, don't be surprised when the outcome is less than optimal.

**PROGRESS REQUIRES MASTERY.** When learning new information, the brain builds on past learning by connecting new info to what's already stored in the brain. How quickly this connection is made, and how well it is remembered, is what determines I.Q. Smart people don't necessarily know more, they are just able to access info faster and with greater consistency, and of course they remember it. Not everyone can be a genius but mastery is achievable by every student. Mastery is when a student has optimally connected new information to old, and remembers it with relatively rapid recall. Brain-based learning research tells us that we should never advance students in a subject until they demonstrate absolute mastery at their current level. Doing so is the root of reading delays and math difficulties. Slowing down and getting it right the first time will save much misery and valuable time down the road. Ironically, it also prevents boredom, the nemesis of all learning.

Now that we understand how the brain learns and the role that brain chemistry plays in the process, we can easily figure out why schooling and learning are out of sync. School is about bringing several same-aged students into a confined space and presenting them with a mandated set of mostly verbal information without regard for any individual student's intellect, interest, genetics, emotional state, or background. Learning, on the other hand, takes place inside the mind of each individual student and is highly contingent upon that person's unique experiences and attitudes.

Schools are not by definition bad. They are by definition poor places to learn. But the news is not all bad. Now that we know the Rules of Brain-Based Learning, it is possible to identify what is wrong with schools and make changes that will promote learning. For example, take the problem of bored students. It does not take a trained eye to see that students in schools are not engaged. One major reason is that they are required to follow a one-size-fits-all degree plan and curriculum with no regard for individual interests or learning styles. While it would be impossible for a school district with tens of thousands of kids to provide an individual lesson plan for each student, it is possible to screen students each year and place them in courses based not on age or grade but on interest and aptitude. This one small change would drastically increase learning.

An ever better example is the lack of feedback and positive interactions between both students and the material being taught. Oversized, lecture-based classrooms leave no time for hands-on exploration or peer-based discussion and debate. This is an easy fix given that teachers say they much prefer to teach in a round table or interactive manner if only their school were designed for such. Smaller classrooms with more teacher freedom to interact and bend the lesson in accordance with the "mood" of the room would increase emotional satisfaction and thus learning.

A final and most telling example is the level of frustration that students report experiencing at school. Students recognize that they are not learning, yet they feel increasing pressure to measure up on standardized tests and end of year exit exams, despite well publicized proof that they lack mastery. The result is large numbers of students graduating high school without core competencies that they will need in college, in their career, and in life. This seems like an impossible situation but by using brain-based learning the fix is simple. We simply do not promote a student who does not have PROVEN mastery.

*We have now identified the primary obstacle to learning: lack of engagement. And we have singled out a viable solution to this problem: customization.*

Armed with this information, we can now start the process of optimizing high school for college admissions and financial aid. And it all starts with optimized learning through custom schooling.

# 3☞

# LEEWAY©

## *A Customized Solution*

Getting into college is a time consuming and emotionally exhausting task, made all the worse by the fact that it happens in the middle of the senior year. On top of Advanced Placement classes, college fairs, football games and prom, a student is required to complete college applications, write numerous essays, collect references, sit for scholarship interviews, and complete last minute standardized tests. And they still have to pass all their classes and graduate!

If students have any level of weakness in their core academics, university is the point where it can no longer be ignored. And senior year is certainly not the time to be fixing such problems. Ideally, any fix should happen before 9th grade.

For all of these reasons, the art of high school to college planning does not begin in the senior year. It also does not begin with perfect GPAs and scholarship level test scores in the junior year. Getting into college and getting it paid for starts with a learning assessment that tells us exactly where the student is in relation to the norms. This should happen prior to starting high school. A valid assessment should include a baseline that proves mastery of the basic core subjects. If mastery is missing in any area, then it must be obtained before the college admissions window begins at the end of 11th grade.

As you might imagine, trying to fix or remediate a high schooler is very difficult. Not only is the brain less inclined to change at this age, but teenagers are highly resistant to intervention no matter how badly they may need it. And, according to the Nations Report Card, which has been reproduced at www.KatheLee.com, they do need it.

64% of students are not college ready,[1] further proving that schooling and learning are out of sync. Yet the current alternative of labeling and holding students back is unhealthy as well.

Based on the **Rules Of Brain-Based Learning**, the solution to this dilemma is clear. Creating a custom learning path is the only way to ensure each and every student acquires mastery before moving forward in school. And academic mastery is the only way to achieve optimal success in high school, which is also the only way to ensure students are ready for college admissions and merit based aid.

While custom learning can be time consumptive, it requires infinitely less time than continually re-teaching the same things over and over as we currently do. Why do students need twelve years of math, six years of World History, or four years of high school English? The answer is, they don't.

In fact, the odds improve when students do not follow the conventional high school curriculum or degree plan. I know this to be a fact, because I have proved it with student after student for over a decade.

*That's right!*

*Students do not have to follow the conventional high school curriculum in order to get into a good college or get it paid for, or to be successful in their careers.*

LeeWay Academy is an independent private high school in Dallas, Texas, that fully embraces the brain-based learning methodology described in the last chapter. At LeeWay Academy, material is never re-taught. Students are taught what they are ready to learn when they are ready to learn it.

To be clear, students are not taught what THEY WANT to learn when THEY WANT to learn it. Students are taught what they NEED to learn when THEIR BRAINS are ready to learn it.

Subjects are only taught once and they are approached conceptually, step-wise, and incrementally until there is clear mastery. Once taught, the student becomes the teacher. We observe them as they either apply what they have learned or teach other students. This is our way of testing them. Pupils find the act of teaching others highly empowering, if not initially a bit nerve wracking. After a few weeks with proper training and support from teachers, students love teaching others. And they learn without even realizing that they are being taught. This works because teaching others is what the brain of a teenager is best suited for. Verbal output of knowledge is ideally suited for the increased integration and faster communication of the evolving teenage brain circuitry. This is brain-based learning.

At LeeWay Academy, students are taught in social groups that are a combination of the students' personalities and the teachers' observations. School is not the time for social experiments. Classes are guided by a knowledgeable teacher whose focus is the students, not a check-off list of material to be taught. Teachers listen more than talk. Their goal is to understand what a student knows, then provide non-judgmental but accurate and objective feedback in real-time. **With immediate and appropriate feedback the brain will learn whether the student wants to or not!** To the brain, learning is a simple process: take in information, process information, store information, test information, receive updated/corrected information, store a corrected version, repeat.

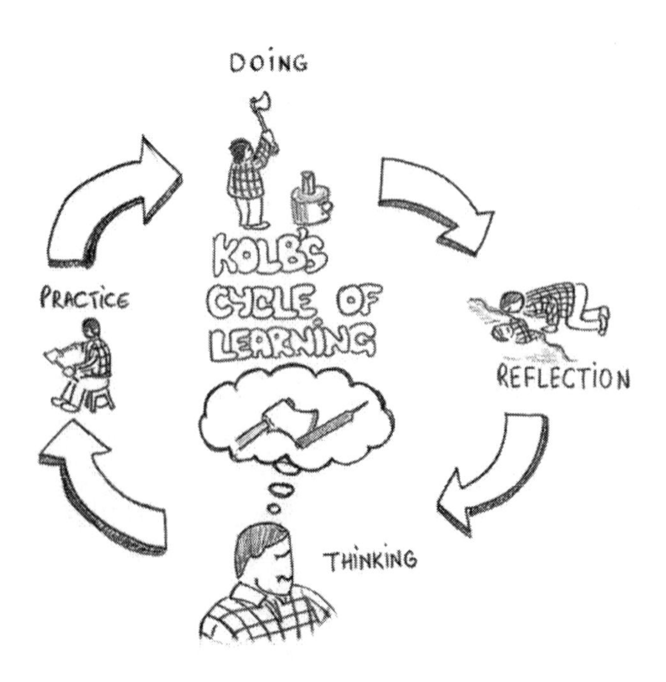

LeeWay Academy class time is broken into small blocks interspersed with quick breaks, thus assuring optimal brain chemistry. Material taught may be auditory, visual, tactile, kinesthetic, or observational, depending on the students and the subject at hand. Teachers are given the freedom to pull from any curriculum that is deemed helpful for any student at any time. This teaches students to optimize their resources, while helping teachers feel valued. It also contributes to both student and teacher motivation. By adhering to the Rules of Brain-Based Learning, LeeWay Academy students not only succeed academically, they are happy.

This all sounds amazing, but does it get students into good colleges and get it paid for? As of the last school year, 100% of LeeWay Academy graduates attended the university of their choice. They received, on average, a 50% non-loan, non need-based academic scholarship for all four years of college. And they regularly reported being happy with their college and later career choices.

As an academic strategist specializing in getting kids into college and getting it paid for, this is music to my ears. For any parent looking for the same, feel free to get excited. Brain-based learning is more than a mantra, it is a transformation in how we think about school. Using brain-based ideals allows us to be more efficient with our teaching thereby leaving more time for exploring personal passions, service to others, and college or career planning; three things that are sorely missing from our current high school curriculums.

I call this educational metamorphosis, Custom Schooling Kathe Lee Style! Custom Schooling allows any student to use all the resources at his disposal to achieve a solid education without burnout and without repetition. Custom schooling allows any student to succeed.

Success is an indisputably appropriate educational goal. But people define success in many different ways. For me, academic success is measured in three sequential benchmarks. If the first criterion is not met then the next one is moot. I often pose these benchmarks to parents and educators in the form of three, straight-to-the-point questions. The answer to all three questions must come from a valid baseline such as the PSAT or Woodcock Johnson. School records can not give us the answers.

My first question is about where the student is psychologically. How he or she feels about life in general. If a student is not emotionally well balanced, if she is not happy, if he does not feel a true connection to the goals he has been tasked with achieving, then our educational strategy is not likely to be successful. Asking this question is critical as evidenced by the percentage of students with documented behavioral concerns. Given the frightening prevalence of drug and alcohol use, overt and early sexuality, and social media influences, we need to be asking if our kids are okay in the way that matters most. I ask the question in this way.

*"Is the student on a path to being an emotionally well balanced adult?"*

The second question is about meeting a very different criteria. We need to know if a student is meeting academic benchmarks. If a student spends 13+ years in the most expensive school system on the planet, then he should at least be on level with his peers. Meeting this benchmark is certainly more important than what college a student might get into or even how much scholarship he will earn. Any answer to this next question must be based on a proven baseline. We can not judge a student on grades alone or even a single standardized test. Once we have an answer to this question, we should not point the finger or try to rationalize away results that we do not like. Parents are especially susceptible to this phenomenon. Instead, we should use the baseline to develop a custom educational strategy and implement quickly, using proven solutions. I pose the question in a purely factual way, making it clear that we are not judging the student as being good or bad but simply answering the question of where the student is academically in relation to others his age.

*"Is the student academically on level*

*with or ahead of his peers?*

*If he is ahead, to what extent?*

*If he is behind, to what extent?"*

The last question can be asked with a focus on college admissions, but I often generalize it. I replace the phrase "life goals" to represent whatever ambition the student may have. For example, I might say "career goals" or "version of a good life" when referencing what the student is trying to achieve. In my office, our focus is usually college related so we usually ask if the student is positioned to achieve *"admission to a good college with non-loan financial aid"*. This is the third and last question we ask on this topic since it is completely dependent upon the first two goals being met.

*"Is the student positioned to achieve his or her life goals?"*

As parents, educators, politicians, and businesspersons, we are obliged to be able to answer a resounding "yes" to each of these questions in order to claim successful educational outcomes. Custom schooling is how I help each of my clients achieve consistently superior educational outcomes which, in turn, produce excellent college admissions and scholarships, that increase the odds of the student actually graduating and having a successful career.

As I have already revealed, my brand of custom schooling is called LeeWay©. LeeWay takes optimal advantage of every resource available, especially dual enrollment. It builds a student's high school curriculum and degree plan around the principles of brain-based learning. It optimally positions students for admission into the college of their choice and makes them highly competitive for non-loan merit-based financial aid. And in my experience, LeeWay results in happy, well adjusted, highly educated, contributing members of society.

LeeWay is a philosophy about learning and how it connects to long term well being and financial stability. LeeWay guides the way I think about every aspect of education. It has opened my mind and my eyes to options and possibilities that have been revolutionary in terms of outcomes.

LeeWay is also a program that exploits one of the most powerful resources available to high school students today. That resource is the subtopic of this book. For most, but not all high school students, the best way to customize high school while optimizing learning and enhancing college admission outcomes is to take advantage of a novel, but far from new, innovation called Dual Enrollment.

Taking college classes while still in high school is usually referred to as dual enrollment or dual credit. This will be a completely new concept for many of you. For others, it may be a familiar notion but odds are a rather murky one. Even for college or dual credit professionals working with students on a daily basis, this commodity is misunderstood and therefore often misused.

Regardless of your current familiarity, by the time you finish this book, you will have a whole new perspective on how to use dual enrollment along with a customized high school plan to optimize college admissions and financial aid planning for any student, regardless of any academic concerns.

The idea of creating a custom educational plan for each and every student sounds daunting. It can be. But our current system does not work. By any report or measure, it is not giving us a good return for our investment. If we redirected every dollar and every man hour currently being invested into our educational system, customization would be possible, and outcomes would improve dramatically. What would such a system of custom schooling look like? A lot like LeeWay.

Compare the case of Nathan R. with that of his peer, Brianna Grace. Both students were seen for private academic advising in high school. They were both from well-to-do families and attending schools with a public record of top rankings in terms of low drop-out rates and quality of the academics being offered. They were equally bright, hard working, motivated, and by all appearances, successful students until they received the results of their first PSAT (Preliminary Scholastic Aptitude Test). This was their baseline.

The PSAT is a standardized test that is taken each year by over 1.5 million high school juniors in hopes of winning the most coveted prize in all of secondary academia, a National Merit Scholarship (NMS). Only the top fraction of one percent of students produce tests scores high enough to earn the status of NMS Winner. This highly normed standardized test, more than any other, tells a student where he is academically in relation to his peers. For this reason, expensive PSAT prep courses can be found in all but the smallest and poorest communities.

Normally, students take their first PSAT in 10th grade. Then counselors and parents use these scores to determine what the student needs to do to earn top scores on the more critical 11th grade PSAT. The proper way to use this test is as a baseline. Take it in 8th grade to spot gaps that can be fixed by high school. Take it in 9th grade to see what the odds are of winning NMS. If the odds are against you then do not roll the dice. Tests taken at the right time and used in the right way can be part of a highly successful college planning strategy.

National Honor Society and AP student Brianna Grace, took her baseline at the beginning of 10th grade and was dismayed with a Selection Index of 162. Given her record of straight A's and a long history of success at her exemplary rated charter school, Brianna expected to be much closer to the 200 point cutoff that is the mark of elite students. Her score put her slightly above par with the national average. Knowing that par in this case was a rather low bar, and expecting so much more of their honor student, Brianna's parents were concerned that their daughter had a problem and started looking for a test prep program to shore up her scores.

Nathan R. took his baseline in 9th grade and was pretty happy with his 159 given that he had never done well on tests in his northern California public school. Plus, he was suspected of having a learning difference. His scores were good for his age but his math score was low. His parents talked to his school counselor about holding him back a year to remediate his math. They also came to see me.

Brianna immediately began a well respected, $3500 money-back guaranteed test prep program that met three times a week after school and optionally on weekends. She was diligent, but the work cut into her extensive AP homework schedule. By spring, she was struggling to keep her grades up. To her credit, she stuck with it and eked out a respectable GPA but not the 4.5 she was counting on to help with college admissions. Brianna continued to prep throughout the summer in lieu of a long-awaited church mission trip and family vacation. She took her final PSAT in fall of 11th grade, and was relieved just to be done. Her score came back in January.

Instead of the 219 Selection Index needed to be a National Merit winner in her home state of Texas, Brianna earned a 189. An amazing accomplishment given her baseline. A twenty-seven point increase on the PSAT is huge. Her hard work produced impressive results but nothing near the number needed to be a winner. She was devastated and angry at her parents for "ruining her life" with a year of nothing but tests prep. Brianna came to see me in spring of her junior year. Mom and Dad wanted a plan for college admissions but it was very clear that Brianna was in trouble emotionally. A quick look at Brianna's baseline PSAT told the story. Her reading score, though higher than the national average, was notably lower than her grammar. To be clear, her reading score was not LOW it was just lower than Brianna's IQ indicated it should have been. This always points to a processing issue. A full learning assessment confirmed that Brianna had a learning difference that significantly affected nuanced reading comprehension. This was a problem. The end of 11th grade is definitely not the time to be addressing such a serious learning issue.

SAT and ACT tests were just weeks away, and Brianna felt she had no choice but to try to score high on those test if she was going to have a shot at a "good college" and the financial aid she would need. Reading delays have a strong correlation to reduced tests scores but Brianna's had never been addressed. Mom decided there was no time to fix the problem so against my advice they opted to invest in more test prep instead.

Over the next few months, Brianna's stress increased dramatically and her behavior at home began to deteriorate. Bri's parents connected her to a counselor at their church with seemingly good results. Her final ACT score was high enough for admission plus she received an $11,000 renewable annual scholarship. Despite a rocky path, Brianna was on her way to college with her peers and a bit of money.

Nathan came to my San Francisco office just a few weeks after receiving his 9th grade PSAT score. Mom was worried about his math delay. I explained that a math gap is common in younger testers since they have not yet completed Algebra 1. Nathan's particular problem with conversions was an easy fix now that we knew exactly what it was. No need to go back and retake any classes. Plus, while Nathan's overall numbers where just average, his highest score was reading, something that told me this student was going to be just fine. The math issue was just a gap that could be addressed in the curriculum by customization going forward. Nonetheless, Nathan was in the doldrums and convinced he would never get into a college.

My first step was to take some time to assess Nathan emotionally, screening for general stress, test anxiety, and any long term potential psychiatric issues associated with his learning environment. Given his mild frustrations, my assessment was an informal process involving a simple conversation. Plus I took some time to help Nathan understand that he was completely normal and would be just fine, an important step to take.

*"In a 2010 survey by the American Psychological Association, 43 percent of 13-14 year olds said they felt stress every single day."* [2]

It is surely no surprise that most students face some degree of emotional distress related to the often difficult task of dealing with feeling that are out of sync with their peers. It is very difficult to balance the stresses of home life and school while simultaneously facing the emotional rollercoaster of impending adulthood. Throw in the added pressure of advanced placement classes, standardized test prep, college applications, deciding on a major which will seemingly determine your entire future, and scholarships, and you have the perfect recipe for setbacks, if not for out and out disaster.

Nathan's custom LeeWay plan included educating him and his parents about their options and helping Nathan select appropriate goals. This offered them a lot of relief. They no longer felt forced to do what the system seemed to demand.

Nathan transferred to a two-day-per-week university model private school that would allow him to incorporate the LeeWay philosophy and program. His baseline had told us where his gaps were. We used the rest of 9th grade to address those gaps. By 10th grade Nathan was ready to focus on mastery of the LeeWay Five Cores of High School.

## The Five Cores

1. *Nuanced Reading Comprehension*
2. *Writing for Clarity and Purpose*
3. *Algebra, Geometry, & Consumer Math*
4. *Critical Thinking for Tests Prep*
5. *Exploration of Passions & Careers*

By 11th grade, Nathan was ready to take the leap into college prep. We had Nathan participate in dual enrollment for his core classes. This freed up 50% of his day which we used for college visits, curriculum based test prep for the SAT (we skipped the second PSAT because it was of no value given his odds of winning NMS), shadowing jobs, and a directed internship. School was actually enjoyable.

By fall of his senior year, Nathan was ready for college admissions with a near perfect GPA, college level classes under his belt, membership in the most respected international collegiate honor society, and a high school resume that was built to impress both college admission officers and financial aid reviewers. Nathan received only $4,000 per year for his academic record but an apprenticeship in lamp making resulted in his winning a Terry Scholarship which equated to a full ride award for all four years of college. These "stackable" scholarships resulted in a cash surplus. Mom was just happy to have no debt. Nathan was thrilled to be going off to the top public college in the state without the hassles that his friends had complained about throughout high school. No AP, no year- round test prep, no late night homework sessions, just admission to a top college and zero college debt!

There are many routes to success. This is a good thing since we are all different and do not want to tread identical pathways. But to reach any goal, we have to be clear on exactly what that goal is. The goal of high school should never be to take a slew of intense AP courses. The goal of high school should not be to compete for tests scores, or complete the most homework, or even to graduate. The goal of high school should be to give each student what they need to succeed in college and life.

For administrators, high school is the last chance to help students shore up core masteries that will be needed to succeed in college and career. For students, high school is the last chance to explore life's possibilities without the emotional and financial demands of adulthood. For academic advisors, planners, and strategists, high school is the last chance to ensure that a student completes the most crucial steps towards a successful educational outcome. For parents, high school is the last chance to set our children on a financially secure life path that is healthy, happy, and emotionally well balanced.

Brianna and Nathan went off to their respective colleges as planned. While Nathan pursued his Bachelor's degree in Arts & Technology with high marks in the Honors College at his university, Brianna changed her major twice and was still dissatisfied. Starting with an ill-advised sojourn into nursing, she eventually spent a semester in both the business school and as a philosophy major. After three years, less than 27 usable credits, and nearly $45,000 in student loans, Brianna took a semester off to reassess her goals. Fortunately, there are many paths to the same goal. Brianna's path led back to me for a custom strategy built around Brianna, not some pre-packaged goal.

When we finally sat down in my Dallas office, it was clear that Brianna would need some outside psychological counseling before embarking on another academic pathway. She was in desperate need of some kind of success, something she had not experienced since middle school. Aptitude testing and some pointed discussions revealed that Brianna was an exceptionally gifted designer of women's accessories. She had not-so-secretly created her own collection of knitted handbags, beaded jewelry, and broached head covers that were in line with current trends. Feeling a failure, but with the weight of expectation gone, Brianna jumped at my idea of her being a personal stylist, a goal she had put away many years before under the notion that it was neither a viable career choice nor an acceptable way to impress her family.

Instead of returning to college as planned, Brianna decided to follow my strategy, which was directed at finding personal success as a stepping stone to education and career success. It started with an internship at a well-staked startup clothing designer in a tony, downtown office. No one famous, just a supportive soul and plenty of opportunity. The first few months were unpaid as she learned the ropes and proved her worth. But by spring, Brianna found herself with a small salary and sitting in Bryant Park between her mentor and the art editor of a Condé Nast magazine at New York's Fashion Week.

The happy ending to both stories is that this May, while Nathan is dressed in cap and gown with braided gold honor cords looped over his left shoulder in preparation for college commencement, Brianna will be in NYC working for good pay on her first fashion layout. Her goal now is to complete her work in New York, return to Dallas to continue her internship, and start classes at the University of North Texas with a major in fashion design. Will she succeed? All we know at this point is that she is finally on the right path to a viable goal that she is personally invested in. I'd say the odds are good.

While both Nathan and Brianna now seem poised for success, the road for Brianna was unnecessarily difficult. A customized high school solution early on could have resulted in the same outcome without the stress, the family trauma, the wasted time, and the debt. Instead of overkill AP courses and tests prep, students like Brianna would be better served by shadowing, doing internships, and starting college classes while still in high school, aka dual enrollment. Freeing up time to explore realistic career options is perhaps the greatest advantage to custom schooling, aka a strategy for success.

4☞

# PREPARE TO BE AMAZED

## A Strategy For Success

As an academic advisor and educational strategist, people come to see me for three reasons, all are directly related to getting into college and getting it paid for. The first reason people contact me is they are worried that their student may be behind academically or may even have a learning difference. They are not looking for a medical diagnosis or educator's label -- just an honest, informed opinion. They want me to assess the problem and guide them to a valid solution.

When time allows, I see such families privately and given my success in this area, parents and educators are understandably eager to hear my insights. While my recommendations are by necessity based on each student's specific history, goals, and situation, I have found certain truths present themselves over and over and are worth sharing with anyone who is interested in helping a student maneuver the often murky waters of high school to college (or career). One such statistic relates to the number of kids who start college but never make it to graduation. Such facts are hard to accept but impossible to ignore.

A second reason people seek my advice is they want to make sure their student is doing all the right things in high school in order to be prepared to succeed in college. Based on the published national drop-out rate, the majority of high school freshmen never manage to complete a college degree. [1, 2] For this reason, I continually consult with public and private high schools and lecture to homeschool groups throughout the country in an effort to spread the word about early baseline assessment and the host of customized educational choices available to any family anywhere.

Without a doubt, the single most useful tool for college planning success is a highly normed baseline test like the PSAT, which is taken by over 1.5 million U.S. high schoolers every October. The right baseline will tell you exactly where a student is in relation to an appropriate norm. In my world, I want to know where a student is in relation to other students the same age or grade. The PSAT tells me this. There are other viable baselines, meaning they are highly normed, so that no matter what is unique about you, some percentage of kids who took the same baseline at the same time had the same uniqueness. Such a test would be truly predictive of how well a student will fare in the college admissions game. I prefer the PSAT 8/9 or the Stanford 10, taken no later than the first semester of 9$^{th}$ grade.

To a trained eye, these tests can predict everything from learning gaps and behavioral differences to the potential for college financial aid. Perhaps most importantly, the right baseline can show us exactly where to expend time, money, and effort over the next few years to position the student for optimal success, both in high school and with whatever comes next, be it college, career, military, or starting a family.

**These tests are not about getting into a great college. These tests are about knowing where a student is academically; knowing what gaps exist so we can create a strategy for getting that pupil on an optimal pathway for a lifetime of success.** While I am highly opposed to early and frequent testing of students, when I am able to see a family privately, I always require that they bring in the results of a solid baseline test. There is simply no better way to identify what needs to be addressed in the curriculum of a student.

The third reason that people take time out of their busy schedule and wait months for a private appointment is that they want to know the secret to getting their student into a top college and getting it paid for via scholarships and grants. This is referred to as non-loan financial aid. It is true that there are some tricks of the trade that are worth their weight in gold. Being able to "read" a student and guide him towards a major or career that is innately right for him is what many clients would call my calling card. But this is hardly a trick.

Good educational specialists must be able to not only connect with students, but be able to understand exactly what a college wants to see on a student's record in order to offer that student admission and top financial aid. They should be able to navigate through the loopholes of a very complex system and be intimately familiar with educational resources that are proven to work yet are reasonably priced. And they should have a fail-proof secret formula for college planning success!

The ultimate SECRET FORMULA TO COLLEGE ADMISSIONS is so poorly kept and so simple that you should never have to pay for it. In fact, I will spill the beans right here in one relatively straightforward proclamation.

# Secret Formula

To get into a good college
and get it paid for,
you need to do three things
at exactly the right time.

**#1**
**(8th – 11th Grades)**

*Build A Perfect College Package*

**#2**
**(Fall of 12th Grade)**

*Apply To Only The Right Colleges*

**#3**
**(Senior Year)**

*Meet Three Key Deadlines*

**October 31st**
All Admission Apps Submitted

**November 30th**
FAFSA and/or CSS Submitted

**December 31st**
All Scholarship Apps Submitted

The SECRET FORMULA sounds simple on its surface but is actually rather tricky even for an old pro with thousands of admissions under her belt. What constitutes a good college package? How does one know which colleges are the right colleges for a particular student? And, why are those three key deadlines so different from what you might find on college websites or admission guide books? I intend to answer each of these questions in a way that is as easily digestible for students, parents and teachers as it is for college personnel. Let's take them one-by-one.

## THE COLLEGE PACKAGE

Before we can start any meaningful conversation on high school to college planning using dual enrollment, I first need to explain what I mean by the term "College Package". The College Package (CP) is everything that a student will submit to a university as part of the application process. This will include a high school transcript, test scores, essays, references, honors & awards, and documented extracurriculars. This could also be called the high school record. The College Package is essentially everything a student did from the beginning of 8th grade through the first few months of 12th grade. The CP will only reflect what is in progress during the senior year, making 12th grade a lame-duck year in terms of admissions.

Quite simply, the College Package will determine if a student gets admitted to a college. The College Package will also determine how much, if any, merit-based non-loan financial aid a college will offer. If getting into college and getting it paid for is important, then building a great high school record, aka The College Package, may be the single most important goal of high school. (Turning out a happy student ranks right up there too!)

Everyone has a College Package even if they are not aware of it. What constitutes a perfect College Package varies somewhat from one college or university to another, but the basic five components of a great CP are fairly universal.

❶

**National Merit** - The first thing an admissions officer will look for is a student's National Merit status. This is primarily determined by the PSAT score in 11th grade. The PSAT selection index (SI) needs to be 200+ to be considered for a National Merit Scholarship. To achieve this lofty goal, students must be good test takers, have spent a good deal of time on a concerted prep program, and produce an SAT with comparable scores. Few students will make this cutoff. To determine who will and who won't we look at the 10th grade PSAT, an ideal baseline that perfectly predicts a student's chances of scoring within National Merit range on the 11th grade PSAT.

❷

**SAT & ACT** - The second thing that matters on the College Package is standardized test scores. For many colleges, certain scores on the SAT or ACT will warrant scholarship offers regardless of what is on the rest of the high school record. A combined score of 1250 on the reading and math portions of the SAT will earn any student a bit of money at many decent colleges. For the ACT, a composite of 25-27 is where aid starts. At top schools, scores will need to be at least 1400 SAT or 32 ACT. One test is not more acceptable than another. Just one good score in either will do the job. There are colleges that base not only admissions but top merit aid on nothing more than these numbers exclusively.

**Grade Point Average (GPA) -** What a student takes in high school is important. Colleges want to see advanced math or science courses. They also like Advanced Placement but only if a class results in a test score of 3 or better. Much more important than what classes are taken is the overall GPA. Having a provable, near perfect GPA in high school is valuable. Many admission rubrics (point systems used for determining admissions) automatically eliminate students who don't make a certain GPA cutoff. For homeschoolers, it can be hard to prove the GPA. AP tests and early college classes are great ways of proving aptitude and college readiness, both of which will get students into good colleges and earn potential scholarships. A GPA of 3.8 or better is nearly mandatory if a student wants to be eligible for top primary merit based financial aid.

**Extracurriculars -** Colleges want to admit students who are going to complete a degree and then go out into the world and do something that matters. To decide if a student has this potential, admissions staff will look at the extracurricular record. They want to see a long, continuous history of competitions, leadership, and community service. Ideally, some of the extracurriculars should be relative to the student's potential major. For example, if an applicant wants a college to give him a 50% scholarship to pursue a degree in business, then that college will want to see that the contender has the potential to be a business leader of the future. The student would demonstrate this by starting his own business in high school, running for office at school, or serving on a community board or committee. Competitions are also important, even more so if an award is earned at a state or national level. Volunteerism is the other thing that matters, not just in terms of hours spent but in relation to whom is helped by the effort. Helping those less fortunate gets attention and attention earns scholarships. For optimal merit-based financial aid, a stellar extracurriculars package is a must. This is easily the single most overlooked part of a students high school to college plan.

**Honors & Awards -** Along the same lines, colleges love winners. Winners are people who make the world a better place. People who have been there and done that. It makes sense if you think of scholarships as an investment that the college is making in a student. Just like betting on a stock on Wall Street, colleges know that some students will be duds so they need a way of predicting who will be the shining stars. Again like stocks, past performance does not guarantee future returns; but a student with a proven history of

> earning honors and accolades, or getting noticed by peers, makes an investor feel confident in their speculation. Colleges and scholarship programs accept and reward applicants who have a solid history of community service, leadership, and awards.

Not surprisingly, better colleges demand a better College Package. In general, if a student is aiming for admission to any of the top 50 universities in this country, he will need to have a very competitive College Package. At the least, he needs to be a National Merit contender, if not an outright winner. He will have proven his academic abilities via International Baccalaureate (IB), Advanced Placement (AP), or Dual Enrollment (DE). He will also need to have a top standardized test score on either the SAT or ACT, be an AP Scholar (have at least three Advanced Placement tests with a three or better on each one), demonstrate a consistently first-rate extracurriculars package that includes a broad base of honors and awards, winning at the national level, and a personal reference from someone of note.

This may sound like a lot, but I can assure you that thousands of applicants have packages of this caliber or better, and they are not even the exceptions. Despite this truth, getting in to college is actually the easy part.

*Getting into college is fairly easy.*

*Getting out of college is the real trick.*

*Getting out without debt*

*is even harder!*

Admittedly, the competition for admittance to top universities and military service academies is fierce. Similarly, if students are vying for top scholarships at even mediocre colleges, they will need, at minimum, great test scores alongside an unbeatable extracurricular record. This is a lot to get done and most students do not make the grade. That is why a serious contender for a top school and top aid must focus on the key components of the College Package and skip all the waste inherent to most high school schedules. Students who manage to do this can easily graduate high school with a top-notch College Package and be a shoo-in for admission to a great college with substantial non-loan financial aid.

## THE RIGHT COLLEGE

The second part to our SECRET FORMULA is applying to the right colleges. How does a student know which colleges are the right ones for him? Again, it is all about the College Package. Not everyone will have a great College Package. The average student's package will be -- just average. But even average students usually have something in their package that would make them attractive to certain colleges. These are the "Right Colleges" for that student. The trick is knowing which colleges have a history of admitting students with packages just like the one that you will be submitting. With this insider information, a student will not waste time or application fees on colleges that are never going to reward his College Package. The way to find the right colleges is through a professional College Screening.

A College Screening is meant to answer the question of *"Which schools are known to financially reward students with packages just like mine?"* The answer could literally be worth a veritable fortune.

When done correctly, an academic specialist will plug all the pertinent parameters into a tested rubric to parse out a list of twenty or so colleges that are a perfect match for a given student's College Package. These colleges should be certain to give an offer of admission. A well-done College Screening will also position a student for a serious amount of financial aid with some degree of certainty. A baseline and a screening are vital.

Of course, the rubric also takes into consideration things like the student's major, geographical preferences, career interests, as well as parental concerns like overall safety, religious leanings, and total cost. With a good College Screening, almost any student can get into college with non-loan financial aid. Hopefully in the future, such screenings will be a standard part of high school. In the meantime, a student or parent can do a fairly good job of screening for colleges using free resources on the internet or through non-profit groups like LeeWayUSA.com

## THREE DEADLINES

The third part to our SECRET FORMULA is the most important -- DEADLINES! You have to do things at the right time. Even students with top College Packages will not get optimal financial aid if they miss the key deadlines. While there are many important dates in the process, three are critical.

**Every student should turn in a completed college application no later than October 31st of the senior year**. This date is essential for everything that comes after. Remember, getting in is just the tip of the iceberg. For example, when a student applies to a college, he is automatically considered for merit aid based on his admission application. This aid is called Primary. Primary aid is a big deal because it is large denominations (approximately 50% of tuition and fees) and is automatically doled out just for applying. But primary aid is given on a first-come basis. So, in general, the later one applies, the less money one gets. Another example is secondary scholarships. These are also big bucks but secondary aid requires separate applications. These secondary scholarship applications have deadlines starting in December of the senior year. If admission apps are not completed by the start of November, then it is nearly impossible to meet these later secondary scholarship deadlines. A costly mistake.

Another key financial aid senior year deadline is November 30th. Every family with an income of less than $250,000 per year should complete either the Free Application for Federal Student Aid (FAFSA) or the alternative CSS Profile provided by the College Board. These forms not only qualify students for federal and state aid, work study, and subsidized loans, they help colleges access overall need. This is important as many primary and secondary scholarships have a need-based component. Not the stringent low income requirements of federal aid, but need based on overall cost of attendance (COA) for a given college. Many families with income over $100,000 adjusted gross income, will forego FAFSA and CSS believing they can not possibly qualify for need, but need is relative to cost. At a high end private school, even top wage earners may find they have need. If in doubt, file a FAFSA.

One last point about deadlines and aid has to do with how money is doled out. Financial aid is distributed on a first come first serve basis. And colleges only have so much money. Once every dollar is allocated, there is simply no more to give. Families assume that once they receive a financial aid offer, it is a done deal. That is simply not the case. If a student applies late in the game, there is a risk of earning a financial aid award that can not be collected due to lack of funds. These things happen at cash-strapped public colleges every year and all because of late applications. Remember, admissions can occur at a variety of times but money will only be awarded when it is available. Deadlines matter. A lot! So know the dates that matter and meet all deadlines. Don't rely on college personnel to know those deadline. Their focus is admissions. Yours is financial aid!

Financial aid that does not have to be paid back has never been exactly free flowing, but recent economic and political changes have made merit-based dollars for college even harder to come by. That's the bad news. The good news is that you have in your hands the most timely, proven, and even personalized insights into how to successfully get a student from high school to college regardless of academic setbacks or how that student stacks up against his peers in the classroom. With only the space and intimacy of these pages, I will share with you my singular go-to tool for achieving all of this and more. That tool is a gift of the mainstream educational establishment most often referred to as dual enrollment. If you are unfamiliar with the concept of dual enrollment or dual credit for high school students, then as the Magic Mirror said to Snow White, *"Prepare to be amazed!"*

# COLLEGE IN HIGH SCHOOL

## The Nuts & Bolts

# 5☞

# TAKING COLLEGE CLASSES

## In High School

As an educational specialist tasked with figuring out how students learn and what they need in order to succeed in high school, I have seen every permeation of educational problem that a student can face. Reading delays, slow processing, loss of attention, bad attitude, bad grades, bad parents, missed deadlines, missed opportunities, and life long struggles with mental illness or addictions are unfortunately a part of my everyday life. The list is long and troubling while the causes are complex and hotly debated. No one has all the answers, but when it comes to motivating and empowering students so they can reach their full potential, nothing works better than success. Success comes from building a customized educational strategy that treats students as the unique individuals they are.

For high school to college purposes, there is no shortage of resources. To earn credits towards high school graduation, students can utilize Advanced Placement (AP), International Baccalaureate (IB), College Level Exam Program (CLEP), Credit

By Exam (CBE), and a plethora of accelerated learning opportunities like university-level online courses (MOOCs), educational co-ops, public and private charters, and the ever growing arena of homeschooling. Among these potentially powerful programs, dual credit (also known as dual enrollment and abbreviated with the initials DE) stands alone in terms of efficiency, customization, and cost effectiveness.

*According to the Blackboard Institute,*
*"Dual enrollment helps a wide range of students*
*to be more successful in college.*
*Students in these programs experience*
*themselves as real college students and gain*
*confidence and skills that can help them to*
*excel academically."* [1]

Once parents and educators understand the power and opportunity inherent to dual enrollment they always ask me, *"Why doesn't everybody do dual enrollment?"* That's a great question. Sadly, the answer is they just don't know about it. So, without further adieu, let me introduce you to the wonderful world of dual enrollment classes for high school to college planning.

## WHAT IS DUAL ENROLLMENT?

In a nutshell, DE is an opportunity for students in high school to earn real college credits while simultaneously meeting their requirements for high school graduation. Dual enrollment may also be called dual credit or concurrent enrollment. Regardless of the name, verify that the program uses sheltered college credits for high school students, as there are other products available that do not work exactly like DE!

*Dual Enrollment allows any high school student to take one class to fulfill two requirements. One class for both high school and college credit.*

## WHAT ARE THE BENEFITS?

The short answer is that dual enrollment saves time, money, and precious emotional energy! Students take one academic course such as math, science, history, English, or foreign language, and receive a bona fide high school credit for that subject along with fully transferable college credits in the same subject. Dual credit classes are college courses but cost only a fraction of what a student will pay later at a university. This fact makes completing two years of college credits in high school the equivalent of a 50% scholarship! That alone makes dual credit worth exploring.

If you are the parent of a teen, you surely know the value of keeping them inspired and constructive. You also know that time is the perceived enemy of every teen. They want nothing more than to get out into the real world and be an adult, even though they have no real understanding of what that means. Dual credit allows them to overlap their last two years of high school and first two years of college which saves time, and motivates the student to keep pushing on just as they are nearing the critical part of the race.

## WHERE IS IT FOUND?

Nearly every community has a dual enrollment option. Federally approved, dual credit courses can be found at nearly all community colleges, as well as some private colleges and state universities. DE is also available on campus at many public and private high schools. A school counselor would be a good resource to learn about options in your area. For homeschoolers, local support groups or any college in the area should be able to furnish information about available dual credit options. For students who do not have a DE option nearby, there are fully accredited online dual credit programs that are available to everyone. A quick web search will turn up a plethora of good options for every type of student from any locale.

## CAN ANYONE DO IT?

Potentially, yes. Every American high school student has the opportunity to take dual credit classes, if not in person then online. The main criterion for admissions is being ready to succeed at college level course work. But there are things to consider before jumping on board. Is the student old enough? While there is not a federal age restriction for starting dual enrollment classes, at many junior colleges a student must have completed an acceptable percentage of his high school level curriculum. This usually means that he must be done with 10th grade, although there are many exceptions. In some states and counties, students may start dual credit classes as early as 9th grade. Each program will have their own rules so do not expect the same answer from different dual credit institutions.

Regardless of age or grade, all students who wish to take dual credit classes must prove they are ready. This means they have to pass a placement exam before they are allowed to start. This is a ubiquitous way of assuring that any student who signs up for a college class is ready to be in that class and has a reasonable chance of completing it successfully. There are many different placement exams available from SAT/ACT to a custom junior college product known as the Accuplacer. Since placement testing is one of the cornerstones of dual credit, there will be much more to say about these tests as we delve into the details of the college in high school option.

A final requirement, that is purely of my own making, is that the student must feel emotionally prepared for leaving behind a segment of their high school life, and for being part of a college environment. The differences between high school and college are massive. Not all students are ready for the change. Some kids are just not ready to give up their friends. On the other hand, many students are chomping at the bit to get away from the pressures and limitations of what they see as an oppressive and intellectually limiting high school experience. For them, DE is like winning the lottery.

## WHAT IS A PLACEMENT EXAM?

Dual enrollment is college. Before a student can start college classes they have to prove that they are academically ready to do college level work. This is done by taking a prescribed exam that assesses how a student measures up in reading comprehension, grammar, arithmetic, algebra, geometry and essay writing. Regardless of a student's age or level of achievement in any one subject, if he or she passes a placement test then he or she is provably ready for college level courses and is eligible to begin taking dual credit college classes while in high school. Trust the placement test to say when to start DE.

## WHAT CLASSES ARE BEST?

Classes that will help the student get into a good college, get it paid for, and succeed once he is there. In other words, take classes that improve the College Package. The best dual credit courses for this purpose are math, science, computing, and foreign language. Core courses like College Algebra, Statistics, Calculus, Chemistry, Physics, and Introductory Programming will usually transfer to any college for any major and they look great on a high school transcript.

Many students will need to start out a bit slower. Core classes that are suitable for any caliber of student and will transfer to most universities include English Composition, U.S. History, American Government, Speech & Communications, Humanities, Psychology, Macro or Micro Economics and lab-based Science for non-science majors. Many DE programs also offer PE, music, dance, photography, multimedia, design, accounting, marketing, and a variety of vocational and college preparatory classes. When available, such classes are a great way to explore interests and possible careers. Optionally, a student who knows exactly which university he will eventually transfer to may want to sync up his DE courses with the official core from that university. But always do this with great caution.

## HOW MANY CLASSES CAN BE TAKEN?

It depends on what the program will allow. Many colleges will limit the dual credit student to two classes per semester. This is to protect the all important GPA. If a student consistently does well in courses, this limitation is often lifted. Regardless of what a college allows, there are some basic guidelines that seem to consistently work. In a short summer semester, one class is enough. In a full semester like fall or spring, two classes are perfect when combined with an otherwise full day at school. An industrious student, or one with minimal academics outside of dual credit, can easily manage three or more DE classes in the long semesters of fall and spring. If starting DE as recommended at the end of 9 or 10th grade, many homeschoolers with flexible schedules can complete their entire first two years of college classes before leaving high school. Many even attain an Associate's Degree.

## WHERE ARE DE CLASSES TAKEN?

It depends. DE classes are found in many colleges and high school, even online. The official explanation says that dual credit classes may be offered in any of three ways: Singleton, Comprehensive, or Enhanced. These terms are rarely used outside of industry but it is worth taking some time to explore the differences between them.

With singleton, high schoolers take classes on a college campus alongside other regular college students following a regular college schedule. Not all students are mature enough for this but then again, social life at a high school can be brutal. Singleton works well if the campus is safe and large enough to have great teacher options.

Comprehensive is where the DE classes are taught by specially trained high school teachers within the high school setting just like regular high school classes. This form of DE does not have good outcomes, probably because such classes just feel like more high school. However, in some cases, DE at the high school is the only option.

For students attending charters, magnets, STEM, or tech prep academies, DE programs are called enhanced. This option may allow students the opportunity to take specialty courses or even lead to vocational certifications such as in IT, auto repair, programming, and allied health. This route is ideal for students needing or wanting early college combined with hands-on or vocational training. This option is not widely available but as parents ask for them, enhanced programs will grow.

In public and private schools, students are rarely directed to DE because AP courses earn schools a lot more money so smart students are usually pushed into AP instead of DE. Some counselors even suggest DE is inferior to AP, making students shy away. Universities and community colleges are now starting to make money off DE and the pendulum is swinging back the other way. But these On Ramps, Early College, and Collegiate High Schools are not actually Dual Enrollment (no matter what the literature says) so beware!

## HOW MUCH WILL IT COST?

Much less than the same college credits taken at a university after high school graduation! Universities are increasingly expensive. Annual increases of 3-5% are now the norm, with the cheapest four year colleges costing $20,000 per year! By comparison, dual credit is considerably cheaper, though prices vary. Costs can range from regular junior college tuition of less than $300 per class to completely free.

Many communities have bond fed programs that not only cover the cost of tuition and fees but in some cases even books and computers are available at a reduced cost. Such communities often have online programs that are available to students outside of the district or state. For students who prefer online classes, these options can be extremely low or no cost. With a laptop and a good WiFi connection, dual enrollment is available to students around the globe. To ensure that the credits transfer to a university after high school graduation, always look for programs that are FULLY accredited.

## WILL THE CREDITS TRANSFER?

Almost always, but it depends on what classes are taken. In America, colleges use course numbering systems. Not all colleges use the same system so they provide equivalency guides to help students compare classes from two different colleges. If you know what college you are likely to transfer to, then get their equivalency guide and use it to pick DE classes that will definitely transfer. Regardless of a matching course number, there are several courses that are required by nearly all universities for nearly all majors. These are referred to as Common Core. Advisers just call them the CORE. If a student takes classes that are considered part of the CORE (explored later), then those classes will transfer. With one exception.

About 20% or so of universities and colleges have specialized curriculums. These are typically, small, private, liberal arts or religious colleges, but a few are well-known, selective universities that do not want a student to take classes anywhere else. Such colleges will <u>not</u> automatically transfer DE credits even if they are CORE. When this happens, a simple one-page petition usually resolves the issue. If the class has a common course number (CCN), transferability is automatic. When there is no CCN then colleges look at the name of the class and credit it accordingly. When a class does not transfer or get properly applied towards a chosen major, the petition process will remedy the problem if done in a timely fashion. Sadly, few people know about or understand the role of petitions. They are important!

## WHAT ABOUT FRESHMAN STATUS?

If you understand the rules and follow them then you will NOT lose your freshman status. Why? Because students in dual enrollment are not college students. They are high school students who just happen to be taking college level courses. For this reason, no matter how many classes they take in DE, they can not lose their freshman status. This is called the Dual Enrollment Loophole. Like most loopholes, there is a flip side. Some of the top 100 colleges in the U.S. will not accept DE credits that were taken on a high school campus. Their logic is that such classes were taught by teachers instead of professors and were thus geared towards high school pupils instead of college students. Fortunately, few universities take advantage of this loophole and it does not apply to DE classes taken on an actual junior college campus.

*No matter how many hours a student completes in DE, he will still be eligible to apply to any college as a freshman applicant as long as no courses are taken outside the umbrella of dual enrollment.*

Of course, not all students will benefit from applying as a freshman applicant. In fact, less than 20% of high school graduates will ever benefit from applying to college as a freshman. The math is very simple. Freshman status is only of value to students who are candidates for freshman financial aid. This is a small and dwindling pool of students.

Most incoming college freshmen do not have either the tests scores or the extracurriculars record that they will need to earn either primary or secondary scholarships. For such students, the goal is just to get in. And getting in, as we have already established, is actually pretty easy, depending on the selectivity rating of the college one is trying to get into.

If they have a great GPA in their dual credit classes, many students may actually be better off applying as a transfer student, in terms of both admissions and money. Transfer students with enough hours and a good GPA are guaranteed admission to many colleges that would be impossible to get into otherwise. At many of these colleges, honors transfer students will receive a nice amount of merit-based financial aid based on their DE record at junior college. Best of all, standardized testing is not required for transfer students with more than 29 credits.

For those few graduating seniors who have managed to attain great tests scores and plan to apply to a university as a freshman, DE credits will not interfere with the plan. Just stay under the DE umbrella and keep your GPA up.

## ARE THERE ANY DOWNSIDES?

Yes. Like with all things, there are ways for dual credit to be misused. The good news is that the potential downsides to dual credit are completely avoidable. First, let me reiterate the upsides.

Students will save time by not having to take classes in high school and then again in college. They will also save money since DE classes are a fraction of the cost of regular college courses. They save themselves from emotional distress, as students feel motivated when they see that the light at the end of the tunnel is closer than they previously thought. For students stressed by the pressures of high school, DE is a life saver.

The first downside is the most serious. Since DE is real college, the student will get a real college transcript. This is a powerful document that will affect future admissions and financial aid. It can also affect what majors a student is allowed into as well as what honors can be earned at college. Unlike a high school transcript, the college transcript cannot be altered under almost any circumstance. Clearly, a college GPA should be taken very serious since it is permanent and can be potentially damaging in often unforeseen and far reaching ways. Even some employers consider GPA when deciding on potential hires.

A second downside has to do with self-esteem. If a student jumps into dual enrollment unprepared, gets a bad teacher and bombs a class, it may scare him away from pursuing a college degree and his transcript will be a permanent reminder of that failure. I have seen more than one student go down this path so I feel it only fair to make note of it. My counter argument to this would be a reminder of the current college graduation rate. The typical student goes off to a university immediately after high school, where he experiences the exact scenario I just described. Only, that student is paying a lot more for the privilege. The bottom line is that all college is serious business and should be treated with caution and excellent planning. Starting out slow with dual credit is an excellent way to do both.

*By spending some time in dual credit,*
*a pupil will gain an exposure to the*
*expectations of college level courses,*
*learn to optimize resources such as*
*great teachers and free on-campus tutoring,*
*and begin to master a*
*post high school environment.*
*Plus, they will revel in the efficiency of*
*taking one class for both*
*high school and college credit.*

If a student is at high risk for failure, I believe he will be better off in the safer environment of DE where the teachers actually invest time in their students rather than the less flexible university setting. At many universities, the classroom instructors are often Teaching Assistants (TAs) to tenured professors, who may see classes and students as little more than a means to funding their research. Having patient, invested teachers is critical to a student making a successful transition from high school to university. If it is true that three out of every four high school graduates will struggle at college, then taking one or two classes a semester in DE makes a lot more sense than jumping into a full course load of six university classes the first year out of high school. From a pure fiscal perspective, if the university failure rate is so high, then why take on the massive debt of a university when dual credit offers a college experience at a fraction of the price?

Studies have shown that dual enrollment significantly increases high school graduation rates. [3] This is great news if you are an educator who has committed your life to helping students succeed. Student polls indicate that 94% of DE students believe that having the opportunity to better prepare for the rigors of university and exploring the college environment before being propelled directly into it, had a direct impact on their success at college. [3] Improved college graduation rates is also great news if you are the parent of a graduating high schooler headed off to an expensive university. I think we can all agree that getting into college is good but graduating is what really matters. Starting out slowly via a dual credit program can dramatically improve a student's chances of being successful at university.

# 6☞

# IS DUAL ENROLLMENT

## The Right Choice?

It's pretty safe to say that nearly every high school student could benefit from an exposure to college level courses before they make the massive non-refundable investment that is today's university experience. But since I'm taking the time to write an entire book, and you are taking the time to read it, I will be a bit more specific.

Having shepherded uncountable high schoolers through the dual credit program, I can honestly say that every one of them benefited in some notable manner. Yet, I must confess that I do not always recommend dual enrollment for every student I counsel. The reason is simple. When I am advising families one-on-one, my process requires me to take a great deal of time to get to know each student's personality, learning style, aptitudes, career goals, and family dynamic. With this information and many years of experience, I set out to build a highly personalized educational strategy that lays out the optimal academic blueprint for each student to follow to college success.

For most students, dual enrollment is a key part of that strategy but sometimes there are better options for a particular student's situation. Since there are a few instances where dual enrollment is not optimal, let's just address these important exceptions right off the bat.

By definition, most students are average in terms of their odds of getting in and doing well at college. But there are extremes on both ends, the perfect students and the not so perfect students. When students apply to colleges, they will be judged heavily on their test scores. Both admission and financial aid will be contingent upon little more than the high school GPA and a couple of standardized tests. Good testers will have a major advantage. The best testers will have an exceptional edge. On the other end of the spectrum, poor testers will get the short end of the stick in terms of getting into top colleges and earning scholarships. For this reason, the absolute best students and the absolute worst students are not usually ideal candidates for DE. Let me define the "absolute best students".

## PERFECT STUDENTS

Most high school students today will take the PSAT in $10^{th}$ or $11^{th}$ grade with the goal of breaking through the 200- point ceiling that will potentially qualify them to become National Merit Scholars. Such students receive maximum consideration from college admission officers. Along with top scores on the SAT or ACT, and a trio of AP tests, these top students are often recipients of the very best academic merit aid available. This money is never loan based and is always given in significant amounts. While the National Merit windfall is not what it used to be, there are still many great universities and colleges that give full-rides to National Merit winners. In my experience, if a student is extremely likely to earn 80-100% in merit-based aid, such as with National Merit, then dual credit may be a misuse of resources, especially time.

Making top scores on standardized tests takes massive amounts of prep. Any hopeful National Merit Scholar will need every second of their valuable time for PSAT prep, SAT II Subject Tests, and SAT/ACT, especially in 11th grade. For top-of-the-line testers, dual enrollment, even if free, is not a good tradeoff, as DE takes time. Time is at a premium for high schoolers and should be reserved for test prep if tests are going to be your ticket to aid. Unfortunately, only a tiny percentage of students will even get close to being a National Merit Finalist.

*Of the 1.5 million students who take the PSAT in their junior year of high school, only 15,000 will receive an accommodation and less than 7,500 will win!* [1]

If only 1% of the students who take the PSAT in 11th grade are going to receive any degree of recognition, then 99% of students are not served by the time and money spent on PSAT prep. The facts are well documented and brutal. Most students are not going to get into college or get it paid for by way of their PSAT and the National Merit Scholarship Program. The odds are sort of like winning a lottery. For the typical student, it does not make sense to throw away a sure thing like dual enrollment for a massive long-shot like National Merit.

*The majority of students would do better to focus their time and money on completing college credits via dual enrollment or taking AP tests to shore up their College Package instead of spending hundreds of dollars and hours on prepping for PSAT & NMS.*

## NOT SO PERFECT STUDENTS

There is another group of students who are also not ideal candidates for dual enrollment -- The Problem Child. If a student has a bad attitude or is such a behavioral problem that he gets kicked out of one high school after another, then sending him to an early college program will not solve the problem. If a student is failing classes, earning repeated detention, or causing a commotion at home, then there is a problem. That problem should be dealt with before risking the post high school GPA by taking courses at a college or university.

When a student acts out, school is a common culprit. Crisis at home is another familiar cause. Such problems are not corrected by jumping into college level courses (or AP classes). They are actually likely to worsen. Regardless of the underlying cause, if a student has a bad attitude, exhibits overt and inappropriate behaviors, or is demonstrating severe stress or emotional strain, then professional help should be sought before any major educational change is initiated. Dual credit would not be appropriate for such students until the underlying problem is successfully addressed.

## IN BETWEEN STUDENTS

### (aka Everyone Else)

When I tell parents and educators that nearly all students should participate in dual enrollment, I get a chorus of excuses for why they plan to wait till university to take college level classes. The most common pretexts are familiar. Many parents fear, *"My kid is not disciplined enough."* Homeschoolers often believe, *"She is too far behind in math."* or *"We don't have time."* Private schoolers fall back on, *"Our school doesn't have a program like this."* or *"He's just not motivated to do school, period."*

These are all very good reasons why a family might benefit from some extremely good academic advising and maybe even professional counseling. But these are not good arguments for not taking advantage of Dual Enrollment. Just because we get off course doesn't mean we stay off course. Dual credit is a great tool for getting back on track. In fact, DE is my go to tool for helping kids who have lost all motivation.

DE is relatively cheap, easier than AP, more meaningful to the student and less time consuming than high school, and the payoff is substantially better in nearly all aspects. The only question is, is the student ready for college level courses?

As I mentioned earlier, there are only three suggested requirements for starting dual enrollment. The ideal DE student is sixteen years of age. He has completed an approved tenth grade curriculum. And he has passed an accepted college placement test such as the College Board's Accuplacer or has a comparable score on an SAT, ACT, or PSAT. If a student can meet these minimum requirements, then he is definitely ready for DE. However, even younger students may be eligible as the rules on age and grade are enforced with less and less frequency.

## AGE

Initial official mandates required that students be 15-16 years of age before they could begin taking dual enrollment classes. This was a good cutoff given that the average college student is 18-24. It would seem rather inappropriate to have 12 year olds thrown in to such a group. This age test was highly enforced for decades but as DE students have begun to out perform regular high school students, districts and states have become more open to expanding the dual credit opportunity to younger students. Today there is an unspoken rule that if a student can pass the required placement test, then he can start dual enrollment. By the beginning of the 2016-17 school year, several state legislatures had passed provisions that mandate younger student be accepted into dual credit programs as long as they are in high school and have passed an acceptable placement.

## GRADE

Dual enrollment began at junior colleges. Since there are only two years of courses available at a junior college, only two years of high school can be "traded-in" via dual credit. For this reason, dual credit is ideal for students in 11th and 12th grades. Starting in 2015, laws began changing to allow younger students admission to dual credit as long as they are provably ready for college level academics. In some states, students as young as 9th grade can already take advantage of dual credit as long as they can pass the placement test. Such laws are extremely new but seem to be the wave of the future.

For now, most programs still require that students be finished with 10th grade in order to start DE. This is reasonable. But it is also an easy restriction to overcome as parents can opt to promote their child to a higher (or lower) grade using high school placement tests like Credit By Exam (CBE). These are comprehensive, individual subject tests that are very difficult to pass but when completed they can prove grade level. It is even easier for a homeschool parent who can simply create a homeschool transcript that says the student is in a certain grade.

While these options are legitimate, they should be avoided unless there is an acceptable placement test to prove the student is ready for dual credit. One would never want to accelerate a student into a college curricula if there is not clear evidence that the student is ready. The best proof is an official placement test. Passing a placement test is exactly the proof that any parent or college should require before letting a student into dual credit.

*Regardless of age or grade in school, if a student can pass the required placement test, then he or she can start DE!*

## PLACEMENT TESTS

As we have just discussed, the best proof that a student is ready for dual enrollment classes is for the student to take and pass all three sections of an official college placement test. Since these tests were specifically created to determine college readiness, and dual enrollment is college, the reasoning makes sense. If a student can pass an official college placement test then he or she is academically ready for college courses even if he is still in high school, under aged, not done with Algebra, or has a learning difference! I feel compelled to add a caveat here.

Not surprisingly, there are those exceptional students who may be intellectually and academically capable of passing a placement test well before they are emotionally ready for a college lifestyle. A child may be an absolute genius but I am never in favor of pushing these younger students into college. Even though they are academically excelled, they are still socially too young to fit seamlessly into a typical college culture. The effects may not be immediate but they will be long lasting.

Younger students may find that both teachers and other students will not always be completely accepting. Such an environment can be unhealthy to the developing psyche. I personally recommend to parents to avoid dual enrollment or early university admissions for all students under fourteen years of age regardless of their academic prowess or seeming social maturity. Psychologically, kids need time to be kids. If they are gifted at twelve, they will only become more brilliant with time. Give them some time to grow. Allow their social skill set to catch up to their intellect. Being precocious is not a valid rational for starting DE. On the other hand, being under the fifteen year cut off should not be an automatic reason not to do dual credit.

Sometimes the question of when to start dual enrollment is not about the child. Mom & Dad are often not ready for their child to go out into the mainstream academic world and be judged. This is especially true for homeschool parents like me who take great pride in the duty of educating our kids but often feel uncertain as to our ability to do so. This is a real fear that keeps some homeschoolers from taking advantage of great options like therapeutic tutoring and dual credit.

As the principal of a private high school, and a homeschool parent myself, I understand the hesitation. But just like with students in public school, homeschoolers come in all shapes and sizes. And just like with public school students, not all homeschoolers are academically successful. But unlike public school students, homeschoolers are likely to be heavily scrutinized by college admission's personnel just because they are different. This is a reality. My best rebuttal to such concerns is don't give it a second thought. You can't possibly do worse than the current public schools! Just going with the averages and ignoring the perhaps sensationalized tragedies, the public school system has not produced good outcomes.

*Look around. In the most expensive public school system in the world, only 36% of student read at or above $8^{th}$ grade level, less than 40% have math proficiency, and nearly 30% drop out without graduating.* [2,3] *How much worse could a homeschooler do?*

## CURRICULUM

When I lecture to homeschool communities, many parents express a concern that their child is not a good candidate for DE because they did not follow a state prescribed curriculum of classes especially in regards to science and math. Instead of a traditional science sequence of Biology, Chemistry, and Physics, they may have focused on hands-on labs or a hodge-podge of science topics in no particular order. While their public school counterparts were learning history over a four year sequence starting with ancient and ending in the modern world, the homeschooled child may have been exploring the ancient Roman and Greek cultures by dressing up and recreating the first Olympics or following in the footsteps of Columbus, literally. My own family has many fond memories of such learning directed adventures in history and science. I would argue that this difference in prior curriculum is a mute point since hands-on learning creates better critical thinking than text-based curriculums and homeschoolers, not surprisingly, have a higher than average pass rate on typical college placement test. So keep using those alternative curriculums and turning out amazing kids!

Math is a different matter. While math should start out with interactive and tactile elements to foster understanding, true math mastery requires discipline and repetition, two things that are no longer in vogue. Most students simply are not ready for college math. Despite this fact, if a student can pass an official math placement test then he is ready for a DE college level math course no matter what his math background is. How can I say this? Because it's true. Consider this.

The average student at any public, private, charter, or magnet school has used a curriculum that has been approved by PhD'd experts as top-of-the-line. Students used this "proven" curriculum for twelve consecutive years, day in and day out. Additionally, they had the benefit of professional instruction via a certified school teacher with a college degree in math.

Clearly, such students have had the gold standard in education, yet according to the official Nation's Report Card, *"Only 26% of 12th grade students scored at or above the proficient level on the National Assessment of Educational Progress's (NAEP) math assessment."* [4]

*That means that barely 1 in 4 students who have "benefited" from a dozen years of professional math instruction and top-notch curriculum can demonstrate readiness for college level math!*[4]

Think about this for just a moment. If the professionals only have a 26% success rate, I think it is safe to surmise that as a homeschool parent or tutor, customizing each student's curriculum to fit his or her needs, and providing nearly one-on-one instruction year after year, then you my friend could not possibly do any worse than the gold standard!

**If an official placement test says that your student is ready for dual credit classes, then do not let any perceived gaps in the curriculum hold him back.**

## EDUCATIONAL BACKGROUND

There is no curriculum or age that assures a student is ready for dual enrollment. Overall, a successful DE candidate should have a normal IQ and demonstrate readiness in certain core subjects. Studies have repeatedly shown that to have a fair shot at college level success, students must have the following skills. Proven mastery of reading comprehension. The ability to write for effect. A comfortable relationship with mathematical concepts through Algebra. And critical thinking skills -- especially those needed for test taking and problem solving.

Reading comprehension is not only reading at a normal speed and being able to understand the actual words that are being read, but being able to fully comprehend the message that the author intends. Students without this skill are at a disadvantage, both in college and in life. Lack of mastery here is much more than just a reading problem, it is a lack of understanding. Long term, such students will have major issues with communications which will often affect interpersonal relationships and career success.

Writing a good paragraph is another skill that will be very useful for students in dual credit classes, which is why essay writing is part of every placement test. Paragraphs are made up of a series of related sentences. Put four to five grammatically correct sentences together in a logical progression and you have not only an effective paragraph, but you also have the basis for every text, email, and official correspondence you are likely to ever send or receive. Essays are often the focus of writing in high school but essays are nothing more than a series of paragraphs, so mastery at the paragraph level is the real goal.

Ironically, having a strong preparatory background in math is not necessary for DE success, as is evidenced by the high number of high school graduates who are not on level in math. But math mastery will make the process easier. That being said, I can assure you that mastery of consumer level mathematics especially as relates to business, purchasing, and legal transactions will be critical in life and will support the type of critical thinking that is more important to math success than either advanced algebra, trigonometry, or pre-calculus.

Critical thinking is the fourth must-have for academic readiness. Any motivated student with a strong work ethic, solid critical thinking, and a reasonable IQ will not only do well in a dual enrollment program but is likely to be a good test taker, which bodes well for college success and financial aid.

Through home school cooperatives and private charter schools, I have been fortunate to teach, counsel, and shepherd hundreds of children through the school process. I have been allowed to research, develop, and test my own custom lesson plans for students of all ages and grades, in subjects ranging from science to math remediation to college test prep to reading & spelling for students with documented learning disorders. I cannot say that I am a curriculum expert. But I will say that I know what produces good outcomes and what does not.

Good outcomes come from using what consistently engages the student. Learning starts with engagement, followed by input, discussion, feedback, then usage, and more feedback. It is this interactive process that produces understanding and retention. Learning comes from novel input combined with immediate feedback so that the brain can properly encode what it is taking in. That feedback doesn't have to be delivered by a professional. It has to be consistent and immediate and non threatening. An education does not come from books and lectures. An education comes from an accumulation, not of information, but of experiences. Learning is being able to fully assimilate those experiences into memories and then weave them together with all the other experiences and memories you have tucked away. Mastery is being able to express those experiences to others. The secret to mastery, and thus learning, is to limit the curriculum to the basics. Minimize homework & lectures. Instead, create space for the student to explore, experience, discuss, and interact with what his mind naturally seeks. Knowledge isn't given by a teacher, it is taken by a learner.

*If a student can demonstrably*

READ

*at an 8th grade level or higher,*

UNDERSTAND

*what is being read,*

WRITE

*a solid, grammatically correct paragraph*

*to explain what was read or heard,*

CRITICALLY ANALYZE

*information for both context and nuances,*

*and demonstrate*

CONSISTENT UNDERSTANDING OF ALGEBRAIC CONCEPTS

*then that student is head and shoulders above*

*most of his peers*

*and is a solid contender for college*

*and the dual enrollment program.*

# INTELLECT

Dual credit is not just for the "smart kids". I have seen numerous students with various documented learning differences (LD) who have completed 30, 40, even 60 plus hours of college credit via DE with success equal to non-LD students. A learning difference is not only NOT a reason to avoid dual enrollment, I believe that DE is the optimal solution for high functioning teens with learning delays such as dyslexia, dysgraphia, processing disorders, attention deficit & lack of sustained focus, or even autism spectrum labels.

In my consulting practice, a good number of students have come to me with diagnoses of Autism Spectrum Disorder or severe Auditory Processing Disorder. With my guidance, these students have managed to complete high school via dual credit. No special classes were taken. These were students who often came from specialized high schools where they were receiving extensive accommodations, and barely passing. But in dual enrollment, they were treated just like every other college student and they thrived. We obviously did not cure their disorder. So, what changed that allowed them to succeed at college level work given their previous struggles in special education high school classes? We customized! For students with any type of learning difference or delay, I always add two components to their college regiment both at the dual credit/junior college level and while they are away at university.

1. **I utilize private therapeutic tutoring on a very liberal basis (2-3 x/wk). And...**

2. **I insist on daily or weekly oversight by a learning partner or Professional Shadow.**

The single major difference between my students with learning issues and the rest of my clients is that the LD students are in great need of help with time management and understanding what is expected of them. This is a service easily provided by a parent but I rely heavily on custom-trained tutors that I call SHADOWS. Through a careful selection process, my staff screens local tutors to find people who are capable of forming positive and trusting relationships with our students. We then train that tutor to shadow our clients through their school week. In the beginning a student might need daily shadowing but very quickly students begin to develop their own sense of rhythm and check-ins are cut to just a few times per month.

If considering dual enrollment for a student who also happens to have some learning considerations, then please don't assume that they cannot or should not do dual credit. Most students with learning differences have normal to above average IQs and are surprisingly capable when out in the real world. It is just the emotionally tumultuous and artificially constructed world of middle and high school where they tend to struggle most. Provide them with the accommodations and assistance they need and they will rise to the challenge. And they will revel in the honor of being treated like a real college student.

Thompson G. was a 17 year old ninth grader at arguably one of the finest schools of it kind, a private institute specializing in students with Autism. He was notably attentionally deficit but he was also very earnest and eager to succeed. His school had held him back once before and was now poised to do so again. Mom opted out and brought him to my office. After less than a semester of private therapeutic tutoring directed at time management, cooperative learning, and reading and writing prep for the DE placement test, Thompson was admitted to the dual credit program at a local university. His two tutors met with him three times per week during his first summer semester course. They spoke by phone daily. By fall, they were able to reduce their sessions to twice per week. By spring, Thompson was using Google calendar with text notifications to manage two classes with weekly check-ins from his adult shadows. Eventually, he only used his tutors to prepare for tests in his most difficult subjects. Assignments were turned in on time and grades were consistently A/B. Thompson completed an Associates Degree in DE before going off to Wake Forest University on a merit based scholarship.

The benefits of dual enrollment are clear and quantifiable. For most students, dual enrollment is a provable win-win scenario. Students win by not having to repeat high school classes once they go off to college. Parents win by getting the first year or two of college at a massive discount. In the case of not-so-perfect students, there is the added bonus of recapturing their verve for life and learning, which is a win for society as a whole. And obviously, the family wins by having a happy, productive member in their midst.

Correction, that makes dual enrollment a win, win, win . . . win!

# 7☞

# GETTING STARTED

## What To Do Now

By now it is clear that dual enrollment is a one-of-a-kind program that should be a part of most students' high school to college plan. Fortunately, it is also a relatively easy resource to take advantage of. Superficially, getting started in dual credit is as easy as one, two, three.

### Starting Dual Enrollment

1. *Complete an application.*
2. *Pass an official placement test.*
3. *Pick classes and enroll.*

*That's it!*

Three relatively quick and easy steps is all that it takes for a student to begin college level classes while still in high school. But these steps are easier at some colleges than at others.

Before starting dual enrollment, a decision has to be made about where to enroll. If the student is in public school then there is really no decision. All arrangements will be made through the school counselor. For private or homeschool students, the parent can go straight to the junior college to kick things off. It will be necessary to do a bit of research about the options both online and in the immediate area before deciding where to apply. Then a few months before the start of a semester, an application should be completed for admission to which ever college was chosen. Once admitted to the college, the student must take and pass an approved college placement test. At that point, official enrollment in classes can begin. Before rushing off to the nearest community college and signing up there are two things that must be clearly understood.

**First, although dual credit is a nationwide endeavor, it is locally administered.** DE is offered at most junior colleges, some universities, and many public, private, charter, and independent schools, as well as some homeschool cooperatives. Each of these will handle things according to their own design. Each student's experience with dual enrollment will be unique to the school or college providing the service. The information provided here is a good guide for newbies but ultimately the administrator at the local DE campus should be the go-to resource as they will have the final word on how the program is governed at their school.

**Second, students can only take in dual enrollment what they have remaining on their high school degree plan.**

This is what we call the CARDINAL RULE. The degree plan is an official list of all the classes a high school student must complete in order to graduate. When starting dual enrollment, students are required to turn in a copy of their official high school transcript. Transcripts are serious documents that once filed, represent a legal record of the student's school progress. This document will show which degree plan is being followed and what classes have been completed up to that point. By having a transcript on file, a college DE officer knows exactly what is remaining on a student's high school degree plan and thus what is needed in order to graduate. The dual credit office is allowed, even obligated in most cases, to limit the classes taken in dual credit to whatever classes are still remaining on the high school degree plan. This core tenant of dual enrollment is worth repeating.

*One may only take in dual enrollment what*
*one has not already taken*
*in high school.*

Dual enrollment students are high school students. They are under the authority of a school district and/or state education agency. These groups may seem all knowing but they are not. They are often overburdened and underfinanced. Even in the best of cases, they are limited by a set of rules put forth by policy makers who are out of touch with the day to day processes. It is important for the parent to remember that they have implicit rights. But these rights often have to be extracted with patience and calm communication. Understanding this before getting started will make customizing more efficient and help the entire process go smoother. One of the main rights a parent has is to have input in regards to their student's transcript and degree plan. Both of these documents will directly affect what classes a student can take both in high school and in dual enrollment. If these documents are prepared appropriately then dual enrollment can be better customized for the student.

## STEP 1

### Complete An Application

The first official step in starting dual enrollment is to complete an application for the program. Before doing this, students and their parents will need to do a bit of research in order to find out what is available in the area. If a town has a junior or community college, there is a high likelihood it will have a full blown DE program. However, don't overlook private colleges and public universities as they often offer dual credit courses even if they do not always have the most choices in terms of teacher and class selection.

Public schools and homeschool groups may offer DE classes but there will be serious limitations in terms of availability and cost. If there is not a local option for dual credit, then consider enrolling in one of the hundreds of accredited online dual credit programs hosted by major colleges and universities throughout the country. A quick Google search should produce a list of both local and national programs that might be a good option for any particular situation. Some of these programs are even free. Since the majority of DE classes are taken via junior colleges, I will explain the process of applying, placement, picking courses, selecting the best teachers, and transcripting grades from the perspective of a junior college.

Starting dual credit begins with a call or visit to the dual enrollment office. That office can make arrangements for the official paperwork that will need to be completed in order to start the enrollment process. The first form required is a college application. The dual credit application looks just like any other college application and is often available online.

Unlike admission for regular college students, there is no competitive element to dual credit admissions. If a student meets the general DE admission requirements, then he will get in. Those requirements will vary from college to college but always involve proving that the student is academically ready for college level courses. Many colleges will ask applicants to meet a two-fold prerequisite.

*The main requirements*

*for admission to*

*Dual Enrollment*

*are a high school transcript*

*and*

*the passing of a placement test.*

A candidate must present an official transcript. If applicable, this document should indicate that the student has completed or is in progress to complete tenth grade. Public, private, and charter schools can readily provide this document.

However, homeschoolers will need to create their own high school transcript. For parents who have never created a transcript before, consider getting a template off the internet.

On page 275, I have provided a sample high school transcript that includes all the important components of an official transcript. This is a good place to start. Chapter 18 provides a detailed description on how to revise a student's high school transcript to properly reflect credits received in dual enrollment. This will become critically important as you start to optimize high school for college admissions.

Transcripts are official documents and as such they can be painfully complicated. For now, suffice it to say, that any transcript presented for DE admissions should look official, be notarized, and clearly indicate what classes have been completed up to that point. The transcript will be submitted at the same time as the application. Once the application is submitted and reviewed, an identification number will be issued and the student will have completed his first step towards starting college classes while still in high school.

## STEP 2

### Pass A Test

After completing the application and getting officially admitted to the college, candidates will have to prove that they are ready to perform college level academics via a standardized placement or admission test. Each college district determines which test or tests they will accept for placement purposes. It really does not matter which test is required as they are very similar to each other and prepping for one will generally work well for all of them.

While prep is not mandatory, many students benefit from the confidence that a few weeks of directed preparation will provide them. A quick visit to an online book seller will produce a long list of current and appropriate prep books for any test a college requires. Better yet, ask the school for a prep guide to their specific test. They may even be able to provide a practice test that the student can use to become familiar with the format and timing of the actual test that the student will be asked to take for placement. Always get informed before acting.

Placement tests are usually available at the college itself on a near daily schedule. They are often free but may cost as much as $30. It will be necessary to contact the DE office or testing center at the college where testing will take place to schedule a date and time to take the test. Appointments are often required. At the testing appointment, the student will need to produce a picture ID and complete the test in private. Testing can require upwards of 4-5 hours since the test does not usually start immediately upon arrival. A well prepared tester will have some type of snack, as well as water, on hand when arriving for the test. While eating during the test is forbidden, going into the test will a full stomach is a great idea. Once the test ends, results will either be given immediately by the testing clerk or scores will be emailed to the student within a few days. If the score is considered "passing" then the student will be allowed to immediately register for classes.

Not all students will need to take the official placement test in order to start dual enrollment as there are a number of standardized tests that can be used for placement. Colleges will often accept a high scoring SAT, ACT, or PSAT in lieu of their official in-house placement test. Even high school exit exams are accepted by some colleges.

Exit exams are grade-based comprehensive tests that many state education agencies require their high school students to take at the end of a school year in order to advance to the next level. These tests are often known by acronyms such as HSPE, STAAR, TAKS, IOWA, DAPE, or TSI. If a student has scores for such a test on file and the scores are high enough, the DE officer may accept them for placement purposes. Once it is clear which tests are acceptable, there is no reason to hesitate. Just do a bit of preparation and jump right in. Placement tests can usually be taken multiple times without penalty so there is no reason not to give it a try to find out if a student is ready to proceed with dual credit courses.

A placement test has at least three sections, often titled reading, math, and writing. Although the test is given as a whole, these sections are generally treated as three separate tests. This means that once a single section, such as math, is passed then that section will never need to be taken again even if other sections remain to be passed. A tester can simply go back and attempt non-passed sections again and again until he is "placement complete."

That being said, if a student fails a section twice, despite appropriate preparation, then he is probably not ready for college level courses. Indeed, such a student should likely be assessed for a learning delay or difference.

While placement tests are comparatively short, cheap, and easy to prep for, most students do not pass all three sections the first time around. This is why there is no longer a penalty for repeated attempts. Pupils should never be made to feel badly if they do not pass their placement test on the first try. Failure is a useful part of life. Feedback from failed attempts can tell an advisor exactly what the problems are. Understanding the problem goes a long way towards finding a solution. Take a placement test and trust it to decide if the student is ready.

## STEP 3

### Pick Classes & Enroll

Now that the application process is complete and a placement test is on file, the student is almost home free. The last step is to pick the classes that he wants to take in a given semester and complete the process of course enrollment.

All colleges have a list of the courses available each semester. This list used to be printed in a catalog but technology has changed things considerably. Nearly all colleges now use an online course schedule that can be found on their official website or by way of a link that can be requested via email from the school's administration. The course schedule will list the name of the class, an identifying letter and number code, the name of the teacher, the days of the week the class will meet, the hour that the class will meet, and the specific location where the class will meet. It will also show if a class is open to enrollment or not. With this information, students can choose their classes.

Once classes have been chosen, the next step is to make it official by completing and turning in an enrollment form. The enrollment form is usually available only from a DE officer, but in some cases it can be found on the college's website. This form must be filled out with the student's name and identification number as well as specific identifying information for the classes to be taken. Both the student and the high school principal or homeschool parent will be required to sign the enrollment form, as well as an admissions officer. Since classes fill up quickly and close with near lightening speed, it is best to handle class enrollment in person at either the college campus or the high school counselor's office. That way, alternative classes can be quickly substituted in the common event of a preferred class being closed.

With the application complete, a placement test passed, and enrollment form submitted, our high school student is officially ready to start taking college classes. While the processes is usually fairly straightforward, these three simple steps can sometimes get complicated. That is part of dealing with a bureaucratic system. The best defense against setbacks is knowledge. Get informed before you start then be prepared for a small setback or two. The application process is straightforward, but placement testing and picking the right classes with the right teachers deserves a bit more discussion.

8☞

# PLACEMENT TESTING

## To Prove Readiness

As we have already established, before starting dual enrollment, it is necessary to prove that the student is ready to succeed at college level course work. Such proof is as much for the student, parent, and high school as it is for the admitting dual enrollment college. For dual credit purposes, proof of academic readiness involves placement testing to determine what level of math, science, reading, and writing, a student should be placed in. Placement tests are not about passing or failing, but rather about making sure the student ends up in the right level of a class.

*You do not "pass" or "fail" a placement test. It just confirms where you are in reading, writing, or math right now!*

Placement is not a universal exam. There are at least three major tests that are used throughout the country for placement.

Additionally, there are several standardized tests that can serve the purpose of placement. Each college determines which ones it will accept and what scores are required in order to be deemed "College Ready".

Since students take a lot of tests during their high school years, and no one wants to make them take any more than are absolutely necessary, it is always advisable to ask the admitting DE program for a complete list of acceptable alternative placement tests. With any luck, the student has already taken a test that can be used for placement and no additional testing will be required.

If taking an approved state placement exam is required, it is important to develop some familiarity with it. The best known placement tests are the Accuplacer and Compass. These tests have formats similar to their even better known cousin, the Preliminary Scholastic Assessment Test or PSAT. While we are on the subject of PSAT, you should know that a good PSAT score can often be used for placement purposes, but of course it is at the discretion of the admitting college. The same is true for the SAT, originally known as the Scholastic Aptitude Test, and the ACT (American College Test).

Just to be prudent, if a student has any standardized test score on file by the end of 10th grade, it would be expedient to speak to someone at the DE college about using that test for placement and possibly avoiding having to take yet another multiple choice, section based standardized test. But remember that the scores will need to meet some serious cutoffs for them to matter. For most students, their PSAT, SAT, or ACT scores will not be high enough to place them into dual credit and they will need to take one of the approved state placement tests.

By far, the most common placement tests used today are produced by the College Board, makers of the SAT, PSAT, SAT II, and AP tests. Their mainstay is the Accuplacer, which according to their website is used by over 1,500 institutions and is designed to test overall understanding in math, reading, and writing. The Accuplacer has been around for many years and has a reputation for being difficult, especially on the math section. Recently, the College Board created a version specifically for Texas that is essentially a reworked Accuplacer. It is called the Texas State Initiative (TSI). These two tests are nearly identical with the latter having higher pass rates on the essay and math sections. The Compass is another well known placement test. It is put out by the makers of the ACT. It is nearly indistinguishable from the TSI or Accuplacer, yet it is notably more passable.

## PLACEMENT vs. STANDARDIZED

If you have never seen one of these test, they are not unlike the SAT, in that they have three sections of reading, writing, and math, as well as an essay component. The major difference between placement tests and the SAT or ACT is that placement tests tend to be computer adaptive tests (CAT). CATs are computer based tests that only show one question at a time and do not offer the option to go backwards. This is important since a common test taking strategy for the SAT is to skip questions that seem hard and come back to them later, as time allows. This approach works well on the SAT where there is a benefit to seeking out and answering the easy questions first since they are worth the same amount of points as the harder questions. On a CAT, however, a tester will need to answer each question presented before moving forward or he will not get credit for that question. There is no skipping of questions on a CAT. Every question gets answered as it is asked and before the tester can progress to the next question.

Placement tests are also different than the SAT as relates to the famous 'guessing penalty' that can be incurred. Historically, on the SAT, when a student guessed and got the answer wrong, a quarter of a point was deducted from the score. Placement tests do not share this scoring characteristic. Getting an answer wrong on a placement test usually does not generate any point deductions, points simply are not added to the total. This allows testers to attempt every question and potentially increase their score without fear of penalty. For Accuplacer, Compass, and TSI, there are no deductions taken when a student guesses so every question should be attempted even if the guess is completely random.

*There is no penalty for guessing on*

*a placement test.*

*Never leave an answer blank.*

While placement tests like the Accuplacer are useful for dual enrollment, they are not a replacement for standardized tests like the PSAT, SAT, or ACT. A good standardized test can provide an excellent baseline of where the student is academically. It can pinpoint gaps and point to learning differences. Placement test are not good baselines. Placement tests are too short, not well normed, and are administered in too wide a variety of setting and manners. The results may be acceptable as a way of deciding what level of math or English class a new college student should start with, but they are not comprehensive enough nor taken by enough same aged students to be a valid baseline. Unlike placement tests which serve one generalized purpose, standardized tests serve three functions.

1. **Taken in 8-9th grade, they are excellent baselines, indicating exactly what a student has mastered and what gaps, if any, should be addressed.**
2. **Taken in 11th grade, they can confirm National Merit status and open the door to great financial aid.**
3. **Taken right before college applications go out, these tests can lead to admissions at top colleges, as well as merit-based aid.**

But a placement test simply tells a DE officer if a student is ready for college level courses, and exactly what level of reading, writing, and math course work that student is likely to succeed at. In as little as 22 questions, placement tests attempt to identity if a student is better suited for College Algebra or the more advanced math of PreCalculus.

While such succinctness is suspect to me personally, it is highly likely that a student will be required to take one of these tests at some point, so it behooves us to understand them and attempt to utilize them in an optimal way. It turns out that when viewed from a high school to college planning perspective, placement tests can be inherently valuable.

For example, since a single placement test can qualify a student to start college level courses, these tests can essentially wipe out a dubious transcript. A passing score on all three sections of one of these tests becomes a get-out-of-jail-free card.

A placement test formally confirms that a learner is above 10th grade level in the key subjects of reading, writing, and math. In some jurisdictions, placement tests have been used to replace the last two years of high school altogether since a number of fully accredited colleges and universities will readily offer admission based on a solid placement score plus a notarized transcript from a parent.

*Yes, you heard me correctly.*
*When a student has passed all portions of a college placement test, she is considered ready for college, which means she is technically no longer in need of high school.*

This is a very provocative loophole to contemplate, but I firmly believe that two years of dual enrollment is a better alternative than heading off to university a couple of years early. Combined with a custom high school program like LeeWay, dual credit can offer a flexibility that is unmatchable.

## PREPPING FOR PLACEMENT

Prepping for a placement test is useful but not required. In fact, I always ask my students to take the test cold the first time around just to become familiar with it. This also serves the added duty of giving me a baseline for that particular test. Many students score significantly higher on their first placement test than they anticipate, but most do not pass all three sections the first time around. Once they have a feel for the test and we know where their problem areas are, we design a 2-3 week directed prep plan aimed at filling in the gaps. Then we retest.

There are two good options for prep. The first one is to download the official mobile app that can be found at www.collegeboard.com. Use this daily for a couple of weeks to get familiar with the test. For students who struggle with tests in general, I would add the step of pulling practice tests from Google and working those questions with some feedback from a parent, teacher, tutor, or friend. It is good to remember that prep is rarely effective when the student sits and works alone.

Placement tests are timed but not always strictly so. We never take timed test as a form of practice. Instead we have the student work practice questions using a feedback teaching methodology (FTM). In FTM, the student reads a question out loud. The tutor (or friend or parent) listens to make certain the student understands the question correctly. Next, the student reads the answer choices and picks the answer that seems most correct. Then the tutor asks the student to explain why that answer is best. The tutor is listening closely to see if the logic is sound. If not, the tutor will point out the flaws in the logic. It is not enough to get the answer right. It is important to understand why that answer is correct.

Since all test prep should focus on learning to think like the test maker, the tutors I train will always ask the student to also explain why the other answer choices are wrong. Then we look for evidence to prove or disprove the student's reasoning. In doing this, the student is forced to see the patterns of how the test was designed. Very quickly, one will realize that there are very discernable and predictable patterns to a test. This is the test makers' mark. With continued practice and feedback, a student will see these patterns quickly and seamlessly.

For placement testing, a little prep goes a long way and most are ready to take their first test after only one to four weeks of review. When a test section is attempted and not passed, a couple of weeks of targeted prep, using the feedback method, is often more than enough to correct the problem and produce a passing placement score for that section.

As previously noted, all portions of the test do NOT have to be passed in a single setting. Retakes are extremely common. In my own practice, the average student will pass the reading and writing sections the first time around, often with flying colors. But the essay portion can be very difficult for students who have not had experience with writing a timed essay from a prompt. The math section presents the biggest problem for the majority of students, even those with excellent SAT scores. Parents are always flummoxed by this reality. I just see it as more proof that what students are taught in high school is not in sync with what is required for college. Fortunately, with the right prep and a good therapeutic tutor, nearly any problem can be overcome and placement can be passed within one semester of starting the process. At least that has been my experience.

Test anxiety is another common cause of poor placement outcomes. In such cases, it is highly recommended to break placement into 2-3 tests and take only one test at a time. This is not allowed in every district but many will do it upon request. This allows a student to experience success in his preferred subjects before being confronted with a nemesis. Eventually, usually after two attempts, all sections will be passed.

Once the reading, writing, essay, and math sections of the placement test are passed, students are considered "placement complete". A student does not always have to be placement complete to start dual credit. In other words, a student does not necessarily have to pass all three sections of the official placement test before starting DE classes. This piece of information is a very powerful tool.

*Being placement complete is not always required. And in the case of math anxiety, it may be optimal to postpone math placement till the end of the senior year.*

When placement is not achieved, the usual culprit is math. Not surprisingly, more than half of students do not pass the math section of a placement test the first time around. With the right type of prep, approximately half will pass it the second time around. Others will need to either complete a lengthy review program at school or home, formally remediate with a professional, or take a developmental math class at the DE college before achieving placement complete.

Failing the math section of the test is not a reason to postpone starting dual enrollment. At LeeWay Academy, many of our students are not placement complete until their senior year when they finally take and pass the math section of their placement test. This is not an accident. We have actually designed our program this way to work to the student's ultimate advantage. Since LeeWay focuses on success above all else, we honor the fact that a large majority of high school students do not have mastery of math at the Algebra level or beyond. So we start DE without pushing to complete the math placement test. We invest a semester or two outside of DE focusing on math mastery work with specialized teachers called therapeutic tutors. During this time, the student takes classes like English and History in dual enrollment. After making an "A" in college level English, confidence soars and motivation for math prep increases dramatically. After a semester or two of specialized math prep using FTM, our students take and pass the math section.

This relaxed schedule not only produces math mastery, something that the majority of high school students provably never attain, it also allows for positive associations about math and school in general. This strategy leaves two semesters of twelfth grade in which the student can complete College Algebra and Introductory Statistics in dual enrollment. These two classes nicely replace the 11th and 12th grade math requirements of any state's high school degree plan. Plus these two classes are all the math that is required for the majority of bachelor degrees at the majority of universities. This type of customization is exactly what makes dual enrollment such a useful tool for high school to college planning. Not every student will need to wait on math placement but for those who do, mine can be a highly beneficial strategy. Waiting on math placement allows my students to develop mastery and get rid of old anxieties related to early math experiences. And it allows them to develop a strong sense of self accomplishment by taking and passing college level courses right away. In no way are they limited by not being placement complete before starting dual credit.

Parents often worry about "putting math on hold" as they put it. They are apprehensive that the student will forget what little math they already know. This is an intuitive fear and one that I shared in the early days of my career, but it turns out to be completely unfounded. The truth is exactly the opposite. By allowing an emotional break from a stressful subject such as math, while instilling a strong sense of achievement via success in college level courses, the brain comes back raring to go and the process of remediation ends up being fast, painless, and successful. If you want to know my personal secret to helping students succeed, you just read it!

*"Learning without any opportunity to share what we've learned, is a little like cooking for ourselves; we do it, but we probably won't do it as well."*

~Mike Schmoker

# 9☞

# PICKING CLASSES

## With Great Teachers

By far, one of the most important decisions any student, parent, or adviser will make in regards to school, be it public, private, college, or dual credit, is related to picking the right classes at the right time and selecting the best possible teachers. This is as true for elementary school as it is for the first year of college. Most parents do not even know that they have a choice about what their student takes once they enter a public, charter, or private school but the laws in this country are extremely pro-parent. As long as a parent is not doing something that is an obvious danger to the child, few courts will rule against a parent's wishes. This gives parents a lot of clout with a school district. The key is using that power judiciously.

Knowing what a student needs at any given time then moving him in that direction should be the goal of any good educational strategy. As a student prepares to start dual enrollment, parents, teachers, and even students need to know which classes to take and when to take them for optimal effect.

Class choice is not the only reason for declining student attitudes and strained GPAs. Picking the right teacher for each class is equally vital since teachers determine student outcomes as much as the student does.

*"The mediocre teacher tells.*

*The good teacher explains.*

*The superior teacher demonstrates.*

*The great teacher inspires."*

~ William Arthur Ward

For students in public, private, or charter high schools, which classes a student can take in dual enrollment is limited by the school district. The choice of teacher will be even more restricted as classes are often taught on the high school campus by high school teachers rather than college professors. This can be either good or bad depending on the individual teachers involved. When there is an option, it should be a top priority to get to know the teachers available and maneuver students into classes with teachers that have proven outcomes.

Public school choices may be limited during the regular school year, but summer sessions are different. Any student can take DE classes during the summer months when regular school is not in session. This can be done with or without permission from school officials but it will require a parent's approval. Obviously, it is always preferable to work with the administration when possible. When the administration will not comply, in many districts a student may choose to become a "temporary homeschooler" for purposes of dual enrollment. Temporary homeschoolers can take dual credit courses with total freedom. For homeschoolers, temporary or full-time, the educational options are significantly greater especially in relation to dual credit. There are three reasons for this.

First, homeschoolers are not at the mercy of state agencies. They control their degree plan and can take any class required for high school graduation, which just happens to match the college core. Second, homeschool students are not swamped with homework and after school activities, which can make it extremely hard to add anything extra. The flexible schedule of a homeschooler is perfectly suited for dual credit. Third, homeschoolers can choose from any DE program, in person or online, without regard for geographical locale. It's a well known fact that some colleges have better environments and class choices than others. And some teachers produce better outcomes than others. Being able to pick and choose to suit a particular student's situation is a big deal when aiming for educational success. Homeschooling allows for just such choices.

Regardless of where or how a family chooses to school their children, there are options for dual enrollment. Regardless of the school system, there is an optimal set of classes that should be taken while in dual enrollment. We refer to this set of optimal college classes as "The Core" because they form the core of what every college student will have to take in order to graduate. Understanding and using The Core is imperative for DE success.

## PICKING CLASSES

Once the application is complete and the placement test passed, the task of picking the right courses can quickly become a dilemma. It will be important to start the process early. Starting early means pupils must be ready to register for classes as soon as the enrollment period begins, about two to three months before the start of classes. Good teachers are actively sought out by students in the know. Their classes will often close within days or even hours of the start of enrollment. Students who wait and enroll in classes after this initial window are likely to end up with not only an awkward schedule but less than stellar professors. Teachers can make or break a GPA, which makes them worth getting out of bed early for.

Following The Core is a fairly simple concept. The Core includes any class that is required for both high school and college. For example, all 11th graders will take an English class. All college freshman will take an English class. Viola! English is a Core class. Same for Math, History, Government, Science, Speech, and PE. The Core is not actually a single list of classes that will work for every student in every situation. The Core is simply a set of high school classes that will transfer to most colleges and be applicable to most majors.

I started LeeWay Academy, an elite virtual high school, nearly a decade ago as a way to help families around the world who wanted to customize their child's high school experience but were unable to because of limited resources or unfriendly laws. LeeWay now caters to students wanting a flexible school schedule; with over half of our students either in or trying to break into the television, motion picture, music, or modeling industry. Their work requires them to travel extensively throughout the school year. This makes a brick and mortar school a poor fit. LeeWay Academy offers such students a top quality education and sure-fire route to college admissions despite their highly irregular schedule and time limitations.

All LeeWay students are tired of non-stop testing and homework. They want to enjoy school again. They are ready to stop stressing and start learning. They choose LeeWay over typical private schools because we have a long-standing reputation for providing an optimal high school experience that allows our students to focus on non-academic pursuits while still getting 100% prepared for college admissions & success.

With few exceptions, dual enrollment, is a big part of that strategy. In fact, dual credit is how we ensure that each student is able to graduate high school on time while meeting the requirements for admission to a top university. Obviously, our clients would not be very happy if they could not graduate on time and with the assurance that the classes they took in dual enrollment would transfer to their final destination university. I use a three-pronged standard when choosing classes to fit into "THE CORE" used at LeeWay Academy.

## THE CORE

1. *Meets the requirements for every state's top high school degree plans.*
2. *Are required courses for most majors at most universities.*
3. *Matches the list that educators report all students should master in order to be "properly educated".*

# THE CORE

Notated with Common Course Numbers (CCN)

## Easy Classes

**Speech 1311 or 1315** – These intro and public speaking classes meet the 3 credit requirement for communications.

**Humanities 1301 or 1315** - Intro to Humanities. Any 3 credits in Survey of Drama, Art, Dance, Music is acceptable.

**Computing 1301+** - Any 3-4 credit course in MS Office, or Intro to a programming language will work.

## Medium Classes

**English 1301 & 1302** – 6 credits of Composition, Rhetoric, & Language in a sequence. Literature is optional.

**History 1301 & 1302** - 6 credits of U.S. History. For transferability, avoid state or world history, and geography.

**Government 2305** – Or any 3-6 credits of an Intro to U.S. Political Science. A second class is sometimes required.

**Psychology 2301 or Economics 2301** - For business or engineering majors, Economics 2301 or 2302 is preferred. ANTH, SOCI, and PHIL are options as well.

## Hard Classes

**Lab Science (Any 2)** – Pick lab-based science classes that are passable. Focus on ones for non-science majors.

**Foreign Language I & II** - 8 credits of any beginning level language. Ex: SPAN, FREN, GERM, JAPN, ITAL, etc.

**Math 1314** - College Algebra or higher plus Intro to Statistics for non engineering, medical, or business majors.

Picking classes from The Core is a great way to optimize dual credit, but not all classes are created equal. It is tempting to take all the easy classes first. Bad idea. Taking a single easy class is an excellent strategy for the very first semester of DE. But after that, a successful student will need to mix it up to avoid ending up with a semester of nothing but "Hard" courses.

Of course, what classes a student takes in DE is not entirely up to the student. It also depends on the degree plan, since students can only take in dual enrollment what they have remaining on their official high school degree plan. This rule makes sense. DE is only for high school students, and high schools operate under the authority of a school district. Every school district follows some type of list that details what a student should complete in order to be eligible for high school graduation. This list is referred to as a degree plan.

Degree plans differ from state to state but not significantly so. Although they are taking college classes on a college campus, dual credit students are always considered high school students, not college students. Therefore, all dual credit students are advised (and often required) to follow their state's default high school degree plan. The exception to this rule is that in many states, homeschoolers may create and follow an alternative degree plan. Either way, any class taken in DE must be on the student's high school degree plan.

With all of this in mind, the best way for a student to select classes to take in DE is to a look at The Core which I have provided. Compare the classes on The Core to your current high school degree plan. Highlight anything on The Core that you have not already taken in high school. What ever remains is a good option for a dual credit class. Start with one easy class then continue in a logical order. The right order will start with a single class that the student is sure to do well in. Then we add a class each semester until he is taking an optimal load for him. Every student is different.

I follow the dictum of playing to a student's strengths. Great readers tend to do well in subjects like English or History where reading accounts for the bulk of the homework. Slower readers or poor writers should avoid these classes until they have been bolstered by a positive experience in a successful subject. If math is a weakness then reserve Chemistry, Physics, and Math courses for a later semester or school year. Perpetually bored or inattentive students will do well with classes that have a strong interactive component like computing, speech, or drama. Such students would be well advised to avoid tedious classes like accounting or math until they have matured as a student.

Any classes taken in dual enrollment will need to be added to the official high school transcript. The official transcript denotes what has been completed in high school, so it is used by DE personnel to determine what can be taken in DE. This is where things begin to diverge significantly between homeschoolers and non-homeschoolers.

The state usually dictates exactly what classes are required to be taken for each year of high school. School districts also limit which classes can be taken in DE by simply not offering anything beyond a few basics. The state and individual school districts will also have some rules about how many DE courses can be taken each semester and who teaches those classes. All of these factors can severely limit which classes a public, private or charter student can complete in a dual credit program. Homeschoolers, in many states, do not have the same limitations.

Being informed before starting out is critical since homeschoolers in the know are often able to utilize some unspoken flexibilities just by talking to their DE administrator in a knowledgeable way. The old adage, "It never hurts to ask" is dancing in my head at the moment.

For the family who customizes through homeschooling, the parents get to determine what goes on the official high school transcript. The parents decide when a student has passed a class, what name to give that class, and what grade to assign. Homeschool parents also have the right to create their own custom degree plan in many states. In such cases, using an innovated degree plan like the LeeWay Distinguished Degree Plan, which we will explore shortly, will be optimal for college admissions and aid. It also allows the parents to control how long their students may remain in dual credit and what classes they may take.

Of course, parents can not fabricate a transcript from thin air or give students credits that have not been earned. But homeschool parents who choose to customize do have enormous power in their hands, and the way they choose to use that power can work for or against their student as they prepare to utilize the dual credit system for high school to college planning.

For example, the typical state degree plan allows for two years of foreign language. If a student has been dabbling in Rosetta Stone's Spanish program at home for the last couple of years, many parents will list a foreign language credit on the transcript for 9th and 10th grades. If this is done, then the student has officially completed the two-year requirement for foreign language and will not be allowed to take college credit foreign language in many DE programs. Why is this a problem?

Most universities require two semesters of foreign language in order to complete a bachelor's degree, unless the student already has two provable years of a foreign language on their high school transcript. The key word here is "provable." Homeschoolers are not easily provable.

Thanks to very family-friendly laws, the homeschool diploma is completely legitimate in all 50 states. A student who graduates as a homeschooler is an official high school graduate and does not need a GED. But the homeschool transcript can not prove the subjects of math, science, and foreign language. This means that Spanish or French taken at home or co-op can not be used to fulfill the college requirements for foreign language the way public school classes can. But dual credit courses can fill this mandate.

*While the home school transcript is mandated by law to be acceptable proof of completion of high school, it is not required to be accepted for placement purposes.*

Thankfully, dual credit math, science, and foreign language will "prove" a homeschool transcript, but only if the student takes those courses through an official dual enrollment program. I will have a lot more to say about these three crucial subjects as we progress through our topic, but as you consider which classes to pick for your students, do not ignore the issue of "provability".

The high school transcript will also determine how long a student can remain in dual enrollment. Since DE was created to act as a bridge from high school to college, it is specifically designed to replace or coincide with the last two years of high school. The rules vary slightly, but under normal circumstances a student will only be allowed to complete a maximum of two full academic years of classes via dual credit. Therefore, the ideal time to start DE is the summer after 10$^{th}$ grade or earlier. This allows students to maximize their time in the program and complete at least two full calendar years of college credits before going off to university.

Public schools will limit the number and selection of classes a student can take each semester, usually a max of two classes per each long semester. Under this restriction, a maximum of 18-24 hours can be completed. For homeschoolers, 60-72 hours can often be attained. With dual credit being free in some districts, it makes sense to go after the max when it is appropriate for the student's specific situation.

My own children completed two full years of college in a free program prior to going off to university. This provided them both with a full 50% scholarship before they even took a single standardized test or applied to a university. If handled right, this is ideal, but such a schedule is certainly not for everyone. Going too fast and taking too many classes at one time can irreversibly damage a student's GPA and set him back emotionally.

Go slow at first. Most students should take no more than one easy class their first semester in dual enrollment. This allows them to ease into the program and learn their way around a college course before jumping in with both feet. After a bit of acclimation, and proof that all is well, consider taking two or more classes per semester for the remainder of high school.

Similarly, start with an easy, enjoyable subject that the student feels strongly about before allowing him to move on to the more difficult courses like lab sciences, advanced math, or certain foreign languages.

## PICKING TEACHERS

If it seems like I'm harping on the topic of good teachers, I am. Teachers matter. A lot! I would go so far as to say that in terms of actual learning, the teacher matters more than all other factors put together. It is not hyperbole to state that one bad teacher or a few unsuccessful classes can sabotage a student's motivation to detrimental effect. I have seen a distressing number of good students leave college and even high school due to nothing more than a singularly bad experience in one class. A passionate teacher can motivate an otherwise lackadaisical learner, while a patient teacher can reach even the most challenging pupil. On the other hand, an arrogant or impatient teacher can ruin an otherwise exciting subject for all but the most dedicated of students.

For most students, DE classes should be taken in person as opposed to online. Studies show that students just do better with live teachers versus online arrangements. Plus, online classes tend to have more homework which is usually a negative. Just to be clear, taking a class with a live teacher does not always mean it will be on the college campus. Many public and large private schools offer DE classes on their own campus with specially trained high school teachers. There are also many homeschool cooperatives that now offer DE classes. Those classes may be taught in churches, local Christian colleges, or even by Skype. One locale is not better than another. The thing to be concerned with is not schedule, or delivery method, or geographical logistics. The number one goal should be to find great teachers!

To find good teachers, use a teacher rating website like www.ratemyprofessors.com. Be aware that these ratings are given by past students and should always be taken with a grain of salt. If you know other students at the college in question then ask them which teachers they liked. If you know nothing about a teacher, consider sitting in on his or her class prior to enrollment. This will allow you to see that teacher in action before committing to his or her class. Students may even schedule a sit-down with a teacher and essentially perform a pre-enrollment interview. When I suspect that a learner is likely to struggle either academically or behaviorally, I put great importance on making sure that he feels some positive connection to his teachers. When a student feels the teacher is relevant, friendly, and caring, the results are stunning. Put time into teacher selection and the payoff will come.

Additionally, as a parent or counselor tasked with helping students pick the right classes, I strongly suggest involving the student in the class/teacher selection process. Don't expect students to actually do the picking. They don't know how yet. But you can teach them as you learn yourself. You can even learn together. Read ratings or sit in on classes then ask your student's opinion. Then listen. This is the perfect time to educate the student so they can take over the entire process of managing their college strategy. But make sure to teach them before asking them to make the decisions. Students may need to be taught to actively seek information and identify resources as well. They will most certainly need to be shown how to use those resources wisely, especially when it comes to picking classes and teachers. Don't assume they know.

I would caution parents and students not to get caught up with over analysis. While it is important to know one's options and consider them in the overall context of one's specific goals, ultimately the objective is a simple one. Success! Always work towards success.

Regardless of how many or how few classes a student takes in DE, it is important that he take courses that are right for him. That means picking classes that he can be successful in. The same is true for picking teachers. The right teacher may not be the one that Mom or Dad likes but rather the one that the student feels a connection to. The right teacher will always be the one that allows the student to succeed. Without success, any school is just a place for busy work.

# 10☞

# THE IDEAL SCHEDULE

## For College Admissions & Aid

As a student progresses through high school, she will be inundated with choices. Sports, music, band, dance, art, robotics, science fair, debate, there never seems to be enough time and everything seems important. While dual credit is an amazing opportunity, it is also demanding and like anything else in inexperienced hands, can produce undesired outcomes. Getting enrolled, passing the placement requirements, picking the right classes and trusting that you have chosen the best teachers, are all major considerations. But all of this work can be optimized even further when a student follows an ideal schedule built around a winning high school to college plan that was designed to maximize dual credit.

For most students, high school is intended to be academic preparation for college, but it must be more than that. If done right, high school should also prepare a student for college admissions, non-loan financial aid, and post-secondary academic success so that the student can graduate with a college degree, get a great job, and live a good life. Just like standardized testing, targeted extracurriculars, and advanced honors courses, dual credit should be an integral part of the high school experience.

The success of any high school to college strategy will be heavily dependent upon doing the right thing at the right time. By necessity, each student's ideal schedule will be somewhat unique, but in all cases there are rules and limitations that will affect when and what a student should do.

## TRANSCRIPTS & DEGREE PLANS

The first major issue that will affect a student's dual enrollment schedule is one we have already covered but is worth repeating again. Students can only take in dual enrollment what they have remaining on their high school degree plan, which is represented by the official transcript. Because of this overarching rule, the original transcript that is filed with the dual enrollment office at the time of admissions into the program is paramount.

Generally, once all graduation requirements are met, a student must graduate high school. High school graduates can not participate in dual enrollment since it is a program for high schoolers. By controlling what goes on the transcript, a school or parent has a good deal of control over how long a student can remain in high school and thus in DE, as well as what classes a student can take. An in-the-know parent can heavily influence the transcript and graduation date.

The degree plan can similarly be controlled. Each state dictates the default degree plan that will be required of all students in all schools within that state. While many states have more than one degree plan option, there is always a default. Let's call it the SDP for State Default Plan. Most dual credit programs simply adopt their state's default degree plan as a guideline to help college advisers decide which classes to allow dual credit students to take. If a college level class, such as accounting, is not part of the SDP, then that class may not be taken in dual enrollment in that state, except by special permission.

The reason this is important is actually a bit of a secret; one that most DE administrators are not even aware of. In many states, like Texas, Colorado, Illinois, and other states with minimum state controls, students are allowed to file their own degree plan with the dual credit office at the time they start the program. [1, 2, 3] The only criteria is that the degree plan filed has to meet the legal standards for an education in that state. But there are many creative ways to produce a custom degree plan and remain in sync with any state's default degree plan.

*A little known fact is that the parent or school can file their own degree plan for dual credit purposes as long as it meets current state requirements.*

Taking advantage of this option can allow a custom homeschooler to take classes in DE that will not only fulfill state requirements for graduation but also count towards a specific future college degree. In fact, taking advantage of little known but powerful rules like making your own high school degree plan is exactly what delineates a custom-schooler from a traditional homeschooler. Even knowledgeable homeschoolers generally just do what public school students do but they do it at home instead of at a public or private school. This is somewhat shortsighted. A custom-schooler, on the other hand, takes advantage of all the amazing laws and resources at their disposal in order to create an optimal educational outcome for the student. This is homeschooling at its best!

For example, most DE students do not take business courses, photography, sculpting, cooking, hospitality classes, advanced programming courses, application math and science, or lessons in dance, music, and art. They do not take such classes because their schools do not have it on their degree plan. But custom-schoolers, like LeeWay Academy, take any or all of these, plus anything else that fits their educational needs.

A great example is vocational courses like engine repair, HVAC, airplane maintenance, cosmetology, or welding. These can be terrific options for students who do not see a college degree in their future or just want to get started in a viable career immediately after high school.

Another reason to take advantage of alternative classes is career exploration. The typical student has no idea what major they will pursue once they are in college. They have even less of an idea about what career they will enjoy. An intro level class in DE is a great way to explore a major before committing.

The LeeWay philosophy encourages optimal use of resources by utilizing a customized transcript and degree plan when starting an early college program like dual credit. However, this must be done within the letter of the law and without offending the personnel involved in providing those services. Once the transcript and degree plan are on file at a DE office, they become part of the official record and are very difficult to change without the assistance of dual credit workers. With that in mind, it is wise to pay special attention to the transcript and degree plan BEFORE submitting them for dual enrollment.

## DEADLINES

The second limitation that governs an ideal high school schedule has to do with deadlines. Full semester dual enrollment classes start in August and January of each year. A student must be admitted to the college, have passed any required placement tests, and be enrolled in classes at least a couple of weeks before classes start. Doing all of this takes time. Starting too late will result in missing an entire semester of courses. In such cases, there is little recourse. An opportunity will be lost.

Getting in is not the only deadline. Once classes start, there are drop dates. Drop dates are the date by which a class can be dropped without negatively affecting the college transcript. **Drop dates are in stone**. There are usually three of them. Miss the first one and there will be no refund for the course that was dropped. Miss the second one and the GPA will be at risk. Miss the last one and you are going to have that class on your transcript for life regardless of the grade or any circumstances that led to that grade. Knowing drop dates is critical since dropping is always better than failing a class!

College admissions happens on a schedule as well. For student's who want to avoid debt, the college application deadline is October 31st of the senior year. No matter what a university reports on its website, by daybreak of November 1st of the senior year, any college applications that have not been submitted, including supporting documentation, are late. Late for admissions? Maybe not. Late for financial aid? Absolutely!

There is more to college admissions than getting in. You also need to be able to afford to attend any college you get in to. While admissions at many colleges is rolling or built around later deadlines than I've stated, financial aid always has some elements of first come, even when need is involved.

*"Rolling" means you can apply anytime.*

*A college may have rolling admissions but*

*financial aid is never rolling.*

*When the money's gone, it's gone!*

To gain admissions to and earn money for college, aspirants should start researching colleges in 10th grade. By 11th grade they should be visiting their top choices and making final selections. By the start of senior year, every student needs a list of 5-7 colleges that they have researched, visited, and will be thrilled to attend if they get accepted. Only if all of this is done at the right time can seniors apply to the right colleges by the October 31st deadline. HINT: Applications should be even earlier if a college's personnel or literature suggest doing so.

The application process has been streamlined by online services like CommonApp.org or ApplyTexas.org. These sites, and many others like them, allow students to fill out one application that can then be submitted to multiple colleges. These programs tell applicants what is needed in terms of essays and supplemental documentation. Then it keeps up with what has been completed. FYI - I ignore the stated deadlines on such websites unless they are earlier than mine.

Despite these wonderful resources, admission takes time. Lots of time! Applications should be started in July and completed by the end of October. By November 1st of the senior year, all college applications should be submitted and paid for. Any required essays, tests scores, transcripts, references, and supporting documents should be in the mail by this date. "Early Admit" students will need to apply even earlier to meet that unique submission deadline.

Two weeks after applications are submitted, it is wise to follow up with a phone call or email to each college in order to confirm that everything needed was actually received and that the application is being processed. This step should be on the calendar of any ideal high school schedule. If all the ducks are in a row, then offers of admission will begin to trickle in by the end of the calendar year.

While waiting for word on admissions, another set of applications will need to be prepared and sent out; secondary scholarship apps. Secondary scholarships are not part of the admission process. They ALWAYS require a separate application. They ALWAYS involve large awards. And they ALWAYS have deadlines earlier than most admission deadlines! Most secondary scholarships have deadlines from November to January of the senior year. These deadlines cannot be met if admission applications where not submitted by October 31st!

If the scholarship being pursued is for something like music, dance, debate, art, or sports, then an interview or audition will be required. Auditions take place on a very controlled schedule as well, again between November and January. To earn an audition spot requires applying to the specific program before December 1st, which requires completing an admissions application before November 1st, which requires visiting and picking college to apply to before September, and so on, and so on. Everything goes back to that October 31st deadline. **Simply put, missing the October 31st deadline will result in reduced financial aid.**

In order to apply by the October deadline, the College Package (admissions record) must be complete by that time. This includes grades, SAT, ACT, SAT 2 subject test, AP Scholars status, CLEPs, IB scores, volunteer work, memberships, references, honors, awards, and of course dual enrollment credits!

The October 31st deadline directly affects dual enrollment planning. Like AP and IB, DE is considered to be a decisive indicator of a student's ability to succeed in college level courses. If the dual credit record is going to be considered for college admissions and aid then it needs to have achieved a degree of notability by the October 31st deadline.

For maximum benefit, dual credit should be started immediately following the sophomore year, or even sooner where possible. This will guarantee a nice presentation of college level success on the university application by fall of the senior year. With this in mind, let's talk about scheduling in a more concrete way by laying out my typical schedule for college bound students.

## MY TYPICAL SCHEDULE

Ideally, I see a client for the first time in 8th grade after they have completed a baseline test. I use their baseline to orchestrate the remainder of the 8th grade year to ensure that any learning issues or gaps are addressed before high school starts. It does not matter to me if a student is in public, private, charter, independent, university-model, or home school.

**My goal is always to get a solid baseline, find any gaps, and fix those gaps before high school gets underway.** A gap is lack of mastery in any of the LeeWay Five Cores (reading, writing, math, thinking, and tests taking). I may leave it up to the individual student, school, counselor, or tutor to determine how to fix a gap or I may personally direct the process. Either way, I ask for a retake of the baseline in fall of 9th grade to find any remaining issues and plan out an overall high school strategy. No other tests are taken in middle school. It is never wise to take tests that do not serve a valid and realistic purpose. LeeWay is a no waste system.

In 10th grade we determine if the pupil is a good candidate for dual credit, or if they would be better served by a National Merit pathway or a remediation protocol. If DE is indicated then we start the application, placement, and transcript process. If all goes well, we start classes in spring or summer of the sophomore year. Many of my clients start earlier. It all depends on state laws and whether the student is homeschooling or in a more restrictive public program. Maturity matters as well.

To some parents, 10th grade seems an early start given that we are talking about college level courses for a fifteen or sixteen year old, but this is exactly on time if you want to optimize DE for college planning, especially if you are concerned at all about the cost of college. Creating the right transcript matters. Filing the right degree plan matters. And the right schedule matters.

If you know anything about me by now, it is that I believe that each student needs and deserves a one-of-a-kind solution for his or her specific educational needs. This belief makes it impossible for me to give a blanket answer to the question of when and how to use a dual credit program for <u>your</u> specific needs. But as an educational specialist, it behooves me to offer a standardized timetable that consistently works well for the typical high school student. Such a docket would have to start with a baseline and any necessary remediation as I just described. It would need to include not only dual enrollment courses but all of the other major components of a winning high school record aka The College Package! A great College Package includes plenty of time for volunteerism, community service to those in need, shadowing to learn about careers, a mentorship to learn a skill, or even a job to earn income and referrals. And of course, it must allow time for researching colleges, going on overnight visits, and completing college & scholarship applications on a schedule that enhances admissions and financial aid.

## Things To Focus On In High School

***GPA*** – *Higher is better but only in relation to the max.*

***PSAT*** – *Early baseline, then NMS if applicable.*

***AP*** – *Baseline in 9th, then one per year till AP Scholar.*

***SAT*** – *Baseline in 11th, then possible final in 12th.*

***ACT*** – *Baseline in 11th, then final in 12th.*

***SAT 2*** – *One or two depending on rest of package.*

***EXTRAS*** – *Serve, Lead, Win, Awards, Societies.*

***PERFORM*** – *Get scouted or audition if applicable.*

After years of assisting private clients as they make the transition into major universities with top aid, what to do and when to do it has become indisputably evident. There are just certain things that colleges want to see.

- In the admissions and aid process, GPA rules! Higher is better but 4.0 out of 4.0 will always be perfect.
- Having one top-ten percentile standardized test score is also on the short list of what a college admissions or financial aid office is authorized to pay for.
- A single Subject Test can show a college that you are gifted in a particular area. When departmental aid is on the line, SAT 2s are sometimes a differentiator.
- Leadership, community services, honors, and awards are as important to the admissions and aid process as GPA and test scores. This is my #1 tool for getting aid!

Years in the making, my Ideal High School Schedule is simply a starting point, not a check-off list, although it can be used that way. The Ideal Schedule is a framework to build a custom plan from. As the situation develops and facts become clearer, a perfect plan should be able to evolve and adapt as needed. For example, great testers may focus more on National Merit than DE until it is evident that they are not going to be a National Merit Scholar. On the other hand, average testers will do more DE and a lot less testing. They will also focus more on outside activities as they will need to be eligible for secondary aid. And finally, poor testers may focus exclusively on DE as tests fall to the wayside. AP will become obviously obsolete, but CLEP may remain an option for some. A winning tactic is always to look at the student and optimize with a focus on success!

# An **Ideal** High School **Schedule**

**8th Grade**

**Fall & Spring:** Baseline PSAT 8/9 then see a strategist. Address gaps, stress, learning issues, behaviors, etc as needed.

**9th Grade**

**Fall:** Baseline PSAT 8/9 & strategy (if not done in 8th). Start extracurriculars via exploration, join clubs, volunteer.

**Spring**: Address gaps. Attain mastery. Try a baseline AP.

**10th Grade**

**Fall:** Final baseline PSAT. Prepare for Placement testing.

**Spring:** Complete DE admissions. Take 2nd AP if indicated.

**Summer 1 or 2**: One DE Class (3 credits)

**11th Grade**

**Fall**: One to two DE classes (3-7 credits). Visit colleges.

**Spring**: Two to three DE classes (6-10 credits). Take 3rd and last AP if indicated, 1st SAT by spring, 1st ACT by June.

**Summer 1 and/or 2**: One DE Class (3-6 credits)

**12th Grade**

**Fall**: Two to three DE classes (6-10 credits). AP classes if needed for GPA & apps. Take last ditch SAT or ACT per differential, and SAT2 if indicated. Complete all college apps.

**Spring**: 2-3 DE classes (6-10 credits). Negotiate College aid.

**Summer 1**: Optional*

***NOTE**: *Summer DE classes after 12th grade are possible.*

As a reminder, The Ideal Schedule is for dual enrollment students. It is not for the one percent of National Merit Scholars who will automatically get in and get it paid for by way of their PSAT scores. It is also not for students who are struggling with notable behavioral or emotional issues; at least not until such issues have been addressed in a suitable manner. The Ideal Schedule will need to be modified for such students.

Additionally, about 10% of seniors are terrific tests takers but will not make the cut-off for National Merit. These students may get an ACT score of 30+ or an SAT score of 700+ on both reading and math. If such students apply to the right schools, they will get primary aid based on nothing more than tests scores and GPA. Honors, AP, and DE will not matter as much for these students. When this is the case, the most important thing to do in 12th grade is to protect the GPA. Taking the wrong classes in college (via DE) or school (via AP) can potentially strain the GPA and knock a student out of contention for top primary aid. Pick classes carefully.

Talented young jocks who hope to play NCAA sports after high school will need to modify as well. There are limitations on how many classes can be taken in dual credit while maintaining NCAA eligibility. The limit is currently two per semester for a total of four per year but this can change. Either way, it requires some obvious adjustments to The Ideal Schedule.

The last group that will likely benefit from modifications to The Ideal Schedule are students planning to attend a very specific college for a very specific program of study. A good example is Massachusetts Institute of Technology. MIT has very tight limitations on transfer credits including DE, AP, IB, and CLEP. Although a simple petition process has often negated this limitation, it is still something to be aware of. Once the target university is known, it would be prudent to adjust The Ideal Schedule to meet that university's specific admission requirements where possible. Just be aware that a student can not really know which college she will end up at until she is actually at that college!

The Ideal Schedule assumes that the student plans to go to college after high school and that she wants to optimize her time and money when doing so. To do this she should start DE immediately after becoming eligible, certainly by the end of 10th grade. She should take one starter class in the summer to get her feet wet, and to gain motivation. Then she can incrementally increase the class load as time and aptitude dictates. She should remain in the program until she completes all the requirements of her chosen or mandated degree plan, and graduates from high school. This is an ideal timetable for the typical student.

The Ideal Schedule will eliminate any wasted classes and will avoid duplication of coursework which is common in the high school/university overlap. The Ideal Schedule, plus good grades and top tests scores, will optimally package a student for college admissions and financial aid by creating a provable GPA in college level courses. The Ideal Schedule will also free up valuable time for the student to invest in personal development, service to others, high level competitions, and career planning. All of which will pay off big time in the race for those ever more necessary yet rapidly evaporating scholarship dollars!

# 11☞

# A PERFECT EXAMPLE

## The Dawson Twins

Robert and Ronald Dawson were fifteen year old sophomores when they came to my Dallas office six years ago. They were the second youngest in a family of seven and had been in a renowned, private Christian school since first grade. They were well mannered, well liked, highly articulate, pleasant to be around, and had made the dean's list at their school for the past six years. Report cards showed them to be academically excelled. Having been under the advisement of their rather expensive school counselor for several years, it was assumed the boys were on track to attend a top university after graduation. Merit scholarships were expected.

Things were complicated a bit when the twins completed a standardized 10th grade PSAT with less than expected results. Everyone agreed it was time for a second opinion. Mom and Dad had recently attended my lecture on the need for timely college planning for optimal financial aid. With a total of seven kids at home, the cost of college was a huge concern for Mr. Dawson. Knowing that financial aid for college is heavily dependent upon top tests scores, Dad quickly realized that Robert and Ronald would have trouble even getting into a good college with their current test scores and they certainly would not be candidates for any financial aid. Their scholarship dreams had evaporated overnight. They needed help.

The Dawson boys were identical twins but could not have been less alike. Bobbie, as Robert liked to be called, was outgoing, talkative, witty and full of ideas about getting an MBA and working on Wall Street. Superficially, he was the embodiment of the perfect student; charming, alert, driven, and articulate. Bobbie was making perfect scores in his AP Science and history classes, and was considered a "math whiz" by his peers. His older brother, by three minutes, Ronald was none of these things.

Ronald was shy, dismissive of his own abilities, and painfully reluctant to look anyone in the eyes. He had no career plans and did not believe himself to be competent in any particular subject. Once I got him to open up, he expressed a clear passion for programming, something he had only explored on his own at home in what little spare time he had, thanks to an onerous university model curriculum. Like his brother, Ronald made top scores at school, but homework took an alarming amount of time and was increasingly frustrating.

While Bobbie was self assured, talkative, and focused, Ronald was withdrawn and completely lacking in direction. They were visually very different as well. Though they were clearly cut from the same genetic cloth, Bobbie was filled out, poised, and one of the prettiest boys I've ever seen, if it is okay to use that word for a young man. Ronald, on the other hand, was the same height but gangly and gawky with a gaunt face, bright red from a fresh crop of acne.

I instantly liked them both but my heart went out to Ronald. To my eye, it was clear that Ronald was just as bright as his brother but some type of learning difference had influenced his social and academic development from an early age. It was impossible to proceed without a lot more information about both boys. I started the long, slow process of getting fully informed.

Dad explained that Ronald had struggled with reading at an early age and was behind his brother academically. He revealed that Ronald had been treated for sensory integration issues and an auditory processing disorder. But Mom impressed upon me that both boys had always made straight As. Ronald just was not a "natural student" as she termed it. He worked hard for every grade and was often frustrated by the fact that his twin did very little for the same top scores. It only took a matter of minutes for me to recognize that the parents' and teachers' assessment of these boys as star pupils was not exactly accurate and certainly not serving the students' needs.

Fortunately, after many years of successful academic strategizing, I have discovered a set of hard and fast rules that are helpful in all aspects of life. These rules have served me exceptionally well over the years; and if my countless clients are warranted in their frequent and lavish praise, then I must give full credit to the fact that I always follow six fixed rules.

I call them my "Steps To Success". They are in a very particular order and begin with a step that is obscenely simple yet rarely achieved. Before making a single observation or recommendation, it is important to spend as much time as needed to gather accurate and pertinent information about the student, the family, and the situation. This takes time. One has to ask short, open ended questions and listen patiently to long, often emotional answers. Seeking clarification and rephrasing what is heard assures that everyone is on the same page. Patience here brings great reward later.

Once I am fully informed, it is time to clarify the problem. Clarity of the problem leads to a more viable solution. Stating the goal clearly makes it is easier to identify resources. Then I simply create a plan, work that plan, and remain prepared to make adjustments to the plan as things inevitably change.

## Steps To Success

1. *Get Informed*
2. *Clarify The Problem*
3. *Establish An Appropriate Goal**
4. *Identify Resources*
5. *Create A Plan*
6. *Follow The Plan (Get Feedback)*

**Never invest time, money, or emotional energy into anything that does not serve a specific and valid goal.*

For the Dawson boys, getting informed was not a straightforward process. School reports were in direct conflict with test results. Mom and Dad were understandably overly emotional and the boys were downright confused. Slowly I managed to glean useful information that I noted in my mental rubric and eventually used to clarify the problem. It became apparent that although Bobbie had excellent grades, they were not actually due to his skill as a student. Bobbie was getting lots of help from Mom on homework assignments and school projects. Along the same lines, teachers had graded him with amazing laxity.

Because of Bobbie's easy going personality, people found it pleasurable to work with him. Between Mom and teacher, a subconscious but very efficient system had developed which had inadvertently artificially bolstered Bobbie's grades for years. It also had the added effect of making Bobbie feel great about himself. His outlook on life was extremely positive, which of course, made Mom even more happy to spend time with him and teachers more likely to assist him.

This is a classic example of positive reinforcement. If Bobbie were to go off to college in a couple of years, without packing Mom in his suitcase, he would be destined to struggle academically and would be at a high risk of dropping out. Ironically, when I pointed all of this out to the parents, they confessed that an older son, with identical issues and personality, had done exactly that. Surprise, surprise.

Frankly, Bobbie was an easy assessment. Sadly, I have seen many students with somewhat similar situations. The real revelation was brother Ronald. Upon further inspection, Ronald revealed himself to be extremely bright just agonizingly withdrawn. His thought processes were much slower than Bobbie's but deeper and produced more accurate and detailed answers. Due to slow processing, Ronald demonstrated a characteristic output disorder that made it very difficult for him to get the complex thoughts in his head out of his mouth or onto paper. In a classic case of negative reinforcement, Ronald's early difficulty with producing output followed by classroom mockery and teacher intervention almost certainly instigated his social introversion. With just a few minutes of person-centered, Rogerian interactions between Ronald and me, it became clear that the student with the real potential in this family was Ronald.

If you are wondering what all of this has to do with dual enrollment or high school to college planning, just go back to my *Rules To Live By* and you will notice that we are on number three. The Dawson Boys presented with one scenario. But after gathering information and clarifying the problem, my recommendations were, by necessity, considerably different than they would have been if I had just started making suggestions based on what was initially presented to me.

It was clear that Bobbie was not the ideal candidate for college he was thought to be. He was also not suited for the advanced classes he was currently enrolled in at his high school. Conversely, Ronald did not just need to work harder as his teacher and parents had suggested. He needed help. What they both needed was a custom plan that optimized what time they had left in high school to get them ready for college admissions, financial aid, and educational success.

My strategy for the Dawson boys utilized a free dual enrollment program in their county. If things were handled optimally, both boys would be able to complete at least a year of college credits before graduating high school. They would also get college ready with the help of professional teachers who were not overburdened with teaching to the test. And they would feel successful while simultaneously addressing problems.

The boys took the exact classes that they would have taken at their private school; but on my plan, they were getting college credit for their effort and they were never bogged down with busy work, which freed up a lot of time for professional tutoring and personal development. My plan created one solution for two very different people. The key was customizing to fit each of their needs. Since the twins are now nearly twenty-two years old and happily graduated from college, I can say with certainty that my solution was the right one for both of these young men.

Bobbie completed a Bachelor of Science in Resource Management from a top university on a partial scholarship. Knowing that he would struggle with the boredom inherent to the typical business degree, I found an interactive internship-based marketing program that was part of the communications department of that college, essentially bypassing the tedium of low level accounting and math classes that sinks so many business majors. Bobbie is happily ensconced in his power position on Wall Street where his outgoing personality has earned him a network of very impressive friends.

Bobbie has no interest in going back for an advanced degree and in a recent contribution to one of my blogs, he wrote that his expectations of college and life were so unrealistic that he is amazed he even made it through a degree at all. Ironically, he has found himself in the role of unwitting career counselor at his pedigree-obsessed corporate office.

Ronald faired just as well but in a very different way. Ronald started dual enrollment very slowly and with considerable personal trepidation. I will confess being very concerned about him. Even with my constant assurance that all he needed were a few tools and the right teachers, Mom was so stressed at the thought of "real college" that she unintentionally imparted her anxiety to Ronald making him even more reluctant to just give it a try. In a stroke of self-proclaimed brilliance, I put both boys in all the same classes for the first year, with the plan that they would support each other.

Their first college class was Humanities in the summer after 10th grade, four weeks of daily fifty-five minute classes that required no essays, no speeches, and no boredom. Intro to Humanities, as taught by Mrs. Parrott, was a series of videos, recordings, power points, and roundtable conversations about the key pieces of architecture, music, paintings, and sculptures from the dawn of ancient times through the colonization of America. For Ronald there were lots of computer-based research and power points that he was challenged to develop. For Bobbie there was the in-class discussions and social elements that allowed him to showcase his personality.

Seeing how vital the class structure and teacher would be, my staff guided the boys each semester in choosing their classes. They carefully selected teachers who would be both engaging and patient. My assistant, Celia, read through the online critiques given by prior students, looking for instructors with lots of adjectives like, *"fun, helpful, passionate"*. She looked for phrases like *"really knows a lot about her subject"* or *"Highly RECOMMENDED!!!!!,* and the all important *"I took it in the summer session and made an easy A"*.

Celia's diligent searches paid off. Finding the right teachers was instrumental in giving both boys a much needed shot of success in their first college level courses. This small but meaningful success begat continual success going forward. For Ronald our plan worked out better than even I anticipated.

Ronald graduated with top honors from a small state school with a degree in video game design. Due to his high grades and unbridled talent, Ronald was offered a scholarship for graduate school and is currently completing his Masters in Computer Science and Engineering at a top grad school in Florida. Ronald emails me at least once a semester to give me an update and thank me yet again for helping him find his path. I point out that he deserves all the credit for his success. I made the plan but he followed through with years of dedication and hard work.

I have dozens upon dozens of students with stories just like the Dawson twins, each of them choosing to trek the road less traveled to achieve their educational goals. Most are clients, some are friends, a few are actually family members but they all have one thing in common. They each followed a customized strategy for high school to college success. They each utilized dual credit optimally which, in turn, gained them admission to a great college along with significant non-loan financial aid. And they did it all without the stress of advanced placement classes, intense test prep, homework-heavy curriculums, or the expense of a private school.

These students were not cherry picked for their high I.Q.s or academic proficiency. Many of them were dealing with diagnosed processing differences, learning delays, or even autism spectrum disorders. What they had in common, besides being my clients and getting a debt-free college degree, is that they combined their last two years of high school with their first two years of college to save money, time, and precious emotional energy. And you can too.

# 12☞

# PLANNING WISELY

## Step-by-Step

When I entered the field of educational advising many years ago, dual enrollment was barely a blip on the academic radar. What to take, when to take it, and how to pick the right classes for a given student was all a matter of trial and error. But over time, patterns began to emerge.

For example, it became clear that taking math, lab science, and foreign language in dual enrollment had major advantages in terms of college admissions and long-term success. Math and science classes are famously difficult at many universities, so completing them in the more supportive environment of a junior college has obvious advantages in terms of a good GPA and maintaining scholarship status. These classes are also what colleges prefer to see on a high school transcript with the honors designation out beside them. DE is honors!

Unfortunately, it became equally clear that many students were not prepared to succeed in college level math and science classes. This is why most public school DE programs only offer easy courses like English and Humanities. Classes that are considered harder, like Math and Science, are heavily discouraged or not even made available at the high school.

These easy classes are certainly good starter options since they are likely to produce success. But once the dual credit student feels successful in real college classes, math and science need to be tackled fairly quickly.

At a university, math, science, and foreign language tend to be GPA killers. So much so that they are often called weed out classes. We all know someone who has had their GPA permanently ruined by such courses. When this happens, some students feel hopeless. In confusion and despair, they change their majors or even drop out of college completely. Since this is obviously something we want to avoid, taking such classes in the safer environment of dual enrollment is the perfect alternative.

DE classes have three major advantages. They have better teacher options. No, not better teachers, just better teacher options. They do this by simply having more teachers to choose from. DE is a safer place to learn. College level classes yet more oversight than a university and less social stress than a high school. And DE classes are infinitely more passable than either high school or university. This results in higher GPAs and higher student self-esteem. To make my point, let me try to place all of this information into a bit of real world context.

In my private advising practice, the college planning process starts in eight grade, earlier if there is a suspected learning difference. Before the end of eight grade, each of my students is assessed academically using either the PSAT 8/9, the ACT's PLAN or Explore, or a CPT 4 with Stanine (we specifically avoid the modified SAT taken in 6-8 grade due to its lack of ability to spot learning gaps). In the case of suspected learning differences, we would ask for a full Woodcock-Johnson (WJIV™) and/or a Wechsler (WIAT®–III). We ask for no more than one test taken at the right time for the right goal, then we use that test to plan an optimal educational strategy. This is our baseline.

Using the results of one of the above tests, a qualified counselor performs a baseline assessment to identify any gaps in the learning. In this way, along with observation and in-class assessment, each student is screened for educational gaps or learning differences. We also work with the parents to identify any problematic behaviors at home or school that might be negatively affecting the student's educational progress. Our approach is, by necessity, a holistic one as it is impossible to separate the student's grades and tests scores from his state of mind or family issues. We never make a plan that only addresses what to take in dual enrollment. We bring in other experts and build a well-rounded strategy for overall success.

With the help of medical professionals, we make sure that any physical, nutritional, developmental, psychological, or emotional concerns are noted and addressed. Certain disorders can take us down a rabbit trail that requires a major slow down in the plan. We may even stop school altogether, but such adjuncts are infinitely better than pushing towards an educational goal without a proper mental and physical foundation.

With the help of doctors, counselors, and therapeutic tutors, any learning differences or gaps are dealt with. We use a combination of counseling, directed therapy, ongoing specialized tutoring, student-led tutoring, and online review. We always target specific problem areas as early as possible. In the best of scenarios, any learning issues that are going to interfere with our strategy are either fixed or under proven control before the start of high school. This assumes a family comes to us early.

When gaps are not fixed before high school, which is too frequently the case, we make sure that those gaps or differences are accounted for and addressed in every step of our strategy going forward. We never proceed into a full blown high school program without a successful solution to known problems. The result would be failure. We want, "Low Stress, High Success!"

*Failure is the most certain way to ensure that a student feels negative about school, learning, himself, and life in general.*

Once high school starts, we run a tight, yet flexible ship, so to speak. We start 9th grade focusing on mastery of our core subjects: reading for comprehension, paragraph writing, consumer mathematics, critical thinking using history & science, and artistic expression. These subjects do not match what you will find in a traditional line-up. There are two reasons for this. The first, we have already established. Traditional curriculum and subject line-up is producing bad outcomes. We need to let it go. And second, years of working with families one-on-one has made it very clear that these are the subjects that students need, want, respond to positively, and that will produce good tests scores and college success. We need to embrace what works.

After addressing gaps, we retake our baseline in October of 9th grade to see if our fixes worked. The 9th & 10th grade PSATs are also our baselines for forecasting college admissions and financial aid success. We do not prep for this baseline and we do not worry about the score. The students know in August that the test is coming and they are told to do their best but not to worry about it. We want to send a message early on that they are not their tests scores. This is exactly the opposite of the intense stress inducing testing pressures that are currently put on students at nearly every school in the nation.

> *"Even when teachers try to minimize the importance of standardized testing, middle school students still feel as though the tests are judging them personally. This raises their anxiety . . ."* [1]

PSAT scores arrive in our office in early January. We look for any residual academic gaps, learning delays, lack of test taking skills, or memory problems. Based on the results of that screening, we either continue to fix problems or customize an off-the-shelf curriculum for the remainder of 9th and 10th grades. While we want mastery of the core, we need gaps closed and problems addressed with even greater urgency. We also never lose sight of any social, emotional, or behavioral concerns as they are the ultimate determinant of success for every client.

By the start of spring semester, all students are working towards core mastery inside their classrooms while working outside the classroom on gaps or remediations with therapeutic tutors that are specially trained to foster understanding using my feedback teaching methodology. We give each student unconditional positive regard and emotional guidance. The aim is to address anything that is likely to hold the student back academically. Math is the most common culprit. Essay writing is next in line. While it is our goal to have all subjects within normal parameters by 10th grade, math anxiety and true learning disorders can linger.

Spring is Advanced Placement (AP) time. For freshman who are good testers and motivated, we introduce the AP test. Only the test! We do not take AP classes.

We suggest to all of our student to steer clear of AP classes in the first two years of high school. Due to the intense amount of non-engaged homework such courses require, AP classes are a sure-fire way to ruin a student's love of learning, plus they damage the GPA! AP courses also leave little time for personal growth or intellectual pursuits outside of school making them an excellent way to ensure that students do not have enough time to focus on the things they will need to focus on in order to be ready for college admissions and financial aid.

Instead of AP classes, our students focus on the AP test. One single test each May. We give them three months of thrice weekly private tutoring in preparation for a specific test. In ninth grade they can choose from AP World History, AP Human Geography, AP English Language, or AP Psychology, depending on their current interests and writing level.

Prep for the AP test becomes a new class. A few weeks into the spring semester, a targeted AP-based review of the subject chosen is substituted for our regular critical thinking course. Classes end 12-16 weeks later just in time to sit for the official exam alongside their peers beginning the first week of

May. The day before an AP test, we set aside our regular curriculum in favor of group chats, Frisbee soccer, and individual walk-and-talks that allow the students to de-stress and refocus their thoughts away from test anxiety. This boosts scores.

This all sounds wonderful, but does it work? Nine out of every ten LeeWay students have scored a 3 or better on their first AP test. That's 80%. And these were 9th graders! Many scored even higher. Compare this to the national averages -- 29.5% made a three, 17.8% made a four, 7.7% made a five. [2] That's only a 55% pass rate.

Of course some students are never going to be good testers. That's fine. Those student can stop AP testing. We may even skip the AP, PSAT, SAT & ACT altogether, opting for an alternative path to college that only requires a dual enrollment placement test like Accuplacer. That is exactly the point of LeeWay, honor the student's natural tendencies. But you need baselines to know exactly what those tendencies are.

The 9th grade AP test is our baseline for the AP Scholar program. Fortunately, the majority do well. For them, we repeat this process in 10th and 11th grades, doing one AP test per year. In this way, we are able to guarantee that all our charges prove their potential and remain competitive for admission purposes as distinguished AP Scholars but without the burnout of AP classes.

Hopefully, it is obvious by now that there is more to the LeeWay program than mere academics. We also want happy, healthy, emotionally well-balanced students. In keeping with this philosophy, most of the summer months (and winter break) are strictly preserved for personal development. We do not broach school, even remediation, during these brief windows of down time. These breaks are not just an opportunity to explore careers, engage in community affairs, compete for recognition, or serve others. Breaks are necessary in order to allow the student's brain to organize and file what it was taught throughout the previous semester or school year. An academic break is also important for good brain chemistry as a smart brain is a happy brain and happy brains need down time! Think of summer break as the brain's vacation from school, but not from experiences.

LeeWay students are not allowed to remain idle during their academic breaks. They must use the bulk of their break in a planned and active manner. We suggest they use breaks to explore their interests and find their passions. To facilitate this, we connect them to clubs, activities, and resources that are specifically matched to them. A student who likes to take pictures will be pointed towards a photography club, local competitions, a community class, or a professional mentor. All of these extracurriculars go on the official transcript. They are equally important to academics. All LeeWay students volunteer or help an underserved community in some way throughout the summer and school year. Some work a job, and many even dabble with starting a business, writing a novel, or putting together a band. Summer is all about personal exploration and mental rebalancing to prepare for the next year of learning.

*When a bar is set for children, and they meet that bar, they are internally rewarded for their efforts & successes. This is how you grow happy, healthy adults!*

The one thing our students are never allowed to do is to sit around and do nothing, or worse, sleep, play video games, or watch TV all day! Staying constructive is imperative at every age but no more so than the teen years. Brains of all ages need structure but none more so than the growing child. Young brains seek novel information continually, but without structure the filing of that information is problematic.

Since the children in question are older teens, we want to empower them to create their own futures. We encourage parents to discuss with their student preferred ways to stay constructive, then post a list of acceptable constructive activities on the refrigerator for everyone to see. This list can be anything from making dinner, to walking the dog, to playing outside, to reading a book, to practicing something that the student is competitive at. The goal is to learn to live a life of meaning and to make being constructive a habit.

If everything goes well, by the end of this process remediation is complete, mastery achieved, and brain chemistry balanced. LeeWay students start the first semester of 10th grade ready to learn. As the sophomore year starts, we begin thinking about National Merit (NMS). We need a baseline to tell us if the student has a chance of winning this coveted honor. If they do, then we focus a lot of attention and resources to make it happen. If the baseline says they do not have a chance, then we are done with PSAT. No wasted resources. We move on.

The October PSAT is our baseline. This one test both predicts NMS odds and it provides a direct year-over-year comparison, which tells us if our fixes worked. It tells us what, if anything, remains to be fixed. When our plan is followed precisely, remediation never requires more than one academic school year and usually just one semester. The success of my methodology is the reason people and schools from around the world now contact us for insights on how to incorporate our ideas into their own programs.

Scores for the 10th grade PSAT will arrive in spring. If the student did well enough to waive the placement test for dual enrollment, they may be allowed to start DE classes early. In a few cases, the PSAT score is so high that we skip dual credit altogether because we know that such students are going to get into top universities with maximum merit-based financial aid if they are handled correctly. This fact shifts our focus from getting the student ready for college level work to getting them ready to compete for maximum non-loan financial aid.

These students are provably well beyond any high school curriculum so we reduce their academic load to core interests, high level critical thinking, and systematic college admissions work. No AP, no IB, no DE, no waste. Just results. They get into a great college with no debt and we have prepared them mentally to excel once they get there.

But these are the exceptional students. For all the rest, our goal for the sophomore year is to be ready for dual enrollment come summer. In fall, we have each student follow a curriculum that directly prepares them for the reading, writing, essay, and math sections of the SAT, ACT, Accuplacer, or PSAT depending on their goals. We do not switch over to a test prep curriculum. We do not add extra classes to our curriculum or require school at nights or on weekends. We do not dishonor our students by forcing them to take timed tests again and again hoping to magically improve their scores. Practice is not learning. Students need teaching in order to learn.

We take real versions of the test being prepared for, and break it out into concrete steps, and then walk our students through those steps in a progressive fashion verifying mastery as we go. When we find a gap we fix it using feedback and engaged interactions. We focus on THE FIVE CORES and require mastery at each step. By the end of the sophomore year our students feel prepared for what is coming.

In early spring, we build a formal transcript, along with a degree plan that leaves room for the student to take at least sixty hours of dual credit courses. We don't really need that many but we like to keep all doors open. We guide students as they complete their applications for admission into the dual credit program of their choice. By March, everyone is either ready for or has completed their first placement test. If any section of the placement test is not passed, then we do focused prep via therapeutic tutoring and have the student retake that section of the placement test in April just in time for summer or fall class sign up. If all goes well, by the end of 10th grade, students are enrolled in their first college class.

In what appears to be an infraction of the summer break rule, our students who do not start in spring will begin dual credit immediately following the sophomore year, in sync with The Ideal Schedule. There are two summer sessions, each being four weeks long. We ask the student to give up four weeks in the summer to ease into college success. It is worth the sacrifice to make sure the student is victorious in his first college class.

We VERY carefully pick the first class and its teacher. We have found that there are three college level courses that are ideally suited for these shorter summer timeframes. They are all Core classes, meaning they can be found on nearly all high school degree plans AND each of these classes is also required for nearly all majors at most universities.

More importantly they are classes that, with the right teacher, can be a great first college experience for a young student, which makes them ideal for our purpose . . . success. In public or private school the first dual credit course is likely to be English Composition I. This is not a bad option for most students. But if your goal is to just test the waters and have a safe voyage into the relatively unknown, three great options are Introduction to Humanities, Speech, or Computer Applications. As always, the teacher is an important factor.

*It is usually safe to start with one of*

*three DE classes –*

*Humanities, Speech, or Computing*

*but only if the teacher is amazing!*

The first DE class is so important that everything else should be planned around it. This class must go well. This is why you are doing dual enrollment in the first place. Success! The teacher must be motivating. The material must be engaging. And the class must be passed, preferably with an 'A'. We want the student to make a top grade in their first official college level course. Nothing could be more motivating. Once a student has this success under his belt, he is excited to take a second class right away, but it is better to take a break for the rest of the summer and to refresh, relax, and stay constructive. Feeling successful is a constant mantra of the LeeWay philosophy.

In 11th grade, our focus takes a major shift towards college admissions planning. We take our first SAT & ACT. We start collecting memberships, awards, and referrals. This is the last year to earn AP Scholar, to do something notable, or bring up the GPA. It is also the last year to visit colleges and decide where to apply. If dual credit is your ace in the hole for college admissions, then 11th grade is the time to earn admission into Phi Theta Kappa (PTK), the international honor society for two-year colleges. PTK is the gold standard in honor societies but is only available to college students who have earned 12-18 credit hours plus have a top GPA. Starting DE later than recommended will usually take PTK membership off the table.

Deadlines are a ruthless reality in the college planning world. For maximum financial aid, college applications need to be complete by the end of October of the senior year. That means that any thing a student is going to do to impress a college must be completed by this deadline. Because of this, 11th grade is the last year of academics that will contribute to the high school record in a meaningful way. But GPA still matters!

**The senior year is all about admissions and aid.** A final ACT in September and/or SAT in October signals the end of testing for most. Awards and honors must be on the record by this time as well. Applications will be in full swing and are due by fall break. Fall of the senior year is hectic to say the least.

In the mist of this chaos, LeeWay students continue in DE but we lighten the load as needed. These honors level classes look enticing on a senior's transcript, which will be submitted with applications and will reflect what is in progress. A typical LeeWay schedule, like the one on the next page, allows our students the time to get it all done without major stress.

# LeeWay Academy's
# Dual Credit Schedule

**10th** - Summer 1 or 2

INTRO HUMANITIES (3 credits)

**11th** - Fall

ENGLISH COMPOSITION I (3)

COLLEGE ALGEBRA or HIGHER (4)

**11th** - Spring

ENGLISH COMPOSITION II (3)

PHYSICS FOR NON SCIENCE MAJORS (4)

U.S. HISTORY I - In Flex (3)

**11th** - Summer 1 or 2

U.S. HISTORY II (3)

**12th** - Fall

INTRO to BIOLOGY or CHEMISTRY (4)

FOREIGN LANGUAGE I (4)

**12th** - Spring

ELEMENTARY STATISICS or ADVANCED MATH (4)

FOREIGN LANGUAGE II (4)

INTRO TO COMPUTING (3)

**12th** - Summer 1 or 2

U.S. GOVERNMENT I (3)

I have used this exact schedule for probably half the students I have advised. This schedule allows plenty of down time yet positions the student optimally for college admissions and financial aid. This schedule allows time for personal development, advanced placement testing, job shadowing, tests prep, and a social life. It allows the student to stick to the rule of doing no more than two to three DE classes per long semester and one in the shorter summer semesters. Yet, it still allows even an average student to complete up to 45 hours of cheap or free core college credits before graduating high school.

This schedule also just happens to review basic Math and English (via DE classes) exactly in time for taking those very important SAT and ACTs. It also reserves harder courses like upper level math, science, and foreign language for the senior year when a student is best prepared to take advantage of them, and the effect on the GPA is negligible in relationship to college admissions and aid, which is essentially a done deal by the time final senior grades roll in. Senior year still matters but if you are going to have a setback, this is the best time for it.

This schedule may appear heavy considering that these are college level courses being taken by high school students. But this schedule is nothing compared to what the typical public or private schooled student is doing in their senior year. We can all agree that typical seniors are doing way too much, so why push a custom schooled student to do the same? They do not need more academics than what is listed on the LeeWay Academy Dual Credit Schedule. More would not serve a valid purpose. They will now have free time to excel in extracurriculars, add college visits, career planning, aptitude testing, admission work, and personal development. Focus on what matters, not busywork. This is how you build a great College Package!

## PUBLIC & PRIVATE SCHOOLS

Obviously, The Ideal Schedule works best for custom schoolers who have optimal control over their schedule and legal options. But public, private, charter, and independent schools certainly want their students to succeed. When approached with the knowledge in this book, even entire school districts have implemented the changes needed to make our Ideal Schedule a reality. When our clients prefer to remain in a public or private school, usually due to their child's network of friends, we encourage them to share the LeeWay philosophy and insights with their school in hopes of facilitating some degree of improvement that might benefit their child.

Do not expect a typical public school to implement LeeWay exactly as designed. Mainstream schools must follow a schedule that is dictated by somewhat dogmatic school administrators attempting to stay in bounds of short-sighted state laws. This does not make the LeeWay philosophy or schedule impossible, but it does require more effort. You will need to start early and plan to educate personnel (graciously) about your goals. I find that most people want to do the right thing. They want to help, especially when a child is involved. But they are not always sure what the right thing is or how to help until someone patiently educates them. Hand them this book and let them learn.

By early spring, high schools have already started the process of enrolling DE students for the following school year. Early planning will pay off. Most high schools do not automatically offer summer DE classes so when following my recommendations, be prepared to make a special request for summer courses. Your school may be resistant initially, but you have the right to this service so be firm and plan to be patient.

Most schools will accommodate this request if asked at the right time in the right way. Private and charter schools are also connected to the dual credit system and will have limitations and rules similar to those found at public schools. Just start early and don't be afraid to push a special request when appropriate.

## COLLEGIATE HIGH SCHOOLS
### (Consider This A Warning)

Dual enrollment has become big business. Even the colleges themselves are getting in on the action. With record numbers of students leaving public high schools in order to homeschool, state agencies have attempted to staunch the exodus by sponsoring a special type of charter school called Collegiate High Schools. Collegiate high schools are often located on a college campus and purport to take optimal advantage of dual credit. They are essentially businesses owned by junior colleges. On Ramps is another such business, only it is owned by universities but administered in the high school classroom.

Without being unduly harsh, these programs sound great but the results have been less than hoped. Some programs have faced audits and even lawsuits. CHSs have only continued to exist because they fill a niche for a small but critical number of students who would otherwise leave the educational system all together. What makes these programs problematic is that they burden students with so much busy work that their college classes suffer and the grade point average (GPA) is often unrecoverably damaged.

These programs may serve a purpose for the right student but there are two groups that should avoid them at all cost. For stressed out students who are already struggling, a collegiate program will only exacerbate the problem. On the other end of the spectrum, for top students with a fair shot at merit-based scholarships for college, joining a collegiate or university managed program would be taking a huge financial risk, as a damaged GPA is the death knell of non-loan financial aid. Real dual enrollment should protect the GPA, not stress the student, be taught at a college by college professors, and allow lots of free time to explore passions and build a great College Package.

Finally, if you are a homeschooler, collegiate schools are rarely a good choice. Regardless of the laws in a particular state, all homeschool families have nearly unlimited power to control their own academic destinies with very little downside. From customized curriculums and schedules to access to resources, homeschoolers are at a major advantage in nearly every way. Whether through umbrella schools or online courses, homeschoolers are in a position to use the dual enrollment program to their personal advantage, playing to students' strengths and navigating around their weaknesses while giving each pupil a completely customized educational experience. It would never make sense to give up that freedom for a collegiate or K-12 program, even if the classes were free, as they often are.

In the end, where someone goes to school is not the real issue. Since there are many types of students and situations, it is only natural that there will be a variety of school options including public, private, charter, and home. My goal is not to direct which type of school people choose but rather how efficiently they use their resources, particularly, the amazing resource of dual enrollment. Following the right schedule makes the process easier and directly affects college success, so plan wisely.

# THE LEEWAY DISTINGUISHED DEGREE PLAN

## What To Take

## &

## Why

# 13☞

# The LeeWay© DDP

# A Universal Degree Plan

Planning for high school to college is about three things. Number one, getting the student ready to academically succeed at college. This entails both an intellectual and emotional component. Number two, building a package that will get the student accepted to a good college and perhaps earn a bit of financial aid. This entails the right combination of test scores, academics, extracurriculars, and timing. Number three, keeping the student on track and motivated to finish successfully, aka Graduate! This is perhaps the hardest task of all.

The most important tool in my college planning repertoire is really just a belief system built upon years of trial and error with a diverse body of clients and unprecedented successes. Every student and every situation is unique. Therefore, any valid strategy for a student must be unique. My tried and true method for getting students into good colleges and getting it paid for is to customize their high school in a way that produces outcomes any college will love. To do this, I first sit down with the student, determine who he is, what he needs, and what it will take to get him where he should be going. Then I build a tailor-made program that is ideal for that student but still meets the legal requirements of his state or school district.

*To help a student succeed you have to first understand his or her needs then meet those needs. The only way to consistently meet these needs is through customization.*

The necessary tools of customization are knowledge, experience, and prior success. The results are praise, personal growth, and continued success. I know this because I have experienced it first hand year after year with client after client. I have also failed. Big time! Thankfully, those failures taught me more than all my successes put together. And most thankfully of all, I stuck it out. If you stick with any quest long enough, you discover some absolute gems.

My prized bauble is a universal guide to what to take in high school to optimally position yourself for college admissions, financial aid, and efficient transit through a college degree. I call it The LeeWay Distinguished Degree Plan©.

The LeeWay Distinguished Degree Plan may well be the most flexible, customizable, broadly accepted high school degree plan available today. The LeeWay DDP meets or exceeds the standards set by all states, and has facilitated admissions to and aid from nearly every major university in the U.S. and much of

Europe for hundreds of my private patrons. As impressive as this is, the LeeWay DDP achieves these lofty goals without the busy work and burn out of a traditional degree plan. The "Low Stress, High Success" motto that graces my letterhead, is not just a tagline, but a truly achievable goal thanks to the LeeWay DDP.

Using the LeeWay Distinguished Degree Plan, students have gained admission to each of the highly selective military academies, as well as the U.S. Coast Guard, Oxford, The Sorbonne, MIT, Berkeley, Stanford, and Ivies such as Harvard and Yale. Even my own children were offered admission and great financial aid to top universities based on the exact same degree plan. More impressively, students who attend university on the LeeWay DDP, tend to actually graduate on time or even early. And when used in combination with my LeeWay philosophy, students graduate without taking on significant college debt, and in a major they feel good about.

The LeeWay DDP came about through more than a decade of research, trial and error, and a bit of very obvious reasoning and logic. As a homeschool mom, I was just looking for a tool to help me guide my own children through high school. I wanted them to be well educated and I wanted them to get into a good college. I also wanted to operate within the boundaries of the law. The state used a degree plan so I set out to make one for my kids. All of this was new to me, so I had to get educated about everything from curriculum to endowments to dual enrollment and college majors to employment trends.

By the time my kids graduated high school and got into great colleges with top aid, I had received quite an education of my own and was considered a bit of an expert in the area of college admissions and merit based aid. Friends and family began using my philosophy and my custom high school degree plan, and when it worked beyond my wildest dreams, everyone began to take notice. That early degree plan was not much different than the version that I am offering in this book. But how it came to exist at all is a rather interesting story,

A local newspaper published a story on the drop-out rate in Dallas, Texas. Over 30% of students were leaving high school without a degree. The article reported on a relatively new program that allowed high school students to take college classes and get both high school and college credit at the same time. This program was improving the drop out rate considerably and the county wanted to have a bond election in order to make the program free to all Dallasites. The national numbers were just as bad which was incredibly troubling to me as both a parent and a taxpayer.

*According to the U.S. Department of Education, "1.2 million students drop out of high school every year. That is an average of 7,000 students every day, 25 percent of the entire population."* [1]

Several years ago, I came across a similar statistic published by The National Center For Higher Education Management Systems (NCHEMS).[2] It stated that only 73.5% of the students who started high school actually made it to graduation.[3] Nearly thirty percent of high school students were dropping out! That was not the worst part. It went on to say that 80% of high school graduates start some type of college program. Yet only 31.4% ever completed a college degree. [3]

I was shocked. Only one in four Americans was obtaining a college degree. This was news to me but it was certainly not a secret among the educational policy makers. The college attrition rate was abysmal and everyone knew it. In an effort to understand the problem and find a potential solution, the U.S. government began collecting and analyzing relevant data. The goal was admirable and the attempt worthy, but as is so often the case, bureaucracy trumped progress.

Psychologist and educational experts began doing exit interviews at universities and junior colleges. They would sit down with students who were leaving college without graduating and discuss why the student chose that college and that major. Then the conversation would focus on the student's motivations for leaving without a degree. The goal was to find a universal reason behind the early exodus. That process is still ongoing, but analysis of thousands of interviews has made it clear to me and many others, that there were, and continues to be, several key problems that drive students away from college before they complete their degrees. It is equally clear that customization, especially using dual enrollment, is a plausible solution to this crisis. Consider the problems.

## WHY STUDENTS DON'T GRADUATE

**Problem**: High schools are not preparing students for the rigors of college level work. There needs to be a bridge added between the two.

> **Solution**: Take classes in dual enrollment while still in high school to ease into college level courses and reduce risk of failure.

**Problem:** Students do not feel invested in the majors they have chosen. They need better understanding of their options before going into a major or career.

> **Solution:** Exploration through non-core classes at DE and outside internships, free aptitude testing at the junior college, and a chance to take core courses before declaring a major.

**Problem:** Students are being burned out by busy work and over testing in high school. By the time they start college there is no motivation left.

> **Solution:** Dual enrollment could reduce both high school and college dropout by decreasing waste. Eliminating duplicate classes would dramatically increase motivation.

**Problem:** The cost of college and associated debt adds financial stress to an already stressful situation.

> **Solution:** Dual enrollment could provide less expensive or free college for up to two years effectively cutting the cost of a degree by 35-50 percent. Instant scholarship!

If the problems are clear, a solution is equally apparent. Conventional high school degree plans promote time-consuming and homework laden AP classes combined with test centric teaching. This leaves little time to focus on real learning, prepare for college admissions or career planning, and self improvement. Conventional degree plans do not lead to success on any level, therefore they need to be replaced. This was my assessment more than a decade ago and it is equally clear to me today.

When I was working to find a solution to the college drop-out calamity, it was clear that to increase high school and college graduation rates we needed to offer custom degree plans combined with dual enrollment and a philosophy of student-centric learning. My logic was simple, the typical high school degree plan was heavily flawed. Someone needed to design a better one. Why not me?

The trick was how to create a perfect degree plan that could easily be customized by any student, family, or school yet produce all the necessary valid outcomes. The right degree plan needed to ensure that graduates were prepared to do college level work. It also needed to result in a high school transcript that colleges would like so much that they would reward the student with an offer of admission, as well as, top financial aid. And it needed to legally graduate a student from any high school in any state. Plus, we wanted students to actually learn & enjoy it.

Basically, I needed a high school degree plan that combined the best of homeschooling with the best college prep programs in the country. And, for efficiency, I needed to do it all within the framework of dual enrollment. This was no small task but the imperative was such that it spurred me to act.

Working backwards, I set the senior year aside for mostly non-academics like visiting colleges, completing admission applications and essays, doing interviews & auditions, attending scholars' banquets, screening for secondary scholarships and completing the applications for same, analyzing financial aid offers, and making final decisions about which offers to accept and which to decline. On top of a couple of dual credit classes in both fall and spring, and a final ACT in September or SAT in October, the senior year was buttoned up.

Continuing to work backwards, 11th grade was clearly the last chance to build a great package that a college would love and reward. Obviously, the junior year should be reserved for a perfect blend of academics and extracurriculars. Academically, we needed proven mastery in all core subjects. Dual credit was the perfect way to do this. We would also need to join all the right clubs, move into notable leadership roles, make a bigger commitment to community service and volunteerism, and take on the SAT and ACT for the first time. Throw in a final PSAT with prep at the beginning of the school year and the junior year itinerary was a wrap as well.

Since dual credit was originally intended to begin in 11th grade, the sophomore year would be used to prepare for eleventh grade. By the end of 10th grade, students had to be academically prepared to pass the placement exam, which covered the core subjects of reading, writing, essay, and math. Sounded like a perfect lineup for the sophomore year degree plan. Now all I had to do was find a curriculum that would produce proven outcomes and be acceptable to the mainstream establishment.

No one wants to run into problems in the middle of the sophomore year, so it was necessary to get a clear baseline in 9th grade and remediate any problems that were found prior to the start of our placement prep curriculum in 10th grade. Everything suddenly seemed to fit. A clear high school pathway suddenly appeared obvious. Now I just needed to know what the government and top universities would expect or require from a graduating high school student.

Like any winning formula, developing the LeeWay DDP was a slow and methodical process but eventually a winning recipe began to emerge.

I called the Texas Education Agency (our local school governing board) to request a list of the mandatory classes for high school graduation. From them I learned two very important things. First, that all classes were "highly recommended but not actually mandatory". This, as you can imagine was a key revelation and frankly one that took me awhile to grasp the true value of. Second, I was told that in my state, Texas, a student could pick from three possible degree options.

❶ The Recommended Degree Plan is for the typical student and very similar to what most of us did in high school. Three years of everything plus a full year for wrapping things up.

❷ The Minimum Degree Plan is for students with math or reading delays and requires a little less of everything.

❸ The Distinguished Degree Plan is for top students who are certifiably ready for AP classes and college level course work. It includes extra science, math, and language courses.

Once we had this information, my assistants and I called a number of elite colleges and came to find out that the distinguished degree plan was highly favored in terms of admissions to their programs. Students using the state's distinguished degree plan were also more likely to be offered large denomination, non-loan, merit-based financial aid, as long as their GPA was top notch and they met all deadlines. Clearly, my custom degree plan had to meet these requirements as well.

Next, we looked at the top 50 colleges and universities in the United States. We identified the general educational requirements that they all had in common. We took the core from the first two years at those top universities and overlapped them with the core requirements for the last two years at top high schools using the distinguished degree plan. Anything on both lists became the foundation for my custom degree plan.

If our information was correct, then such classes would be fairly universally accepted for both high school graduation and college credits, making them highly efficient choices. This set of core classes was formulated into a official degree plan format and labeled the LeeWay Distinguished Degree Plan©.

As students began to graduate high school following the LeeWay DDP and headed off to colleges around the country, we continued to research what worked and what did not. When our students applied for admission to colleges and got their letters of acceptance or denial, we would speak to the admission officer at each college to find out why the vote went the way it did. When students received top financial aid offers devoid of loans, we would actually meet with financial aid officials at that school to find out why the student earned such great aid. When a student was rejected, we wanted to know why. From this feedback we fine-tuned the LeeWay DDP until it evolved into something that consistently worked for most colleges.

The LeeWay DDP, as presented here, is the cornerstone of every high school to college advising that we have done in our offices for the past decade. In some cases, obvious changes are needed to meet the specific legal requirements of a particular state or foreign country but far more often than not, we use the LDDP just as it is.

The many private, charter, and homeschool groups that we work with, feel that the LeeWay DDP is best used as a "Check Off" list. In ninth and tenth grades, they make certain that each student completes the LDDP requirements based on the class name and grade level. To clarify, in 9th and 10th grades each student will do one English, one Math, one Science, one History and so on, exactly as noted on the LDDP. The specific curriculum used or topic of that English or Math or Science course is left up to the individual teacher or school.

There is no reason to dictate Biology in 9th grade and Chemistry in 10th. What matters is that a bona fide Science course is done in both 9th and 10th grades and that the student benefit optimally from those courses. This allows for maximum customization while insuring that all core subjects are mastered. Students are not forced to learn what is being offered but rather they are taught what they are ready to learn. Teachers report that students, as well as themselves, are less stressed and more engaged. Students report feeling more connected to learning and having less negative thought about school overall.

For transcript purposes, once the student demonstrates mastery in a core freshman or sophomore class, that class will be denoted by a letter or number grade. It will also be appropriately designated as honors if the volume or level of work was in keeping with an honors curriculum. AP is honors, as is DE. If an advanced placement test was taken in a subject then the AP designation will be given to that course. When presented this way, your transcript will have all the info a college needs to assess your student for admissions. Throw in the proper balance of extracurriculars and you have the basis for great financial aid. Not accidentally, the LDDP frees up an enormous amount of time for these critical extracurriculars.

I recommend that everyone use the LeeWay Distinguished Degree Plan as a guideline. For public school, it can tell you if your counselor has you on the right track. For private schools, it will tell you where to stand firm since you have some flexibility. And for custom schoolers, it will guide you straight into college and financial aid with minimum muss and fuss if you can give up the old beliefs and just trust the plan. Don't over think it. Allow the LDDP to be what is needed for a particular student when it's needed. If the LDDP calls for a science course in 9th grade then pick any science related subject that the student can engage with. Pick any curriculum that imparts the information the student needs to learn. It is not necessary to study Biology just because you are in 9th grade and everyone says Biology is for 9th graders. You do not even have to use a textbook based course, or a certified instructor. It simply needs to be science . . . and it does need to lead to mastery of a core science knowledge. Feel free to play fast and lose with the subject and curriculum but be very rigid with the schedule, consistency, and feedback methodology.

Whatever science subject you pick, do that "class" until the student proves mastery in that subject. Then, assess a grade, check off the 9th grade science box on your LDDP, and move on. Do not be tempted to do more than the student will benefit from. You have more than enough to get done over the next four years. It is never wise to make unnecessary work for yourself. Plus, what message are we sending to the pupils when we pour copious amounts of time and energy into objectives that end up not serving a valid goal or producing positive outcomes?

# LeeWay© Distinguished Degree Plan

## ☐ ENGLISH (4.0 Units)

| | | |
|---|---|---|
| 1 | English 9 | ☐ HS 9th - Fix Issues |
| 1 | English 10 | ☐ HS 10th - TSI Ready |
| 1 | English 11 | ☐ ENGL 1301/02 or AP Lang |
| 1 | English 12 | ☐ ENGL 2322 or AP Literature |

## ☐ MATHEMATICS (4.0 Units)

| | | |
|---|---|---|
| 1 | Math 9 | ☐ HS 9th - Fix Issues |
| 1 | Math 10 | ☐ HS 10th - Get TSI Ready |
| 1 | Math 11 | ☐ MATH 1314* |
| 1 | Math 12 | ☐ Any DE Math* |

*Any DE Math is acceptable. Higher is better.

## ☐ SCIENCE (4.0 Units)

| | | |
|---|---|---|
| 1 | Science 9 | ☐ HS** |
| 1 | Science 10 | ☐ HS** |
| 1 | Science 11 | ☐ DE Lab Science* |
| 1 | Science 12 | ☐ DE Lab Science* |

*Any DE Biology, Chemistry, Elem/Conceptual Physics, Geology, Astronomy, Enviro Science, Anatomy. I prefer non science major.
**Any engaging science at home, coop, or school will fit here.

## ☐ SOCIAL STUDIES (4.0 Units)*

| | | |
|---|---|---|
| 1 | History 9 | ☐ AP H.Geo/W.Hist. or HS |
| 1 | History 10 | ☐ AP E.Hist/W.Hist or HS |
| 1 | History 11a | ☐ HIST 1301 or AP* |
| 1 | History 11b | ☐ HIST 1302 or AP* |
| .5* | History 12a | ☐ GOVT 2305 or AP* |
| .5* | History 12b | ☐ ECON 2301 or AP* or PSYC 2301 or AP* |

*Any history, economics, philosophy, psychology, religion, sociology, can go here. CLEP can replace AP, DE, or a class.

## ☐ FINE ARTS (1.0 Unit)

| | |
|---|---|
| ☐ .5 Any Fine Art | ☐ HS or AP |
| ☐ .5 Any Fine Art | ☐ HUMA 1315* |

*Intro to Art, Music, Dance, Drama, etc. Must transfer.

## ☐ FOREIGN LANGUAGE (3.0 Units)

| | | |
|---|---|---|
| 1 | Any Language | ☐ HS 9th or 10th |
| 1 | Honors FL ** | ☐ AP, CLEP or DE 1411 |
| 1 | Honors FL ** | ☐ AP, CLEP or DE 1412 |

*Two semesters of college level work in same language
**Must be same language.

## ☐ PHYSICAL EDUCATION* (1.0 Units)

| | | |
|---|---|---|
| .5 | PE 1* | ☐ HS |
| .5 | PE 2 * | ☐ HS |

*PE, Fitness, Health, Athletics, Band, Dance, Cheer

## ☐ SPEECH (0.5 Units)

| | | |
|---|---|---|
| .5 | Speech | ☐ HS or SPCH 1311/15* |

*Competitive Speech & Debate does not go here.

## ☐ COMPUTING (0.5 Unit)

| | | |
|---|---|---|
| .5 | Typing/Comp * | ☐ DE, HS, AP, CLEP |

*Intro to MS Office or Programming. AP Computers is an option in 11th or 12th grade. Typing/keyboarding is another choice.

## ☐ ELECTIVE COURSES (4.5 Units)

| | | |
|---|---|---|
| .5 | Any Elective | ☐ DE, AP, CLEP, HS |
| .5 | Any Elective | ☐ DE, AP, CLEP, HS |
| .5 | Any Elective | ☐ DE, AP, CLEP, HS |
| .5 | Any Elective | ☐ DE, AP, CLEP, HS |
| .5 | Any Elective | ☐ DE, AP, CLEP, HS |
| .5 | Any Elective | ☐ DE, AP, CLEP, HS |
| .5 | Any Elective | ☐ DE, AP, CLEP, HS |
| .5 | Any Elective | ☐ DE, AP, CLEP, HS |
| .5 | Any Elective | ☐ DE, AP, CLEP, HS |

Electives Can Include: Driver's Ed, Robotics, Volunteering, Job, Computing, ACT/SAT Prep, PSAT Prep, Clubs, Mission Trips, Summer School, Church, Developmental Courses at DE, Remediation, TSI, WorkStudy, anything from Co-op, or community service hours and shadowing. This is the ideal place to try out subjects at DE or use your extracurriculars.

**Colleges prefer this degree plan. As you complete a requirement, check off a box.**
**When you have checked all the boxes then you are ready to graduate Distinguished.**
**Everything in red should ideally be taken via Dual Credit or as an AP test.**
**When there is more than one option, they are in order of idealness.**
HS = Classes done at home, co-op, private, or public school.

www.kathelee.com

# HOW TO READ THE LEEWAY DDP

Hopefully this document is fairly self explanatory. On the LeeWayDDP, the first section is titled ENGLISH. There are four rows under this section. Each row represents a school year. The first row is ninth grade, second row is tenth, etc. When a student graduates high school, he should have a total of 4.0 English credits. What counts as a credit? That is up to the parent or school district. In the case of dual credit, a one semester class is equal to 1.0 credits and it is "Honors" level.

A student should complete 1.0 credits of English in both 9th and 10th grades. This class is usually done at the high school (HS) or via homeschool (HS). No that is not a typo. HS can stand for high school or homeschool depending on your situation since the results are the same regardless of where you choose to school. A class is considered HS even if it is online, at a co-op, or with a tutor. This is all homeschooling. And it is all high school.

Ninth grade English is usually done via HS, but in exceptional cases it may be completed by way of an AP tests or as a dual enrollment (DE) class. Likewise, ninth grade Mathematics, is usually best reserved for high school or co-op instead of AP level math or even dual credit math

In 11th grade, things change. Most classes are now available through dual credit, and many are available as AP and CLEP test. If a class can be completed via DE, AP, or CLEP then it should be. It would not be efficient to take such a class at school or home, since it would only have to be repeated at college a year of so later! Since efficiency is motivating, cost effective, and logical, efficiency is our goal.

The HS, DE, AP, and CLEP designations are listed beside each subject in order of preference. They are simply suggestions but should be followed when possible. If one of these designations is not present, that is because that option is not optimal for that subject in that school year.

Note that there is often a college course number listed beside a subject. A good example is "ENGL 1301" in the 11th grade row under the section titled English. This is a Common Course Numbers (CCN). In this case, it indicates a freshman level college English course. When a CCN is listed, it is because that course is the optimal class to take in DE for that school year. So ENGL 1301 is the optimal way to fulfill your 11th grade English requirements. MATH 1314, or College Algebra, is the optimal way to fulfill your 11th or 12th grade math requirement.

When a specific CCN is listed on the LDDP, it is important to confirm that the DE class or CLEP test that you are choosing is equivalent to the numbers given. Only a dual credit English class that is equivalent to common course number ENGL 1301 can be certain to transfer to a university. The class titles and common course numbers have been meticulously chosen for exactly this purpose. Pick your classes carefully.

## HOW WE USE THE LDDP

When a student comes into our offices, we use a digital version of the LeeWay DDP that allows us to check off what has been completed. We use the student's current transcript to document what that student has already completed. We do not ask which curriculum was used or how many days, weeks, or months went into a class as this is not necessary information. The class may have been completed at school, at home, in a co-op, or online. Either way, the amount of credit earned will be the same as noted on our sample DDP and will be equally valid.

Sometimes a parent or counselors will get hung up on whether or not a student has taken an "official" version of a class like English, Math, or History. We caution against over thinking the meaning of the word "official" when working a student's degree plan. While there are rules, they are not clearly defined in most cases leaving much open to the parent or teacher's interpretation. This is particularly true of what constitutes a class in 9th and 10th grade. The question to ask is what did the pupil learn, not what class did he take.

People often lose sight of goals when faced with rules. But in this case, the rules and the goals are not mutually exclusive. Fortunately, using the many alternative school laws in America, anyone can achieve the goal of preparing their student for academic success, without breaking the rules. There is also no reason to overload a student with insane amounts of homework, or dogmatic, boring, busy-work laced curriculums like those our students are currently using.

## THE GOAL vs THE RULE

The **goals** of high school are to prepare our charges to perform at a college level and succeed in a career. This is true in all but the most extreme of cases. The **rules** for high school vary. At worst, the rule is to do exactly what the state says with no room for individuality. At best, the rule under numerous and varied alternative school laws is that the parent determines the curriculum, which includes the amount of time spent in a subject, the material covered, location of the class, and qualifications of the instructor. In between these two extremes is where most of us will operate, in terms of the rule. But the goals do not change even though the goals and the rules are often at odds. Here is a simple yet astounding truth that can bring the goals and the rules back into sync. A gentle warning, it will be a while before the true power of this fact sinks in.

*If a student can prove mastery of a certain grade level by way of an acceptable standardized test, then that student has legitimately completed all classes in that grade level even if no time was invested in that specific grade level.*

To be clear, I am stating that as long as an acceptable test shows the student is academically above a certain grade level, then that student has legitimately completed all required course work in that grade level even if no time was invested in that grade level beyond the time spent taking the test(s).

Which test? End of the year exit exams created by various state education agencies. The nearly ubiquitous SAT created by the College Board The equally accepted ACT. And Credit By Examination (CBEs), which public schools use to give a student credit for a class when the situation arises. All public high schools use CBEs exactly as I am describing. If public schools are doing it then surely it is an acceptable practice. But it doesn't really matter. The bottom line is that these tests determine when a student has reached academic milestones, so they can and should be used for grade placement and to test out of courses.

Some educators cringe when I make this statement, but standardized tests are either valid or they are not. State and federal governments say these tests are valid for placement and graduation purposes. Colleges say these tests are valid for admission purposes. Financial aid officers say these tests are valid for determining merit based aid. The evidence is overwhelming that standardized tests are valid so why not use them accordingly.

Another cringe-worth fact is that from a college planning perspective, the classes a student takes in 9th and 10th grade are highly flexible. Science 9 can be watching an intriguing *Nova* series over several weeks or raising beetles in a favored tree-house. As long as it is denoted as Science 9 and the grade is favorable, you are good to go. Whether Biology is taken before Physics is not that important. What is important is the name of the class and the grade earned. These matter a great deal since every student who applies to a college must have a full high school transcript showing that all required courses have been completed going back to 9th grade.

The required classes that many colleges prefer to see on a transcript are exactly what are listed on the LeeWay DDP. That is what makes it so ideal. The method of fulfilling these required courses is the "outside the box" part. Take a deep breath and consider this fact. How a student fulfills a particular class is up to the parent and the school. For public schoolers, options are more limited but parents can petition for personalization in many classes. For private schoolers, the options are much broader if you consider the old adage, *"The customer is always right!"* For custom homeschoolers, the sky's the limit. Parents control the curriculum. The real trick is proving the student has mastery, which is the whole purpose of tests.

If a course is accredited then mastery is assumed (obviously inaccurate, but it is the rule). If a course is not accredited, then a standardized test score will be needed to prove that the grade given in that course is accurate. This makes standardized tests very powerful. If such tests say a student is above 10th grade level then he is done with 10th grade! If he can prove himself via such a test then why should he be required to continue taking classes that are meant to prepare him for those same tests? He should not.

In the case of otherwise great students who are not good tests takers, standardized test scores will not prove college readiness, but great students who don't test well can shine in dual enrollment. What better way to prove college readiness than to have a full compliment of core college classes already completed when you apply? This is exactly what makes dual credit classes and their corresponding official GPA so very powerful in the college admissions process, especially for homeschooled students, whose transcripts are always held up to a higher scrutiny.

# DEALING WITH PROBLEMS

## Common Pitfalls & Fixes

# 14☞

# A SPECIAL WORD About Math

The LeeWay program uses the LeeWay Distinguished Degree Plan and Dual Enrollment to help students graduate from high school while simultaneously preparing them for college success, as well as for optimal admissions and financial aid. LeeWay has been proven by thousands of clients over the past decade. But even with the best of plans, there are students who will struggle with one subject or another at some point.

When problems do arise, LeeWay is easily modifiable to accommodate, or even prevent the majority of problems that typically occur along the high school to college thoroughfare. Yet there are a few tricky curves in the road that are so common that it is prudent to proffer a special word or two.

For reasons that we can easily assume, the subjects of math, science, and foreign language tend to be most problematic overall. In high school, these subjects, especially math, tend to foster strong negative emotional associations. At the college level, these subjects require more tutoring than their counterparts and have the common side effect of lowering a student's GPA. And at all levels, these subjects create confusion and discourse about what schedule, curriculums, and methodology will produce superior outcomes. High schools are at a loss as to how to deal with this conundrum. They simply keep changing curriculums and teaching methodologies year after year hoping that something will suddenly change. But these subjects continue to be a special problem. When building an ideal high school to college plan, parents, teachers, counselors, and advisers must give special consideration to these realities.

Perhaps because a majority of people feel an intense frustration about their ability to understand and execute mathematically formulations, the subject of math single-handedly accounts for more school setbacks than any other factor. This makes math a major contributor to the educational anxiety that many students report feeling. Not to make light of the issue, but a quote attributed to author Rick Bayan puts the math predicament in pretty clear perspective.

*"Math Anxiety: An intense lifelong fear of two trains approaching each other at speeds of 60 and 80 mph."*

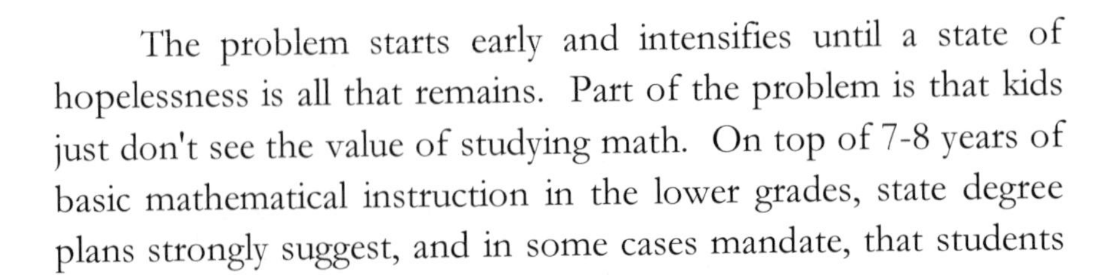

The problem starts early and intensifies until a state of hopelessness is all that remains. Part of the problem is that kids just don't see the value of studying math. On top of 7-8 years of basic mathematical instruction in the lower grades, state degree plans strongly suggest, and in some cases mandate, that students follow an aggressive sequence of training in higher order math. Starting in 8th grade with Pre-Algebra, students will take one year each of Algebra 1, Geometry, Algebra 2, plus a senior math course. Advanced learners will start the above sequence earlier and complete Trigonometry, Pre-Calculus, and Calculus. This latter sequence only makes sense for a small fraction of learners, yet a large majority of students are being pushed to meet this unrealistic goal. [1]

Why is this a problem? Because taking these classes does not produce math mastery. Seventy-five percent of students were required to complete an Algebra II class in 2009.[1] In that same year, based on ACT scores, only 42% were college ready for math.[2] This means that the majority of high school students are taking math courses without feeling or being successful. This is always a problem.

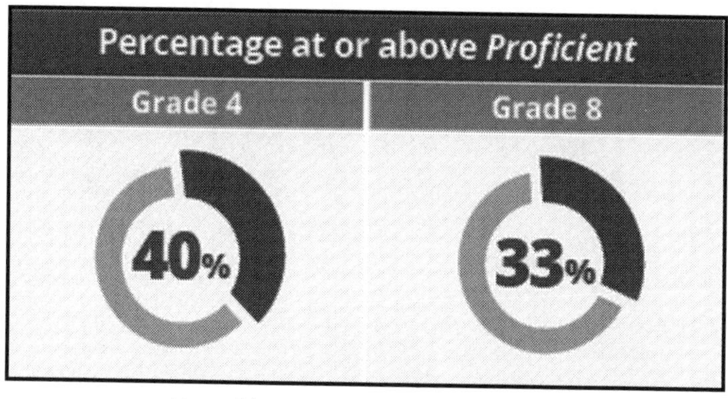


*http://www.nationsreportcard.gov/

In contrast, LeeWay calls for a baseline at the end of 8th grade to determine where students are mathematically before they even begin high school. For the 67% who will show a notable lack of mastery in basic mathematics, as shown in the diagram above, we do not move forward on a traditional path. We also do not go backwards. We do not repeat the last year of math or hold students back a grade. We actively screen for gaps and fill them in using a proprietary mastery-based process. When this is done successfully, students are ready to move on. Not before.

For the 33% who prove mastery on their baseline, LeeWay continues them on to Algebra, Geometry, and Pre-Calculus, plus DE math as soon as possible. Such students are clearly math capable and should go as far as possible in this subject. These may be our doctors and engineers! This also has the added benefit of allowing precocious learners to bound ahead without the constraints of a system that requires teachers to teach down to slower pupils. I have seen amazing outcomes when like minded students are placed together with the right teacher.

This is also true for lagging students, of whom only a tiny percentile will ever be great at math, or even like it! Most do not need advanced math. But they do need to be proficient in consumer math and personal finance. They also need to complete the math required to get a college degree: College Algebra and Intro to Statistics. Fortunately, these two courses are available through dual enrollment. Once any gaps are fixed, even mediocre students are ready to leap the hurdle of their DE math courses and get a college degree.

On top of getting their high school and college math completed simultaneously, fixing gaps causes students to feel empowered. Frustration wanes and interest in learning returns. When a student is held back for re-teaching, it de-motivates and increases a type of emotional stress that drives students away from learning. We need to demand a system that no longer expects every student to study Trig, PreCalc, or Calculus.

Students need to be taught what they are built for and what will help them achieve a successful career and/or personal life. Math is always a part of the success equation. Calculus is not.

The one personal plea I would make to every parent, teacher, and school administrator reading this book, please put your students' needs first. Make it "OK" for them to focus on life-oriented math such as consumer applications and personal finance in lieu of Trig and Pre-calc. Teens desperately need to know the ins and outs of buying a home, saving for college, negotiating a car loan, and managing savings. Don't just make consumer math available. Make it equal. Better yet, make consumer math preferred!

*For 80% of teens, consumer math will be more valuable then algebra or calculus. Don't just make consumer math available in high school, make it the preferred math!*

---

At LeeWay, we accept the fact that the majority of entering freshmen will not have math mastery. For the few who do, we follow a traditional math sequence. For the many who don't, moving them forward would not be sensible. We get a baseline. See what is missing. Then we fix it, using a hands-on, linear, step-wise, low repetition curriculum focusing on individual math concepts and testing skills. We use a customized math curriculum, developed at LeeWay Academy, that focuses on three things: mastery of functional math to use throughout life, preparing for standardized testing, and re-associating the subject of math with success and love of learning. Once these three goals are met and placement is passed, we use the last two years of high school to complete one course of College Algebra and one course of Introductory Statistics in dual enrollment.

The student has now completed all high school math requirements. The student has also completed all the math he will ever need to achieve a bachelor's degree assuming he does not plan to major in engineering or medicine. These majors require a good deal more math, which should always be made available to any motivated student who wishes to push through.

The natural rebuttal to my plan is, *"If the student wants to become an engineer, nurse, or doctor he won't be prepared for the college level calculus class that he will be required to take."* Actually, in the majority of cases, he will be significantly better prepared than had he continued through the traditional series of math courses. For starters, he will have mastery of core math, something only 44% of high school graduates can claim. This core mastery will increase his odds of success as he moves into more advanced math if he should choose to do so. And his renewed positive attitude towards the subject will dramatically enhance his potential to learn overall.[3]

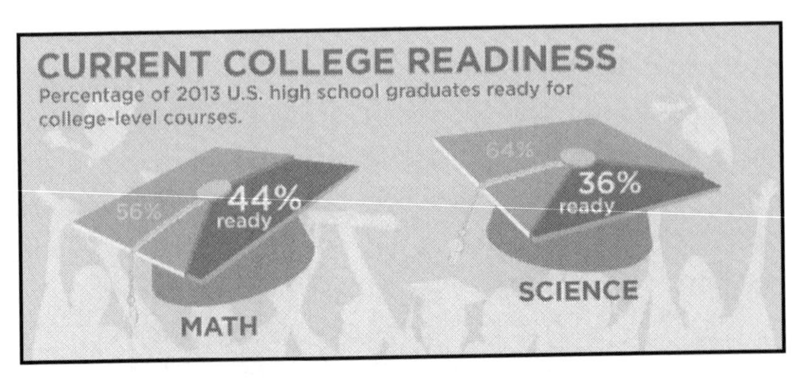


*https://www.nms.org/AboutNMSI/TheSTEMCrisis/STEM

Of course, the majority of college undergrads are not going to complete an engineering or medical degree[4] and therefore will never need the upper levels of math that school administrators and paid tutoring corporations are promoting. So why pressure high school students towards such an unachievable and unnecessary goal? What is the payoff besides stress and a national fear of mathematics?

We've all heard the standard refutation that if more kids did upper level math in high school, then more of them would complete engineering and medical degrees. We have decades of evidence that proves this simply is not true. I will concede that if more of them MASTERED upper level math in high school then more of them would compete for such degrees, but until we can assure mastery, we need to change the expectation.

By my logic, if most students top out at Algebra 2 in high school, as studies indicate, and the normal college math sequence begins with Algebra 3, aka College Algebra, then why not move directly from one to the other? Why not start College Algebra in dual enrollment immediately following Algebra 2 in tenth or eleventh grade? The transition between the two would be highly efficient and fairly seamless. I know this for a fact because this is exactly what all LeeWay students are advised to do and the results have been stellar for over a decade!

To start college, all students must take a placement test. Scores on these tests reveal that "*Only 31 percent of students demonstrated the level of science expertise needed to succeed in entry-level college courses, and more than half were not prepared for college math courses.*" [5] But just being college-ready may not be a worthy benchmark, since one-fourth of students who test ready still do not succeed in their math classes.

*"Students deemed college-ready in a subject have a 75% chance of passing a first-year college course in that area."* [5]

This is largely due to the practice of advancing students to the next level before they are fully competent in their current one. Students know they are not ready but parents and teachers have a prescribed sequence to complete and dutifully move students from mathematics to pre-algebra to geometry on a rigid annual schedule without confirmation of mastery. Each year they get further behind until once students reach college, where they can pick their own classes, they try to avoid math altogether. The end result is that many fail to graduate due to this one insurmountable stumbling block. [6]

If used correctly, the LeeWay program using dual enrollment can help students finally break through the math barrier to obtaining a college degree. But success will likely start with a failure because most students will fail the math placement test their first time out. Failing a math placement is not a reason to avoid math classes or dual enrollment. But it is a call to arms for educators to find new ways of approaching math, which is exactly what we have done at LeeWay.

Based on the results of a baseline and the answer to a series of progressive questions, we guide students to one of three paths by the end of 10th grade. One path is not better than another, they just lead to different places. If we do our job well, they all lead to success as defined by the individual student. And success is our only real goal.

## ➊ Math Path One

For students who struggle in math, dislike it, or had trouble with placement, we recommend a one semester applied statistics course taught by a Therapeutic Tutor. The applied nature of theses classes seems to allows students to find a connection. Then we start a slow emersion into a college statistics class using dual enrollment. In some cases, we quit while we are ahead and bypass math in dual enrollment, choosing to focus on vocational programs instead of a typical college degree.

## ➋ Math Path Two

For those who struggle and barely pass placement, but either enjoy math or feel strongly about completing college, we take a Developmental Math (DMAT) course that directly syncs up with the DE math sequence. One semester of DMAT allows for entry straight into College Algebra. If all goes well, they will also complete one semester of Introductory Statistics and be done with college math. In some cases they will choose to work hard and show dramatic improvement. When this happens we merge them into the Trig, PreCalc, Calculus sequence after a passing grade in College Algebra.

## ➌ Math Path Three

For students eager to major in Science, Technology, Engineering, or Math (STEM) subjects, we focus on prep for placement testing. Our goal is to get into DE level College Algebra then move on to PreCalc. If a student can manage this, then they are ready for Calculus I when they arrive at university. We stay with this plan as long as the student is passing each class. We provide as much tutoring as needed to assure success and we carefully pick teachers that are proven to facilitate learning. Following this process, precocious learners will be ready for advanced math their first semester at university and be able to complete an engineering, science, or pre-medical degree in the prescribed four years.

One of these three math paths will work for every student. Only in rare circumstances has a student needed further customization. The biggest problem is that most students just do not pass the math placement test their first time around. This makes students and parents think they are not ready for DE. But if the student can not place into College Algebra in 11$^{th}$ grade, why are they taking Trig & Pre-Calc in high school?

Happily, placement tests are cheap, can be taken repeatedly, and prior attempts do not affect college admissions as they are not part of the official record. Sadly, many students who do not pass the math section after their first try, will predictably return to their old math course and keep chugging along for another semester hoping to "fix" their math problem. Homeschoolers make the same mistake by remaining in math classes at home or co-op in hopes of eventually mastering their math nemesis. This simply does not make sense. If it didn't work the first 10 years why would it work the last two? Clearly, it will not!

Take my advice. If your student does not pass math placement the first time around, instead of going back to what you know does not work, spend a bit of time and perhaps money on some directed mastery work entwined with placement prep. Use a book of basic review like Barron's *E-Z Math* and go through the concepts incrementally with a good tutor who can motivate as well as explain in a way that the student can grasp. No homework, just daily progression. Make it quick and succinct. Aim for mastery. Once placement is complete and college math classes are underway, something has truly been accomplished and it all counts for both high school and college credit!

Unless a student's math is taken in DE or proven by CLEP or AP, it won't be efficient. Any upper level high school math courses taken at home, co-op, or school will have to be repeated once the student reaches college. The realization of this fact is a common reason students report when dropping out of college or leaving STEM majors. **It is de-motivating to work so hard through four years of high school math just to be told that it will all have to be repeated again at college.**

Placement testing for math is always stressful. Understanding how placement works will help prepare for this nemesis. When students take the math placement test, their results will place them into one of three categories.

## High Placement

These are exceptional students who are ready for PreCalculus, Trigonometry, and Calculus. These students should start with the highest level DE math class they are placed into. My client, Tristan, stopped public school math after 10th grade because his PSAT score placed him in the 99th percentile for math. I had him take the Accuplacer, which placed him into Calculus 1. He took it at a local junior college via DE and passed with a grade of 92. He then took Calculus 2 with a similar result. By the time he started at university, he was ready for Linear Algebra and Differential Equations . . . two full years ahead in his Mechanical Engineering degree.

## Middle Placement

These students are still above average and will place into College Algebra, which is the ideal. They should complete one semester of College Algebra and then follow whatever path fits their intended major. For some, that will be Trig or PreCalc and for others it will be Statistics. This takes care of the $11^{th}$ & $12^{th}$ grade math requirements for high school as well as the math requirements for many college degrees.

**One note of caution:** A few universities will not give financial aid without the word Calculus on the transcript. In such cases, consider taking an online, one semester Calculus course like the self-paced www.MathTutorDVD.com. This would preempt any problems with financial aid. The senior year would be the best time for this. This would be in addition to any math taken at dual enrollment.

## Low Placement

These students are the norm since well over fifty percent test into this category. Low placement students are required to prep and retake placement. Or they may opt to take a developmental math course before going on to College Algebra.

DMAT is a special class specifically designed to prepare students for admission into College Algebra. There are multiple levels of DMAT, each one only marginally harder than the last. Placement into the highest level of DMAT would be a strong indication that the student just needs to review with a tutor then retake the placement exam.

Students who test into one of the lower levels of DMAT are likely to need a full mastery program before embarking on any regular math class at either college or high school. In a few cases, math has such negative emotional associations that professional help is needed to win the war against this terrifying adversary. But the fight is necessary if we are going to help students succeed in high school and college.

*"Teaching should be such that*
*what is offered is*
*perceived as a valuable gift*
*rather than a hard duty."*

~Albert Einstein

# 15☞

# MANAGING Science & Foreign Language

Just like with math, public schools have a required sequence of classes in science and foreign language. For science, it is usually one year each of Biology, Chemistry, and Physics, plus one advanced science course. For foreign language there are two options. Basic degree plans call for two years of a single language. Most distinguished or honor's degree plans require a third year of the same language. Homeschoolers often follow the same science sequence, perhaps assuming that they are required to do so. They are not! State laws vary but as suggested earlier, under the protection of numerous umbrella programs there is no reason for a custom-schooled child to follow anything other than an optimal strategy.

*By now, what is optimal should be fairly obvious. Take what is required to get into and succeed at a good college.*

Take courses that engage the student and help shore up any academic weaknesses or build on known strengths. Take classes that have friendly, helpful, motivating teachers that are known for making a subject interesting. In short, follow the LeeWay Distinguished Degree Plan and use The Ideal Schedule.

It is surely no surprise to learn that math, science, and foreign language are the most problematic in terms of maintaining a good GPA. They are even referred to as weed-out classes since they are known to reduce college rolls. Taking and passing these subjects in dual credit is a way to avoid the typical freshman GPA slump. It can even reduce college dropout.

If a student has limited time in DE then these three subjects are my sole focus. One math, one statistics, two lab sciences, and two semesters of a single foreign language is the goal. Some or all of this is ideal. Regardless of the major chosen, most students will have to complete these six courses in order to receive their bachelor's degree. These six classes will also fit onto any good high school degree plan. I say do them once and do them in dual credit so they never have to be repeated.

We have already delineated the critical and off-putting role that math can play in the educational process. While science and foreign language are much less problematic, they are of special concern and are persistent stumbling blocks in both the college admission process and the road to graduation.

## SCIENCE

Science is not hard. Taught correctly, science is the most engaging, enlightening, and exhilarating subject on the roster. So say I, but over three-fourths of all third graders report it being their favorite subject as well. [1]

Until middle school, the majority of students make high scores in all areas of science.[1] Unfortunately, by high school, the pendulum has swung in the opposite direction. After four years of hardcore, lecture based, math-heavy high school science classes, few students pursue a pure science degree at university. [1] It's not that students have lost interest in science by the time they get to college. They just don't stick with a science major once they enter college.[1] It seems sad that so many students begin college with a science based major in mind, then end up switching to other majors out of frustration.

*"19.8 percent of students believe they will choose science, a higher percentage than for any other discipline. In the end, however, only 7.4 percent end up majoring in it."* [1]

In college, the goal can quickly change from obtaining a coveted degree to just survival. In order to maintain scholarships, students must keep their GPA at a certain level. This puts enormous pressure on them for grades, which in turn erodes enthusiasm for classes that threaten their grades. This is a shame considering the real-world value and long-term career possibilities inherent to the subject of science. [1]

An obvious solution is to take science once in high school and have that class count for college. No repetition. There are other reasons to love science in DE. Remember, college courses are only 16 weeks long compared to a full school year at a high school. A highly focused, 16 week course with a great teacher can actually reinvigorate an interest in a science-based career, while allowing a student to earn an 'A' in a core science!

Should you do science in DE or as an AP test? According to a recent article in Psychology Today, just because a gifted student can take on "nearly anything" in high school, does not mean that he should. This is particularly true for AP level science classes. The sheer volume of work is enough to sink even the most diligent of students and it can turn students off of science altogether. After three to four years of non-stop AP homework and testing, is it really surprising that students decide to cut themselves some slack when they arrive at college?

There is nothing complicated or stressful about how to do science using dual credit. The LeeWay Distinguished Degree Plan suggest 4 credits of high school science with at least 2 of those being done in DE. Remember that colleges require completion of two lab-based science courses in order to obtain a bachelor's degree (outside of STEM majors). Depending on the major chosen, any DE science credits will meet this criteria as long as they have a lab component. This means that a student can study whatever area of science engages his imagination in one semester increments. Be it Geology, Astronomy, Anatomy, or Biology, Chemistry, and Physics, it will fulfill both the high school and college requirements for science.

The ideal way to handle science would be to complete two years of high school science in 9th and 10th grade and then take any two lab-based science classes while in dual enrollment. This would allow for a transcript that shows four provable and accredited science courses, two of which would be at the honors level, aka dual credit. If the courses chosen were of interest to the student, and great teachers were selected, then the final grade should be noteworthy. Great grades combined with honors courses are to universities like honey to a bee.

Obviously, at the college level, science gets a bit more difficult. Depending on the teacher and subject, a DE science class can be downright hard and not all branches of science are equally appealing to every student. So how does one know which dual credit science class to pick for a given student?

*The best dual credit science class for any*
*student is going to be the*
*easiest one offered in which the student can*
*feel engaged and actually*
*learn something*
*yet still get a valid college credit*
*that will transfer to a university and apply*
*towards the chosen major.*

That little prescription is a good subtitle for this book. To put it another way, pick the two science courses that will not ruin the GPA since GPA will matter big time come application & financial aid time! And follow the student's interest.

In most cases, I would avoid the temptation to take courses designated for science majors. This can pose a major risk to the GPA and is unnecessary. Many of my clients are planning a career in an allied science such as nursing. They are told by college counselors, as well as nursing school admissions personnel, that any science class taken must be for science majors or else it will not transfer to their nursing program. This is absolutely not necessarily the case. It is accurate in terms of the rule, but it simply is not what actually happens.

This is a case of what people say versus what people do. There are definitely rules to college admissions and credit transferability, but I have had literally a hundred students get into various nursing programs using dual credit non-science major Biology and Chemistry, all with no push-back at all. In every case, these courses were not required to be retaken and full credit was given. Over more than a decade, I have never had this particular process fail. Why? What an allied health program actually wants is two semesters of Anatomy & Physiology. Biology is usually just a pre-requisite for Anatomy. So students take Biology in order to get into A&P. But Biology for non-science majors will usually get you into A&P, so why take science major Biology, which is going to potentially damage the GPA?

But let's assume that the nursing or STEM program that YOU are applying to does require the harder Biology for science majors. That does not change my recommendation to avoid the harder version in dual enrollment.

*Dual enrollment is about finding academic success, learning to love learning again, and building a strong academic record that college will reward when you apply.*

Take the non-science major version in DE. It only costs one semester of time. It counts as high school Biology and it perfectly prepares you for Biology or chemistry for science majors if that ends up being required later. Following this route requires no extra work but it protects the GPA and allows the student to be in a college level science course that actually feels doable. Having success in a college level science course will also encourage him to move forward with his STEM plans when he arrives at university. Motivation is always a good thing.

To be clear, I strongly suggest taking the easier versions of all science courses in DE regardless of intended major. This will protect the all important GPA while providing excellent preparation for the harder version if it is required at a later time.

Dual credit students are not limited to Biology, Chemistry, and Physics. They may take Astronomy, Environmental Science, Nanotechnology, Marine Science, Forestry, Nutrition, Anatomy, or Geology, as well as a few unusual options at some junior colleges. Not all options are available at each college but it pays to ask. If something sounds interesting then go for it. Just like with math, science classes may alternatively be taken via AP or CLEP if the student is a good test taker and prefers this route. The main thing is to get college credit science done while in high school to avoid weed-out courses at university.

Try not to get too focused on whether or not a particular university will eventually accept the science classes chosen. If a class is taken at an accredited college then it will be transferable. How it will be applied is a different matter. Occasionally, a formal petition will be required in order to have a certain class credited towards a certain major in a preferred manner but the petition process is quick, free, and works more often than not. I personally have never had a petition fail but I will concede that I am always a bit anxious that it might.

I personally try to follow the prime rule of doing what is best for the student. I trust that everything else will fall into place. I always plan for optimal outcomes while I focus on overall success for my student. I don't worry about problems until they arise. I trust that I can fix them as needed. I'm not ignoring potential pitfalls, I just find it a complete waste of energy to invest time on a problem before it even exists! Science won't be a problem if you handle it with dual enrollment.

## FOREIGN LANGUAGE

Speaking of problems. The rules for foreign language (FL) in high school and college can be a challenge.

Although few Americans are bilingual, polls show that fluency in a second language can pay big dividends, thus learning a second language has long been encouraged. Most high schools have foreign language requirements that must be met prior to graduation. Not coincidentally, colleges expect to see two to three years of the same language on the high school transcript.

Ideally a student would complete two years of a single FL while still in high school but regrettably, low scores in math and reading have required more class time to be taken up with remediation in these subjects causing many students to complete high school without the pre-requisite two years of a language. When this happens, colleges have a mechanism in place for making certain that a proper FL education is attained. They require such students to take two full semesters of a single foreign language before they can graduate from college. Plus there are many college majors that have their own FL requirements that go above and beyond what is required in high school. To recap, the rule is this.

*A student must either prove completion of two full years of an accredited foreign language in high school or complete two semesters in college.*

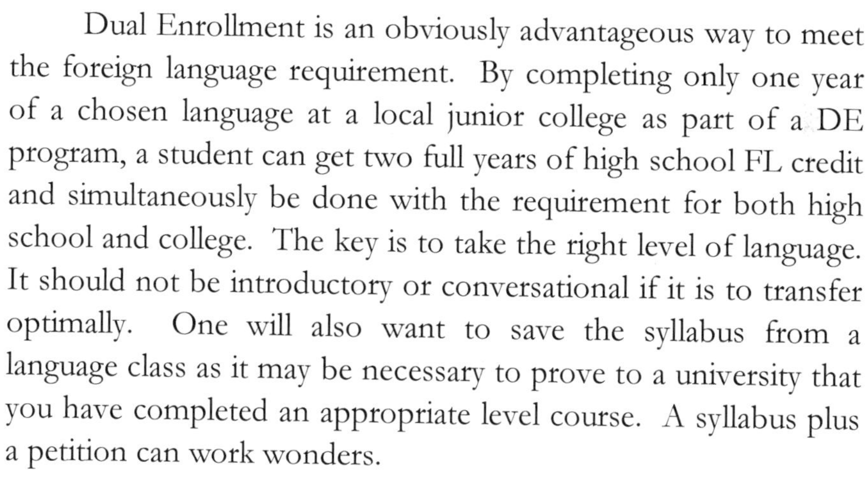

Dual Enrollment is an obviously advantageous way to meet the foreign language requirement. By completing only one year of a chosen language at a local junior college as part of a DE program, a student can get two full years of high school FL credit and simultaneously be done with the requirement for both high school and college. The key is to take the right level of language. It should not be introductory or conversational if it is to transfer optimally. One will also want to save the syllabus from a language class as it may be necessary to prove to a university that you have completed an appropriate level course. A syllabus plus a petition can work wonders.

AP is an option. A great test taker can study a language at home, online, or via international travel, then sit for the AP test in that language at the end of any school year. If the score is 4 or 5 then both high school and college credit is awarded. But few students are ready for an AP test in a foreign language. This is where CLEP can really be an asset. The CLEP test is much shorter and easier to prepare for than AP, making it a great choice for testing out of FL. Just make certain that the college in question will accept the foreign language CLEP chosen before spending time and money on prep and testing.

Lamentably, the foreign language requirement cannot be met by taking a homeschool class. (Unless the program is accredited, which is rare.) This is because a FL class must be fully accredited in order to be accepted by a college. Many of my homeschool clients challenge me when I make this statement. It can be a hard concept to grasp. But as a homeschooler myself and an expert in helping homeschoolers get into and out of college, I can assure you that this statement is accurate.

Yes, homeschooling is completely legal in all 50 states. With four major variations on how homeschoolers are supervised, laws are clear about the legitimacy of home schooling. In many states, it is equally clear that the diploma a home school parent gives their graduate is equivalent to the diploma from an accredited public school in most states. [2] It is equally true that colleges love homeschoolers and accept their transcripts with relatively consistent ease. However, almost all colleges will reject claims by students who purport to have completed a legitimate foreign language sequence at home or co-op unless the student is prepared to test and prove mastery of that language.

This is where DE can be a boon. By simply waiting until the senior year of high school, then completing two quick semesters of a single foreign language in DE, homeschoolers can add two years of legitimate and provable foreign language credit to their high school transcript and be done with foreign language in both high school and college. This method is a simple, cost & time effective way to prove that a student has fulfilled their high school and college language requirements.

Most public schooled youths are required to complete a documentable and accredited foreign language sequence in high school. If they do so, then they do not have to take a language at college as part of the matriculation agreement. So the FL rule is less problematic for kids in public or private school. I might even argue that a full two years of language in high school, with the same teacher and curriculum, is more likely to produce some degree of proficiency than just two semesters at DE.

For any student who does not complete two years of provable, accredited courses of the same foreign language while still in high school, he needs to be prepared to take these classes once he arrives at a university.

# 16☞

# SOLVING PROBLEMS

## The LeeWay Recovery Plan

*Without success a student is miserable.*

*Miserable students can not learn.*

*Students who can not learn are miserable.*

*It is a self-perpetuating cycle.*

*When a student feels successful, he will learn, he will graduate, he will get admitted to a good college, and he will get it paid for!*

*Don't let your students be miserable.*

The first goal of the LeeWay Program and the overriding theme of the entire LeeWay Philosophy is SUCCESS. Humans need to feel successful to be healthy. An important but distant secondary goal of LeeWay is learning.

Knowledge is necessary for a full and happy life, but knowledge at the expense of success will be squandered. The final goal of LeeWay is for the student to graduate high school and get admitted into the program of his choice without significant debt. While important, over-focusing on this singular goal ignores the bigger picture. Students need to feel successful, and in some unique way each of us can succeed.

When it comes to working with students, I like to accentuate the positive, but there are situations that dictate otherwise. Not to put too fine a point on it but some kids have real problems. If the problem is one of substance abuse, declining physical or mental health, or problematic behaviors that are affecting the learning environment, then appropriate professional intervention is warranted.

**Fixing these life problems should always take precedent over everything, including school.** But what is the right move when the cause of these problems is school itself? Personally, I would not hesitate to remove a student from college or high school if the environment was even remotely exacerbating such a problem. And frequently, this is the case.

Students go to school because, for various reasons, they have to. And we send them so that they can learn. But what happens when they do not learn? What happens when the stress created by their educational environment creates behavioral or emotional problems that interfere with their learning?

At least half of the students who come to see me for college planning have signs of a learning difference or psychological distress. Some are aware of their problem and have taken steps towards repair. Others are at a complete loss to explain why they do what they do and feel the way they feel. They just know that something is not right. Such students, if left in their current school settings, will continue to decline academically and/or struggle emotionally. It is imperative that these students be identified, sooner rather than later, and offered a viable solution.

If a child is in elementary when problems arise, there are wonderful opportunities available. From intensive phonics training for dyslexia, to sensory integration therapy for input/output dysfunctions, to cognitive skills training for processing disorders, to speech therapy for language acquisition disorders. If you suspect your younger pupil has an issue then get an assessment, develop an Individual Education Plan (IEP), and start personalized treatment.

*Before the age of ten,*

*almost any treatment works if it is*

*individualized, frequent, short but intense,*

*and performed by someone to whom the*

*student feels a connection.*

**Treatment should be implemented early and consistently if the student is going to achieve permanent improvements.** Young brains accept treatment very well, the key being early intervention and consistency!

Research now shows that in the middle school years, recovery is still possible thanks to the ability of the brain to physically change itself during these critical years. High performance brain training (HPBT) by specially trained therapeutic tutors or cognitive neuroscientists can result in a reversal of the memory, mastery, and behavioral problems so common today. [1] Instead of creating brains that can shovel in fact after fact, tutors using HPBT are creating young adults who know how to think critically. Reasoning skills and physical learning are the missing components in education. Without them students feel lost because they are lost. The net result is frustration and dropout in the high school years.

Over the past decade, a special area of adjacent research has developed in my Dallas office. Smart, motivated, seemingly successful students with no previous indication of a problem show up with an abrupt educational crisis related to an abrupt psychological crisis. Dealing with a teen that has a sudden diagnosis of bipolar, anxiety, or oppositional defiance, is not easy, especially when a few weeks earlier he appeared to be thriving in every way. But it happens more often than you might think. We are seeing them in record numbers.

I would like to say that these students get started on proper treatment and continue on down their academic road while barely skipping a beat, but that just is not the case. Providing an educational strategy for such students has required me to develop a whole new level of open-mindedness. But so far the results have been rather remarkable, so let me elaborate

The LeeWay Recovery Plan is an HPBT program specifically created for older students struggling with their current educational goals. Just like with each of my private clients, we design a customized strategy that takes the individual into foremost consideration. In seven steps we get students back on track and headed in a viable direction. The process has been so requested and so successful that I am sharing it here for the first time in a highly abbreviated format. It is my hope that even this short overview will be helpful for parents and practitioners alike.

## THE LeeWay Recovery PROGRAM©

For a student in crisis, my first step is to meet the student and listen, really listen! I ask open-ended questions about school, life, passions, etc. In this way, I can identify the stressors that have triggered the crisis. There is always a trigger. Once we identify the offending stressor, we remove it. The most common stressor is school, or more accurately, pressure and failure at school, so we actually stop school in a carefully planned manner. We withdraw from all classes and stay at home just like with any other illness. **This is the decompression period.**

Next we seek medical and/or psychological intervention to temporarily correct brain chemistry. Then we start professional counseling to address faulty thinking and develop appropriate coping skills. We work towards success and avoid failure at all cost. The last thing a brain in crisis needs is another failure. Instead of school, we focus on therapy, rest, and service to others. **This is the healing period.**

When things have stabilized, we reintroduce the stressor (school) using well-trained, hand-picked therapeutic tutors to implement our HPBT program. We train the parents to support our efforts at home which offsets some of the cost. This is the most likely time to have setbacks. **This is the recovery period.**

If all goes well we eventually start dual enrollment using the LeeWay DDP. We use Shadows to oversee the student and act as partners to the student and family. All of this, if done in a timely, systematic fashion, appears to lead to normalization. **We call this process The LeeWay Recovery Program©.**

To be clear, there is no one-sized-fits-all way to administer The LeeWay Recovery Plan. It absolutely must be adjusted to fit each student's specific situation. And it should take the parents, the school, and the student's home and social environment into consideration. That being said, when students are referred to me by a specialist citing a psychological or behavioral concern of some type, my go-to system is LeeWay Recovery.

To reiterate, the first step is to get informed. I start with a one-on-one advising session that includes both of the parents and the student. If there are specialists already involved then I include them only after the fact. Teachers, school administrators, and other professional may need to be involved in future sessions but this first get-to-know-the-student-and-situation session is just for the family, the student, and myself.

We sit down at a table and we just talk. I listen carefully to everyone. I give prompts to get them talking then sit back and let them have their say. I ask questions to clarify what I am hearing. I give feedback in the form of reframing, and I constantly clarify meanings. Occasionally, I will summarize to reinforce that I am listening and to ensure that we are all hearing the same thing. These are all aspects of active listening and are intended to manage the flow of communication and increase the amount of information I receive.

I never judge what I hear. I am only interested in facts. Later, I will use these facts to define the situation, clarify the problem and get everyone on the same page. After I have all the pertinent data, we begin the seven step process, the LeeWay Recovery Plan. It has consistently led my families to the academic or emotional recovery that they are seeking for their student, so I trust this system. But the road is never an entirely smooth one. In fact, I tell everyone up front to expect setbacks. No reason to worry or panic, just assume setbacks will happen and trust that the system works. I always say, build a plan, work the plan, trust the plan. Here is the plan in a nutshell.

1

## REMOVE THE STRESSOR

When a student has a worrisome behavior or attitude related specifically to the learning environment, then THAT learning environment is a problem. Our first step is to remove the stressor aka The Superficial Problem! We literally remove the student from his current school even if just temporarily. There are very few exceptions to this rule, but since part of the healing process is empowering students to take control of their own lives, we always defer to the student on when and whether or not to leave school. The pupil will sometimes beg to stay in school despite even the most egregious situations.

Be aware that many students can see that their current educational environment is emotionally toxic or even physically dangerous but they are fearful of what will replace it. They may also be afraid of being perceived as a loser if they "run away" from it. No one likes fear. A student may initially opt to stay in school if given the choice. Leaving lifelong friends is not an easy option. Information is critical in helping students make a healthy decision. Once the decision has been made, we then have to decide when to pull them out.

If the student is in clear distress then we recommend removing them immediately, otherwise we wait till the end of the current semester and follow a planned process of withdrawal. A major life skill that students need is learning not to just quit or run away from a problem but to plan to overcome or work through or around it. It is never healthy to try to overcome something while down and out. Step away, rebuild, then tackle the problem from a position of power.

## PROFESSIONAL INTERVENTION

If the student is in crisis then we advise starting individual, and possibly family, talk therapy with a professional of the family's choosing. This can be a psychologist or a trained member of the community or clergy. The final choice should be the student's but parents may have to set parameters related to cost, distance, etc. We defer to the student as much as possible since we know that if he or she does not feel a safe and near instant connection with a therapist then the results will not be good. Studies indicate that this one factor accounts for the end result more than all other factors combined so it should not be taken lightly. Watch for a spark between student and therapist.

We often suggest that the family also seek a medical evaluation and consider any recommended treatment, even prescriptive medications to temporarily, artificially restore brain chemistry if appropriate. I am generally adverse to medications except in life threatening situations, but they can be a valuable adjunct to the rest of the plan, at least in the short-term. I believe that it is important to look for doctors who understand the value of older, safer drugs and short term dosing. Medications are usually only optimal during the acute phase of recovery since long-term use is known not to be curative.

I have also seen that certain meds consistently have better results than others. A good doctor will prescribe what has consistently worked for his clients then finagle the dosage till it works for the student. Good doctors will never push the latest and greatest or continue a med past six weeks if it is reportedly not helping or causing unwanted side affects. Do not stay with something that is not working, but don't give up till you find what works. Meds can be weaned, with the help of a medical professional, when the student is feeling a strong sense of emotional security and behaviors have clearly moderated. Therapy may continue indefinitely and family counseling may be added after individual therapy has yielded results.

## BUILD SUCCESS

Once the student has left her old school and started therapy and possibly medical treatment, the decompression period, she will need a short period of time to heal. This is a critical period where the brain chemistry is righting itself, initially through artificial supplementation then more naturally due to having the stressor removed and having learned healthy ways to deal with anxiety, anger, or pain. During this time, our only goal is to correct brain chemistry and build a strong sense of success.

For most, it starts with helping others. Nothing feels more rewarding than to see your personal effort pay off, and immediate pay off is the very best kind. We use volunteerism liberally. Nothing difficult, just show up and ladle out the soup. Walk a dog. Pet a cat. Read to little kids after school. Play the piano at a nursing home every other day from 1-2 pm. There are as many ways to achieve this goal as there are students.

At home, the student is given lots of leeway but still required to abide by fair but firm parental rules. The first week or two is very relaxed in terms of rules. We want the student to decompress fully before we start rebuilding them. In a few weeks, when the healing phase starts, discipline will become critical. But fairness and understanding will remain valuable throughout the entire recovery process, especially in the beginning.

Academically, we are doing nothing more than meaningful tasks at home during these first stages. No schedule, no set chores, just participate and be a part of the family. That may mean helping with dinner or bathing little sister. It could be walking a pet or sitting and holding mom's hand. It should be peaceful. If the student is not in major despair, then she may take non-academic classes like cooking, stained glass, photography, programming, etc. No grades are given. No bars are set. Participating is its own reward.

As soon as we feel the student is emotionally ready for some artificial pressure, we introduce them to a private, therapeutic tutor trained in HPBT techniques and Rogerian theory. We do not do a baseline. We just start with the basics.

Testing at this stage is counterproductive to our goal of helping the student feel successful. Instead of a baseline, the tutor will focus on overall reading comprehension, paragraph writing, consumer math & personal finance, and critical thinking for tests taking. These are exactly the same grade appropriate classes we teach to our regular LeeWay Academy students.

When the student is strong enough and there is no risk of harming the student emotionally, then we will get a firm baseline via an in-house test like an online Stanford 10. This lets us know exactly where the student is academically in relation to her peers. Ironically, most of our students have such great success with their HPBT program that their baseline is above average which serves to shore up their success. With a solid baseline and a great attitude, students are ready to make academic progress.

4

## RESTART SCHOOL

After one to twelve months, the decompression & basic healing periods will be completed, a baseline obtained, and an educational strategy constructed. It is now time to restart schooling. Classes can be either at home, in a homeschool cooperative, in a specialized school that the child feels good about, online, or with tutors. Some students go back into public school but they do so with strict guidelines and a very active support system of tutors, mentors, advisors, and therapists.

Our four core subjects will now be expanded upon. We will include grammar, hands on science, and historical literature and explorations. Having mastery of reading comprehension, writing, math, and critical thinking will allow us to very quickly get the student back on track and caught up with her peers despite having taken extended time off school and an apparent light load upon return. This is critical, as we do not want the student to feel behind, which will only create more anxiety. We are not pretending since it is well known that students use only a fraction of their school time for actual learning. Studies show that regular classrooms only get 10 minutes of learning for every 55 minutes of class time. So when we miss a few weeks of school we are only missing a few hours of learning!

Research has proven that the most effective way to treat anxiety is by exposure with extinction. This means that, when your brain is chemically ready, you will need to be exposed to your stressor, in a safe environment. The student will need assisted calming in order to overcome an innate, anxiety producing reaction when reintroduced to their stressor. This is done with lots of patience and therapeutic tutors.

My preferred curriculum for this stage is one we have been experimenting with at LeeWay Academy since 2009. It is still a work in progress but students respond well to the method and our success rate for college admissions is too good to ignore. Our method is built around the known realities of how the brain actually learns and retains information. It follows the rules of brain based learning.

**Engagement -** If the brain is not emotionally engaged in a positive way then new memories can not be formed. Without proper encoding, retrieval is difficult. The student must like the teacher and be engaged in the material at the moment of input if he is going to learn optimally.

**Input -** Information has to go into the brain. All input should be in a format that is in sync with that student's brain. To point, if the student is tactile then information must have some tactile component. All input should be handled by a teacher that the student has a connection to and feels good about.

**Repetition -** Once shown something (input) the student must repeat it. This is where the brain builds a synaptic connection for that specific piece of info; a micro-burst of daily repetition of the info just taught. More practice equals stronger connections. Stronger connections equals better retrieval and usage.

**Feedback -** The brain must prove that it understands the info. No pressure, no timing, no grades. Just toss out questions directly related to the material learned and listen to the answers carefully. Correct faulty logic as you hear it. Students need a give and take conversation about WHY the answer is right or wrong and HOW to make the answer right if it is wrong and vice versa. No judgment during this step! Just ask why, then give feedback.

**Practice -** Now that we have proof that the info is in the brain correctly, that info must be used regularly in order to make those neural connections permanent. This is where homework comes in. Minimum repetition every four days is enough to seal the deal.

***Beware:** *If you are doing an hour of homework and it is wrong then you just grew a strong neural connection to inaccurate information. That is a huge thing to overcome. Don't drill until the info is stored & processed properly.*

To enhance engagement, all teaching is ideally done with three students at a time. They do not have to be the same age or on the same grade level. This is mastery learning and grade has little to do with true mastery. **LeeWay tutors are allowed to use any curriculum they feel is right, at any given time, for their group of students.** They tend to use the reading and writing sections of the Accuplacer, PSAT, and ACT as a guide then pull from workbooks and the internet for supplementation. We never use timed test sections or work against the clock. This is stressful without producing learning. A bad combination.

Instead, the teacher introduces the section (input), explains any core concepts and fields questions (feedback). Next, students will work a handful of questions on their own (repetition). Then the students explains why they chose the answers they did and why the other answer choices are wrong (more feedback). The teacher plays devil's advocate and challenges the student's logic until the student begins to recognize the obvious patterns in the material (learning).

Students work reading, writing, and math sections for no more than 30 minutes each, three to five times per week (practice), followed by 15-30 minutes of feedback. They work the pages linearly, one concept at a time. They always focus on mastery and do not move forward without it. For critical thinking, they do 10-30 minutes daily with constant feedback.

Students in recovery should never be handed a book or worksheet and sent off to do busy work, even if they ask for it. Feedback is not only critical for brain based learning, but conversational give and take between the student and the tutor fosters a love of learning and gives the student a chance to truly interact with the material alongside a supportive adult. To augment static curriculum, we add in online readings, YouTube clips, library books and videos, even related games and television shows. All of these interactive components spark interest and give a fuller understanding of the material. It also distracts from the test prep focus of the program.

Due to the high demand and an ever more limited schedule, I only work with high school students. For this reason, the LeeWay Recovery Plan is academically aimed at completing the placement test for dual credit. This gives the student a valid and achievable goal, it avoids busy work, and it can be done anywhere with any teacher with just about any curriculum. It also takes very little time daily, thus freeing up a good deal of time to spend with family, perform community service, seek social outlets, and focus on therapeutic interventions and emotional healing.

5

## START DUAL ENROLLMENT

As soon as the student is emotionally stable, behaving well at home, and the tutors report the student is ready for testing, we have the student take a placement test for dual enrollment. They do not fail. **We never progress a student until we are certain they will succeed.** We cannot GIVE them success but we can tell them when they are ready to get it on their own, show them how to achieve it, and reward them for it.

**To Review**: When we are tasked with recovering students who appear lost, we take them out of school -- be it public, private, charter, magnet, or home! We do not do academics while a student is in crisis. We give them a short break to de-stress while they see doctors, start therapy, and possibly medications. We focus on health.

When they are completely stable emotionally, we start casual home schooling with therapeutic tutors who teach them placement test prep in lieu of all other academics. We do not teach the tests, we teach core mastery of what will be needed in order to do well on the math, reading, and writing TSI test.

We do not assign homework, we guide the student through input and repetition on a near daily basis using an interactive feedback teaching methodology. We schedule the remainder of the student's time to include explorative extracurriculars such as clubs, recreation, career planning, and possibly even family therapy to rebuild relationships. The goal of "time way" is simply to de-stress, begin working towards a valid and doable academic goal, and explore what the future has to offer.

As soon as the student is able to pass the reading and writing section of a placement test, we enroll them in their first dual enrollment class. We pick their teacher carefully and give them enormous support outside of class. We also start them in some sort of group class or club for socialization.

**A Quick Side Note:** In these extreme cases, I recommend dropping all high school academics in lieu of college placement test prep. To be clear, I am not advocating "teaching to the test" as it were. We are teaching for success and the student feels successful when they ace a college placement.

We avoid busy work. Busy work feels like a waste to the student because it usually is a waste. We honor the student's feelings at all time. This is a key message we want the student to receive -- life can be what ever they make it.

We avoid remediation. Remediation makes a student feel like a failure. Test prep feels liking working towards a goal. The LeeWay Recovery Plan is about success. Instead of remediating, we focus on targeted learning. We review what the student should have already learned while looking for gaps to fill in.

We use placement testing to tell us where the student is. If placement shows that she is ready for college then we let high school go and let her move on with her life. That means we start dual enrollment. If it shows that she is not ready, then we get her ready -- slowly, patiently, and without making her feel that she is doing anything other than REAL school.

Once DE starts, we go slow. I recommend only one class during the first semester in dual credit. The class should be on campus if possible, as opposed to online. It should be with a great teacher in a highly passable subject. Humanities is a personal favorite but ultimately the scholar should decide. The goal is success in an academic environment. This is what the recovery student needs more than anything else at this point.

*Making a passing grade in one or two classes in a college setting with a great teacher in an interesting and passable subject is the best medicine money can buy.*

6

## STAY CONSTRUCTIVE

During the first year on the LeeWay Recovery Plan, the academic load is very light so the challenge is to help your students remain constructive during traditional school hours. This helps them feel in sync with their peers and is important to the healing. It is never good to let a student just sit around at home watching TV, talking on the phone, and playing video games (after those first critical days of de-stressing). The idea behind the decompression phase of LeeWay Recovery is for the student to get out from under the stress of an oppressive educational environment. This is not intended to be a time of irresponsibility or laziness.

We ask parents to brainstorm with their students to find ways for them to stay busy. They volunteer, take music or art lessons, join clubs, mentor others, explore careers through on-the-job shadowing, be creative, invent, work, be physically active, etc. They will need opportunities for leadership, community service, or group competitions. This is what makes an emotionally secure, independent adult. They need doable goals to achieve on a very regular basis. Check out local homeschool co-ops, community recreation centers, or even start your own family meetup group. The key is to stay involved in life!

When you leave a public or private school, there is often a strong sense of aloneness. Do not let this become entrenched in the student. Make sure to include a regularly scheduled social outlet such as a weekly co-op class, club meetings, or team activities with the same group of friends. Skipping this one step can set the recovery back in ways that are difficult to explain yet very real. Just bear in mind that people need to belong. This is where getting informed and validating will have a big payoff. Find out what your student wants. Guide but do not push. Let them find their own connections but take this opportunity to make sure the connections your student chooses are healthy ones. And never let them remain idle.

7

## NORMALIZE

After one full successful semester of dual enrollment, most of my students have de-stressed enough that they are able to reduce or get off all medications with the assistance of their physician. They also are usually ready to reduce their therapy schedule to a maintenance level. When this happens, the student is ready to start a regular high school dual enrollment schedule using the LeeWay Distinguished Degree Plan. We also ask them to remain in whatever extracurriculars they feel good about. We want them to continue to stay constructive. We want them to slowly begin to explore colleges and career options so that when they graduate, on time, they will be ready to take the next logical step which is often to go on to college.

Among the clients who come to me with stress related problems, by the end of the first year on The LeeWay Recovery Plan, each student is basically unrecognizable and my staff gets a flood of additional referrals from families and physicians asking us to help someone else they know. We tell them the same thing I am telling you right now. Listen to your student. Take the time to really get to know them. Find out what is causing them to feel stressed, then address it in a systematic way. Perhaps even consider using The LeeWay Recovery Plan.

# COLLEGE ADMISSIONS

## Getting In
## &
## Getting Money

# 17☞

# GETTING INTO COLLEGE

## The Admissions Game

Up to this point, I have been introducing you to the dual enrollment program and giving you a number of solid reasons why it should be part of any high school to college plan. Now comes the fun part – using DE for college admissions.

Dual credit can be used in a variety of ways. Obviously, it is an amazing stand alone resource that can be used for straightforward high school credits. Instead of taking classes in high school then again at college, a student can take one dual credit class and get both high school and college credit.

Dual credit can also be used as an emotionally safe way to gain mastery in the core subjects of reading, writing, and math. If timed right, it can be used as synchronous prep for PSAT, SAT, or ACT. ENGL 1301 and MATH 1314 are perfect prep classes.

When used strategically, dual credit can be a tool for restoring a passion for learning, or even as a way to help a failing student recover his equilibrium. I have seen many a distressed teen recover fully using DE and the LeeWay Recovery Plan.

DE can be used to prove college readiness, or a way to escape the stress of a school system that is focused on schooling over learning. DE can be a mechanism for earning honors without the overkill of AP and IB courses or DE can be used for optimal efficiency. I personally value efficiency above all else, which makes dual enrollment my golden fleece. And since the goal of high school is to prepare a student for college and life success, the next few chapters are aimed at laying out optimal ways to utilize dual enrollment for any student.

How does one use DE to get into a great college? How does one use DE to earn non-loan financial aid? How does one use dual credit for psychological wellbeing to increase overall success? How does one use DE to get free college credits? The answer is simple. Use the SECRET FORMULA.

*Build A Perfect College Package*

*Apply To The Right Colleges*

*Meet Three Deadlines*

It really is as simple as one, two, three. Any student that does these three things in the right way can get into a good college of their choosing, can potentially get at least 50% of the cost of tuition and fees paid for by way of primary aid, can optionally earn the other 50% plus room and board through service-based secondary aid, and can graduate debt free. This is not just for elite students, although being a naturally good tester certainly makes the entire process significantly easier. I am saying that absolutely any student of any caliber can get college paid for if just one ideal is honored. Follow the SECRET FORMULA!

## BUILD A PERFECT COLLEGE PACKAGE

The first step to getting into a good college and getting it paid for is to build a great College Package (CP). You may remember that the CP is everything a college will see when the student applies for admission to a college or university. It is essentially the student's academic & extracurricular record.

The College Package is more important for freshman applicants than transfer students. This is because freshman applicants have more (but not necessarily better) choices for financial aid. Understanding freshman vs. transfer status is a first step to benefiting from any college planning tool. Freshman applicants are treated differently than transfer applicants.

The baseline tells us whether or not a student's College Package is likely to make him primary (merit-based) scholarships. If his CP clearly does not or will not get him aid, then I recommend he focus on a transfer route to college. Something we will talk about in detail in a later chapter. But if the baseline indicates that his College Package does have the potential for primary aid, then we follow my SECRET FORMULA and put most of our time, money, and precious emotional energy into improving his College Package. We start this in 8th grade.

*The better the College Package,*

*the better the college a student can get into*

*and the more non-loan aid he can get.*

A college will consider an applicant's record going back to the beginning of 8th grade. For this reason, credits in math, science, and foreign language from the last year of middle school are often used to round out the high school transcript. On the other end of the spectrum, the College Package will be a wrap by the beginning of 12th grade. (The CP does include the senior year but in a very cursory way since college admissions is completed well before senior grades are reported in late spring.) With admission applications being due by October 31st of the senior year, only academics through 11th grade are of note. But extracurriculars and testing can continue through the summer and into the first couple of months of twelfth grade.

Every student wants and needs a great College Package but earning one is not always easy, mainly because many students are just not great testers and tests are disproportionately represented in the College Package. PSAT, SAT, ACT, AP, SAT2, all play a major role in the admissions process. At some colleges, they are all that matter. ☹

GPA is another biggie. GPA is usually part of financial aid eligibility. As such, it is pre-built into the rubric that colleges use for admissions. We refer to GPA as an inflexible data point, meaning that it is hard to change and hard to overcome once it declines. GPA is directly tied to the choice of high school degree plan. More demanding curriculums produce lower GPAs in general. Think about how difficult AP classes can be. Is it any surprise that they can lower GPAs overall?

On top of great test scores and a high GPA, awards & honors will be expected along with volunteerism, leadership, and competition, aka extracurriculars. This forms the trifecta of college admissions: tests, grades, and service.

Think about it from the colleges' perspective. They only have so many openings each year. More students apply than there are openings for. Colleges need a way to pick students who will truly thrive at their school and actually graduate. Like any other business, colleges need to get a return on their investment. That return is a successful graduate who goes out into the world and makes it a better place, hopefully making a name for himself, and his alma mater, along the way. Colleges try to figure out who these "winning" students will be and offer them admissions and aid. Only a top percentage of all applicants will win a paid trip to college in the admissions game. What do these winning applicants have to do to score such a windfall? A lot!

A great College Package is intimidating and not easy to come by. A top university's ideal applicant will be a National Merit winner. He will also have a 750+ on the reading and math portions of the SAT or a 34 on the ACT. He will be an AP Scholar with at least three AP tests with a score of 3 or better. He will have a solid 4.0 in DE, and be a member of Phi Theta Kappa, as well as a member of the National Honor Society. He will also have a referral from someone of note, plus three or more years of outstanding community service and leadership. An extracurriculars resume full of volunteerism along with several state or national awards will be expected as well. And even this amazingly excelled student would not be assured an offer of admission from the top fifty universities in America!

This is no exaggeration. The competition for spots at the top 50 colleges is fierce even for the best of students. Fortunately, there are a lot of really amazing colleges and universities that are not on that rather politicized list of top colleges. This is why applying to the right college is the second step in the SECRET FORMULA.

*The college dream is possible for every student of every caliber as long as they have something special in their record and apply to a school that will be attracted to that something.*

Everyone is special in some way. Being an ideal candidate is not realistic for most students. So a better goal is to just be the best YOU that you can be, then find a school that likes the YOU that you are. There is a unique path for every student. Find it. Follow it! Sure, we can spend years in high school trying to mold a young man or woman into what top colleges will want, but will they be happy when they get there? Would it not be better to support and encourage our young men and women to develop into the best version of themselves that they can be then send them off to an educational institution that is in sync with their aptitudes, interests, and learning styles?

Whichever route is taken, students will need to build a College Package that is competitive for the caliber of schools they hope to gain admission to. The way to achieve this goal is to look at the College Package Check Off List on page 250, and figure out early on what is doable for a specific pupil, and what is not. Then help that student focus on being remarkable at the things that are doable for him.

If the student is a proven tester, then set his sights on scoring big on the PSAT. A great PSAT could result in a NMS. National Merit is always a priority when possible. But if the student is not a good tester then it would be a silly waste of resources to go after National Merit. All the expensive, time consuming and soul draining test prep in the world won't get a poor tester to the lofty goal of NMS. And would he even thrive at a college full of students who did not have to work so hard to win such a coveted admission? The adage of a big fish in a little pond is coming to mind. Only in this case, the student would be a guppy swimming with the sharks!

Students who do not test well should put their eggs into the dual credit and extracurricular basket. The payoff for aid will be equally excellent and the outcome is likely to be better. The student will almost certainly be happier and high school will be less stressful for everyone involved. Every student would be well advised to focus on just what he or she can realistically achieve then apply to a college that will appreciate what that student has achieved. Put another way, be yourself then look for a mate that will love you just the way you are. The resulting union is much more likely to be a happy & successful one!

## CrowFly©
## College Countdown Tool

A College Countdown List is a must have for high school to college planning. I use such a list, along with a constantly evolving algorithm, in my office every day to customize our client's high school strategies. I call my list CrowFly.

Thanks to a decade of successes that has surprised even me at times, my office is bombarded with requests for personalized advising. I can only see a fraction of the families who contact me. There simply are not enough hours in the day. For years, the running joke in our Dallas office is that they need to find a way to clone me. As that option is many years down the road (presumably), my brilliant husband, John, decided to engineer a solution. A sort of digital version of me.

As a computer software specialist with twenty years of developing technological solutions to real world problems, John came up with the idea of creating a virtual Kathe. The results were better than expected. (I'm starting to believe that he may actually be able to "clone" my thought processes some day!)

He and his tiny team set about to design an online tool that could ask a student the same questions that I would ask, then run the answers through a proprietary algorithm, which they dubbed ***The Kathe Formula***. Just like my real brain does, the Kathe Formula's algorithm calculates what steps a particular student should take in order to have a successful high school to college outcome. Since our aim is always to get into a good college and graduate with no college debt, success was easy to measure. John's program worked and we use it every day in our office.

The Kathe Formula is still a secret tool that we only use in-house, but it wet my whistle for something to share with my clients. I put John back to work. What he came up with was a web based subscription product that parses out a grade-specific "To Do List" for each year of high school. CrowFly users (student & parents) are transported through a secret link to their own private high school to college planning tool. Monthly email and text reminders nudge students to check in and get informed.

CrowFly essentially delivers a reminder from me to the student of exactly what that student should be doing to stay on track for graduation and college admissions with financial aid. If followed religiously throughout high school, CrowFly will get any student into college and get it paid for.

CrowFly is constantly evolving. In the beginning, information was simply doled out on a 30-day basis with minimal fanfare. Three little things to do right now. But people need motivation so each month, additions such as personal messages from me or video chats have increased the usability of the program. Another addition, though still in the early stages, is added student accountability, which allows a parent to track a student's progress and see that progress online.

When used correctly, CrowFly allows a family or high school counselor to plan a child's high school classes, tests schedule, volunteerism, leadership, competitions, college visits, scholarship applications, college admission apps, essays, interviews or auditions, in exactly the same way I would do it in my office. But with CrowFly, they can do it without the time and expense of seeing me personally. My publisher and benefactor, a non-profit organization called LeeWayUSA, makes CrowFly available through their website and mine as part of their "Premium Content" that also includes live chats with me, my continually updated blog, and copies of this book.

The KatheLee.com website allows parents, counselors, and students to try a full fledged version of CrowFly for free when they signup using my name as a promo code. This is my way of allowing anyone to check out this continually improving, one-of-a-kind resource. With CrowFly, any student can succeed.

CrowFly is available for students in 9th, 10th, 11th, and 12th grades but I personally think it is invaluable for juniors and seniors. I rest a little easier knowing that all the people who cannot get in to see me personally can still stay on target for graduation, admissions, and financial aid just by using CrowFly. My students say it's almost like having me right in their inbox.

## College Package Check Off List

- ❑ **PSAT/National Merit Scholar**
  - Winner, Finalist, or Semi-Finalist
- ❑ **Tests Scores**
  - SAT: 1390--1450 (super scored)
  - ACT: 30-34 composite
  - SAT II: 700+ in any subject test
- ❑ **Honors Curriculum**
  - AP Scholar – Three AP tests with 3+ on each
  - Dual Credit – 18 hours with 4.0 GPA
  - Calculus – In Progress for 12th grade
  - 3.8 GPA overall or Top 10% of class
- ❑ **Awards & Accomplishments** (Extracurriculars)
  - Leadership – Do something outstanding
  - Volunteerism – 200 hours over 4 years
  - Competitions – Win at state or national level
  - Associations – Honor societies, memberships, etc.
  - Awards – Be provably notable
  - Recognition – Get publicly noticed for helping others
- ❑ **GREAT Referrals -** Must be from someone well known; either in your chosen field of study, important to the admitting college, or internationally famous.

By the end of high school, every student should have everything on this list accomplished if they want to be a competitive candidate at a top college or for top financial aid. If you're reading this book then you know this to be true and you even know why, but will you remember exactly what to do or when to do it? Now you can become a KatheLee.com Premium user with direct access to CrowFly, and let this amazing College Countdown Tool guide from the beginning of high school through graduation and college admissions. CrowFly knows exactly what to do and exactly when to do it. So you can relax and just wait for your next set of simple instructions.

When it comes to building a College Package, few students can do it all. Most should not even try. A better goal would be to allow each student to progress in a way that is natural for him, then use step two of the SECRET FORMULA to match his final College Package to colleges and universities that have a history of admitting and giving aid to students with packages just like the one he ends up with!

## APPLY TO THE RIGHT COLLEGES

The College Package wraps up in 12th grade with a final SAT/ACT in early fall just in time for applications by the October 31st admissions deadline. This is the point where step two begins; apply to the right colleges. To do this requires knowing which colleges will look favorably upon a CP like the one under consideration. This requires a College Screening.

In a College Screening, we collect all the information for a student's record. Then they will ask the student for a list of personal parameters. This will include things like how far the student wants to be from home, size of campus preferred, geographical location, religious preference, etc. Then we define a set of parameters related to demographics, freshman retention rate, alumni network, study abroad opportunities, cost, financial aid qualifications, graduating class indebtedness, and graduate school admissions. These are all data points on our rubric.

Once we know a student's package and personal parameters, we plug it all into a proprietary system that scans hundreds of colleges and universities to determine which ones have a history of accepting and financially rewarding records like the one we have in front of us. The resulting dozen or so colleges should be a perfect match for our student. These are the colleges we recommend that our student visit. Then based on our client's feedback, we pick five colleges to apply to. We pick one dream/reach school, one default school, and three additionals. More is allowed but three is minimal.

Performing a College Screening without a professional college advisor or strategist is not difficult. It will just take a good deal more time since as of this writing there is not a reliable program or system available to the public to do what our proprietary product does for us. Notwithstanding, a college screening can and should be done.

To run your own College Screening, build a list of the parameters that matter to the student. Then factor in all the components of that student's College Package. Decide what is most important, getting in vs. getting money vs. personal experience vs. some other factor that is particularly pertinent to the student or family. This is the Focal Point. Then take a list of all colleges you want to consider and remove any college that do not match the Focal Point. What remains is a list of viable colleges. Now, start comparing the viable college list with the overall parameter list.

The results of this comparison will be a list of a dozen or so colleges and universities that deserve a much closer look. Pay them a visit. Call ahead and arrange to sit in on classes. Meet with professors in a major of interest. Have a sit-down with financial aid to confirm that they are indeed likely to reward the CP that you may be sending their way. With all this information, you are ready to pick five plus colleges to apply to come October.

In my practice, we have specially trained staff who do nothing but College Screenings since this is a crucial step in the admissions and aid process. **Ironically, a College Screening is more important than either test prep or AP classes, but less than ten percent of students will ever get one.**

## MEET THE DEADLINES

The third step to a successful college admissions strategy is to meet three key deadlines. This involves taking the right tests at the right time, completing all applications by a preferred deadline, and submitting ALL financial aid applications by December of 12$^{th}$ grade. All of these deadlines assume that the student is not wanting to be a "junior admit", or planning to take a GAP year or be a super senior. Junior admits need a different schedule and have much earlier deadlines.

The biggest deadline, outside of college admissions, is what tests to take and when to take them. The following deadlines are what I personally recommend to the majority of my clients, but there are many factors that would cause me to make adjustments. If you are unsure which modifications to make then spend some time at KatheLee.com or let CrowFly guide you.

## The Ideal Test Schedule

- ☐ *Stanford two years in a row in 6-7th*
- ☐ *PSAT 8/9 in 8th or 9th to find gaps*
- ☐ *Baseline AP in May of 9th*
- ☐ *PSAT in 10th to predict National Merit*
- ☐ *Second AP in May of 10th*
- ☐ *Official PSAT in October of 11th*
- ☐ *1st SAT in December of 11th*
- ☐ *1st ACT in Feb - April of 11th*
- ☐ *Third AP in May of 11th*
- ☐ *SAT 2 Subject Test in June of 11th*
- ☐ *Last SAT in August of 12th*
- ☐ *Last ACT in September of 12th*
- ☐ *Last SAT2 in October of 12th*

Many high school counselors, and of course all test prep centers, will recommend testing earlier and more often. In short, don't! In fact, some of the tests on my list can be eliminated for many students.

For example, most students will not need SAT2 Subject Tests since most colleges don't require them. Unnecessary testing should be avoided! Over testing early on creates a lot of anxiety associated with the testing process, constructs an inaccurate picture of the student's potential, and sets the student up for disappointment down the road. Waiting and optimizing is a proven ploy that will produce optimal outcomes. Testing is deadline number one.

The remaining two deadlines are for applications and financial aid. No matter what a college publishes in their admissions material, absolutely all college applications should be completed, submitted, and paid for no later than end of day October 31st of the senior year. The reason for this will become obvious as you read on. Note that in some cases, freshman admissions deadlines will be even earlier, but never later!

Two weeks after submitting an application, an email or phone call should be made to the college to confirm that everything was received and processing is underway. Once this is confirmed, a request for an admissions interview is in order. Not all schools honor an interview request but if the student is going to participate in sports, art, music, dance, debate, or the like, this is the point at which a request for an audition or interview should be made. Do not get hung up on the word "interview". We usually just ask for a "sit down" with admissions, a department head, or financial aid for the purpose of helping the student get connected to the school. In reality we are getting admissions, a department head, and financial aid connected to our student. Admission applications is deadline number two.

Secondary applications will be needed in order to get scholarships based on community service and the extracurricular resume. These applications must be submitted by their individual deadlines which begin as early as October and are effectively over by the end of February. This is one of the main reasons that we are such sticklers for the October 31st admissions application deadline. If you do not have an admissions application on file by this key date, scholarship deadlines become impossible to meet.

The final financial aid deadline is February 15th. Notice that this is the FINAL FINANCIAL AID DEADLINE. That means everything else is done by this point. In order to receive a fully vetted offer from a college in the critical March financial aid window, all students should complete either a FAFSA or CSS Profile no later than midnight on February 14th. The FAFSA is a free federal aid application and is ideal for state schools or for families with less than $100,000 adjusted gross income. The not free CSS Profile is better reserved for families with high incomes, especially at expensive private schools where a high cost of attendance (COA) can make even a relatively well off student, needy. FAFSA is now available on October 1st so don't put it off till the last minute. Financial Aid is deadline number three.

College is outrageously expensive and increasingly so every year. Even if students live at home for all four years, a bachelor's degree from the cheapest public university will cost a minimum of $20,000. This number is deceptively low. The average bachelor's degree actually costs over $100,000 at pubic schools and $200k plus at private universities. [1] The majority of this cost is paid by parents from savings and retirement accounts, or it is taken on as debt by both the student and the parents in the form of student aid and parent plus loans.

The college debt problem in America has clearly reached a crisis level with many families and experts questioning the value of continuing to send students off to college at all. If you have a student in 7th, 8th or 9th grade then you absolutely must start thinking in terms of what you can do now to make high school pay off for college, especially in relation to college financial aid. We know that most families do not have a plan. But even those who do can find their plan sorely lacking once the time comes. Once high school starts, time will speed up in a way that is unimaginable to first timers, so start early.

College planning is a big picture business that requires a holistic approach. You can not hope to offer someone appropriate advice if you have not first learned about that person. My advising strategy always begin with getting to know the entire family situation and analyzing that family's resources. Just a casual but focused conversation so that I can collect relevant information. Then I build a plan that allows for easy adjustments as new information becomes apparent. My process is best explained by sharing the story of Emily, an eleventh grader at a well respected private school in Chicago, whose father had contacted me for a private consult.

Emily was my first client of the new school year. A bubbly 11th grader with reportedly glowing grades and active memberships in all the right clubs. This is exactly what her parents wrote in their email asking me for an advising appointment. Her father was a commercial airline pilot and her mother a professional stylist to some well-known celebs. Both parents went to good colleges and wanted to make sure their daughter followed in their footsteps. They had prepared financially by contributing to a 529 plan for over a decade, plus their combined salaries were enough that they felt they could come up with about $10k per year for Emily's education without having to dip into savings. But recent events had shaken their faith in their plan.

The concern was that Emily would end up with the same financial woes as her older brother. Emily was the second of three children. The oldest, Michael, had gone off to an out-of-state school three years earlier and did not get the amount of financial assistance he was promised by the counselor at his well-regarded private high school, despite his better than average tests scores and time consuming AP classes. Michael was now a year away from college graduation and had already signed off on $37,900 in personal student loans. His parents had paid about twice as much out of pocket as they had originally planned creating a shortfall for Emily. Mom and Dad wanted to avoid these pitfalls the second time around.

Their task for me was two-fold. First, make sure that Emily would qualify for admission to Northwestern, an elite university in Evanston, Illinois, with a stellar program in journalism that everyone agreed was the perfect major for Emily. Second, figure out a way to get the more than $40,000 per year Emily would need in order to pay for her upscale college experience. I immediately assured them that no one could guarantee admission to any particular school but other than that, I felt confident that I could fulfill their request.

## ACADEMIC ADVISING 101

**Step 1: Assess & Plan** - Where was Emily academically? Had she taken any standardized tests? What were her test scores? Was this with or without prep? What classes was she taking at school? How were her grades? What clubs was she in? Had she won any awards? What had she done that was notable?

As I asked each of these questions, the answers were typically superficial. According to everyone at the table, Emily was a top student, made nearly straight As, and was a great tester. They had no doubt that she would get admitted to a top college, and scholarships were a given. I asked for her records.

In reality, Emily was a very typical student. She had a 3.73 unweighted GPA at her elite high school. She was in Advanced Placement classes but had not scored anything higher than a 2 on any associated tests. Her PSAT showed a selection index of 162 despite an after-school intensive prep program that her parents had paid serious money for her to attend. This was a respectable score but nothing close to what she would need for Northwestern. She was on student council, a member of Key Club, with no independent community service. In short, Emily was not a good candidate for admission to Northwestern and she would certainly not be in the running for scholarships.

Let me be clear. Emily was not a bad student. She was actually above par as compared to the national averages. She had several unique merits in that she was a cheerleader, member of the debate team, and very involved in competitive gymnastics via her school. Unfortunately, the work load of her AP classes and sports practice made it difficult for her to do anything outside of her school related activities.

Emily was not interested in leaving her current high school, despite the hefty annual tuition, so I was forced to work within the confines of that school's degree plan and transcript. With two years remaining before graduation, I had to find a way to work with the limitations that existed. It never really worries me to have so many obstacles because I know that there is a path for every student, and I have learned not to expect that path to always be a smooth one. I built a plan for Emily that accommodated all of these realities.

**Step 2: Build The College Package** - I took some time to speak with the administration at Emily's school. After a bit of negotiation, they agreed to replace Emily's degree plan with the LeeWay DDP, which we customized to meet a couple of specific requirements in their district. Since Emily's AP classes were time consuming but not producing good test scores, we removed those from her schedule. With the freed up time, we added two dual enrollment classes that fall. Fortunately, she did so well in dual credit that we added a total of three courses in the spring semester with the enthusiastic blessing of her school counselor and parents. We did one more dual enrollment class in the summer via an online program, since her school district did not have a summer DE option. Emily reported being happy.

Due to pressure from her school and against my advice, Emily prepped for and took the PSAT in 11th grade. As predicted, her final number was only slightly better than her first. Throwing good money after bad, with encouragement from a school counselor, Emily's parents put out nearly $1,700 for a top SAT prep program from a respected organization. Even after four months of prep, her SATs barely broke 550, something her PSATs clearly predicted. Disillusioned and none the richer, everyone agreed to stick to my strategy and focus on the things that Emily could naturally excel at.

Knowing that Emily was likely headed to Northwestern University, since that is what the family had specifically hired me to make happen, we went online to get a list of CLEP tests that Northwestern would accept. Using tutors, Emily prepared over the summer and took a CLEP in her least favorite core class, hoping to avoid it in college. The therapeutic tutor we picked did such a fantastic job that Emily scored high enough on her CLEP to get credit for both sections of U.S. History. It was a major motivation to Emily to know that she would never have to take a history class again. Emily felt that the results were well worth giving up four weeks of her summer for. She loved not having to take any History her senior year.

**Step 3: Focus On Extracurriculars** - Outside of school, Emily followed a very personalized plan of extracurriculars, which we fine-tuned to coincide with career exploration. After learning that her writing interests were specifically related to movies, movie stars, and all things Hollywood, we arranged for Emily to work as an unpaid intern at an online blog. Seeing her first story in print was all it took for Emily to get on the bandwagon and take the reins. Without prompting, Emily submitted several pieces to national publications and actually got a byline. We also arranged for Emily to shadow a local newspaper columnist and movie reviewer. By Christmas of her senior year, Emily was in L.A. at a movie premiere with the movie critic who had taken Emily under her wing. To say that things were improving would be a huge understatement.

**Step 4: Manage Time Well** - That same fall semester, we kept the load light so that Emily would have time to write her articles, travel with her mentor, complete some college visits, get her applications in by the October 31st deadline, and work on applications for secondary scholarships. After visiting a dozen or so colleges, Emily fell in love with the NYU journalism program and everything shifted to meet this new and lofty ambition.

Knowing that she would need an interview and a quality portfolio in order to have a shot at such a great school, we stopped DE that fall and further reduced the time she was required to spend on school by implementing a work study program that allowed her to have half days off to focus on her writing work. Motivated by her newfound independence and the reality that her dream was actually a possibility, Emily poured her heart and soul into an amazing portfolio that she broadcast by way of a professional website.

**<u>Step 5: Apply To The Right Colleges</u>** - By the first major deadline, the application window, Emily had an amazing College Package despite middle-of-the-road test scores. If she applied to the right colleges, Emily would be a shoo-in. A key factor was that the right colleges would need to be willing to overlook weak test scores. So we performed a proprietary College Screening to come up with 16 colleges that were sure to love Emily's College Package sans test scores. We reserved NYU as a dream school, knowing it was a long shot at best.

In the end, Emily applied to eleven colleges including NYU and Northwestern. She got an offer of admission from all but three. Thankfully, NYU was among the acceptance offers! They were heavily swayed by her impressive portfolio and 4.0 DE record. But getting in was just the beginning. NYU is a pricey school and without winning test scores, Emily was not a candidate for many of the larger scholarships that she would need. Using a few tricks that you will learn about in the next chapter, we negotiated an acceptable financial aid packet at two of her top choice schools. Then we left the final choice of which college to accept firmly in Emily's hands.

Emily is now in her second year at NYU and Mom and Dad are thrilled to have their college budget back under control just in time for their youngest to start down the college planning road. They have already started working on my plan by moving their younger daughter to a three-day-a-week alternative school that frees up time for her to optimize dual enrollment when the time comes. And knowing that this student is also not a great test taker, they have replaced time demanding test prep with targeted extracurriculars. Plus we have started some therapeutic tutoring which just might make testing a better option when the time comes for this last child to head off to college.

As Emily's story so aptly demonstrates, dual credit is not just a chance for students to take free or cheap college classes while still in high school. It is not just about the efficiency of taking one class and getting credit for both high school and college. Or about motivating lackluster students by taking a year's worth of classes in one semester. These are all just perks of the program. Dual credit should be the core to any efficient high school to college plan when you want to make the most of all the tools at your disposal and increase the odds of your student having a successful transition to a great college with solid financial aid options.

# 18☞

# TRANSCRIPTS

## The Art Of Reporting

The high school transcript is created, maintained, and otherwise administered by the school a student attends. For homeschoolers, this means the parents. When applying to colleges, the transcript will be the main source of information about a student's College Package, which is everything that students are asked to submit to a college when they apply. Different colleges will want to see different things.

## WHAT COLLEGES WANT

- ↑ GPA
- Top 10%
- ACT 27+
- SAT 1400+
- AP Scholar
- 18 Hours DE
- Math at DE
- Science at DE
- Calculus
- 3 F. Language
- Top Awards
- Several Clubs
- Competitions
- Great Essays
- Honor Societies
- Leadership
- NMS Finalist
- Legacy Status
- Memberships
- Top References
- Service Record
- Subject Tests
- Volunteerism
- < $90k Income

A highly competitive candidate for admission and aid will have all of this and more, and nearly all of it will be reflected to some degree in the academic record as represented by the official high school transcript. The transcript is the most important document in the student's repertoire. To optimize dual enrollment for admission and aid it will be necessary to understand how to make and use a transcript.

For students in public, private, or charter schools, the transcript, just like the degree plan, will be automatically handled by the district. And, just like with the degree plan, the product the district turns out may not be in the student's best interest. Unfortunately, a public school transcript is not easy to augment or change. But it is not impossible. For families committed to tailor-made schooling, supervising the creation and maintenance of the official transcript is imperative even for public schoolers.

Creating transcripts is not easy, which is why the numerous apps that pop out a formatted document in minutes is alluring but ill advised. Turning out a transcript optimized for college admission and financial aid borders on rocket science. Knowing the proper words to use, optimal presentation order, and what to highlight takes a bit of expertise.

**The transcript is the main and most powerful demonstration of a student's academic abilities.** As such, universities pay very close attention to the what, where, and when of reported classes, credits, and grades. It is important to denote DE, AP, IB, and CLEP courses in the most advantageous way. How rank is achieved or how GPA was calculated can be critical. Homeschoolers have the added problem of trying to create a transcript that won't get discounted by a college admissions officer. Homeschooling may be completely legal but old prejudices die hard. Straight 'A's without great test scores or DE is often suspect on a home school transcript.

On a transcript, it is the little things that matter. Just the formatting can make a big difference. How things are named will matter even more. There are many rules, not a lot of instructions, and plenty of places to go wrong. In order to create an ideal high school transcript, one first has to understand the high school credit system. Then one has to be able to legally manipulate that system in order to give a college what it wants in an applicant without misstating the facts.

The high school credit system is controlled by various governing boards. For the most part, it is standardized throughout the U.S. Take another look at the LeeWay Degree Plan. You will see that each high school class is worth either 1.0 or 0.5 credits. A full school year in a core course like English, Math, Science, History, or Language is always valued at 1.0 credit, unless it is an Advanced Placement class in which case it may be worth up to 1.5 credits. If students only complete half a semester of a full year course, or they only complete half of the work required for a 1.0 credit course, then they get only half of the credit or 0.5. The same is true for non-core classes.

Non-core, elective style classes like art, music, PE, economics, psychology, or computing are only valued at half a credit and are generally only one semester long. If the course is designed to continue for both semesters, the credit is still the same, only 0.5. If students only complete half of the coursework then they only receive half of the credit or 0.25. There is no hard and fast rule about how long a class has to be, how many days the class has to last, or even what curriculum must be used. The parent or school district will decide this.

Oh, there are rules. Lots of them! But they vary from state to state and even district to district. To remain in compliance with the local or state school boards, a family will need to get educated about the specific guidelines available in their jurisdiction. Start by asking the state school board for their official guideline, but double check everything.

Once credits are earned, how they go on to the transcript is rather formulaic. If a pupil completes a legitimate course that has been either approved by the parents or accepted by the school board then that student gets a corresponding credit on his transcript. The name of that class will be determined by the school or parent. The grade will come from the supervising teacher or parent. Current public school naming and grading convention is in sync with how colleges expect to receive such information. For parents who choose to optimize their transcript, remaining true to these conventions is wise.

*Homeschoolers should assign credits according to the system used by public schools. It is similarly wise to use a common naming codification.*

When parents build their own custom transcript, classes may be named and credited as the parents see fit. But when a college receives a transcript with unique naming conventions or an odd crediting scheme, a well-intentioned college admissions clerk will try to assign conventional names and somewhat randomly apply credits based on some default degree plan or prior experience. This is rarely favorable for the applicant. In the case of classes like bible study, Worldviews, and Crossfit, it would be better to go ahead and convert the name prior to sending out the transcript. Bible study could become Theology. Worldviews may become History, Western Civilizations, or Social Studies. Crossfit should become PE or Athletics.

Many homeschoolers and small private schools harm the admissions process by veering from a proven standard. This is done either in ignorance or in an attempt to control how a college perceives their students' high school record. This should only be attempted by someone with a lot of experience and proven results.

## HOW TO MAKE A TRANSCRIPT

There is a right and wrong way to make a transcript. The first thing that every good transcript needs is a header. This includes things like the name of the school, contact information, student info, and ID numbers. (Never put the student's entire social security number on a transcript or any other document!)

After the header, comes a section that highlights the current status of things such as planned date of graduation, cumulative credits earned to date, current GPA, and rank. Another section should feature honors and awards including memberships, leadership positions, and only the best tests scores. All of this is on the first page. Think of the transcript as the start of a college scholarship application, because that is exactly what it will become when it is submitted for admissions.

The final and main section of a transcript is an actual list of classes. This is often on a second page. Classes may be listed in several ways but in general there should be a school year for each class taken, amount of credit assigned to each class, and the final grade for each course. It is best to list classes in an English, Math, Science, History order that is the same for each school year. This makes it easy for an admissions officer to quickly see progression within a single subject. The individual course grade should be clearly denoted as well as a cumulative grade for each semester or year of study.

If an AP or IB class or test was taken, then the AP or IB designation should be present on the transcript. This can be added before the class name or in a separate column that might also be used to show honors coursework. For example, dual enrollment classes are harder than typical high school classes so they warrant the "Honors" insignia, along with an asterisk to indicate that the class was taken at a specific college. It is not helpful to add information like how many weeks the student was in the class, who taught the class, or what curriculum was used, although this info may be requested at some point so it is prudent to keep a separate record in case it is needed.

The two things that confuse people most on a transcript are the GPA calculation and how to apply specialty classes like DE and CLEP. If you add up all the grades received in a single semester then divide by the number of classes, the resulting number would be the GPA for that semester. If calculated in this way, the resulting number would be an unweighted GPA.

A weighted GPA would give more weight to harder classes. For instance, a grade of B in an AP Calculus course would be worth maybe twice as much as an A in Typing. The idea is that some classes are inherently harder and require more work than others so they should carry more weight. Weighting is only allowed when the student takes classes that are unique such as AP or IB. Most schools use a 4.0 scale and colleges generally prefer this model since it is easily understood. Regular classes on this scale would look like the first column. AP, IB, and honors classes could be represented on a weighted 5.0 scale like the second group in the chart below.

## Honors Weighting

| Grade | Regular | Honors | College |
|---|---|---|---|
| A | 4.00 | 4.50 | 5.00 |
| B | 3.00 | 3.50 | 4.00 |
| C | 2.00 | 2.50 | 3.00 |
| D | 1.00 | 1.50 | 2.00 |
| F | 0.00 | 0.50 | 1.00 |

Which scale is better? Well, perfect is always perfect. Everything else is a shell game where nobody wins but the cup shuffler. Stick with a 4.0 scale. If it is favorable to do so, give weight to harder classes but make sure to denote what made them hard like the fact that they were taken at a college, involved a massive test that few kids survived, or were part of a very difficult curriculum overall. Transparency is what will pay off. I personally almost never weight a GPA but there are certainly times when it is advantageous to do so. A student with a majority of AP, IB, DE, or other honors levels courses may qualify for a perfect 4.5 or 5.0 under a weighting system. In such a case, it would be appropriate to add weight.

## ADDING DUAL CREDITS TO A TRANSCRIPT

The confusion about how to represent dual enrollment credits on a transcript is due to the fact that there are two transcripts that reflect DE credits. There is the high school transcript, and there is also a college transcript. The official college transcript includes all DE classes attempted, whether passed, dropped, or failed. If a class is passed, it will be assigned one to four college credits and will be named according to some version of the Common Course Number (CCN) system.

CCN is a combination of the subject, its grade level, and the number of credits a class is worth. Take the example of freshman English. It will have a lettered prefix such as ENG or ENGL followed by a three or four digit number like 130 or 1301. This number means something. Reading from left to right, the first number tells us the level of the course. The second number tell us how many college credits the course is worth. A class labeled ENGL **1**301 would be a freshman course worth 3 college credits. MATH 2**4**02 would be a sophomore class worth four credits. At the end of each semester, a college transcript will be issued clearly noting the class title, grade, and college credits awarded. When a student applies to a university, this college transcript will be required along with an official high school transcript. They will not be the same as they do not serve the same purpose.

The whole point of dual enrollment classes is that they receive two sets of credits, one for college and one for high school. On a college transcript, math, science, language, and computer courses are likely to be worth four credits, while everything from history to philosophy will be worth three. PE, private music lessons, and some art classes are often given just one or two credits. Students, parents, counselors, and high school administration have no control over how DE classes are credited on the college transcript. The responsibility of creating a college transcript rest solely with the college where the classes where taken.

The high school transcript is a completely different instrument. It is the responsibility of the school district or parent. DE classes on a high school transcript should be represented in high school credits, not in college credits. This means that even though ENGL 1301 is worth three college credits, it is only worth 1.0 high school credits. The grade on a high school transcript should be in sync with the one on the college transcript with one change. Colleges usually just give an A, B, C, D, or F as a grade. But it is advantageous to show a number grade on the high school transcript, especially when that number is 89.9 or the like.

This is a good time to just stop and think about the goal of your high school transcript. Colleges are going to use your transcript to determine if you are the kind of student that would fit in well at their university. A transcript can tell the college several things, all of which they need to know in order to determine best fit. They need to know if you have actually completed the basic courses required for graduation in your state. They need to see if those courses were the same caliber of courses that your peers took so they can compare apples to apples. They need to see if those courses were special in some way. Were they modified to accommodate a learning difference or handicap of some sort? Were they more difficult than classes taken by other students, meaning were they honors level, IB level, AP level, preAP level, or actual college classes taken at an accredited college such as through DE? All of this paints a picture of the student that an admissions officer will use to determine if the applicant should be offered admissions.

Take a look at the sample transcript on the next couple of pages. This composite transcript has been optimized specifically for college admissions.

**If a student were starting dual enrollment instead of applying to a university, the transcript would be optimized in a very different way.** Since students can only take in dual enrollment what they have remaining on the transcript that they submitted to the DE office when they enrolled in the program, the ideal transcript that will get turned in to the DE office at enrollment will show exactly 6.0 credits for 9th grade and 6.0 credits for 10th plus any 11th grade courses that are in progress (IP) at the time of admission into a dual credit program. There is no reason to put anything extra on a DE transcript since it is strictly for DE and is almost never in sync with the final transcript that will be sent out for university admissions. Our sample transcript here would get me into a lot of great colleges but would not be good for DE!

Notice that our optimized transcript is two pages in length. This is not mandatory but it usually aids in clarity. The front page is for key information about the student and the high school, while the second page is reserved for classes and grades. This particular transcript is broken out by school year. It could just as easily have been broken out by subject. Neither way is more optimal than another. Again, the key is to make the entire document highly readable so that an admissions officer can quickly and accurately assess the caliber of the student. It must also be notarized and have the signature of a school official.

# SCHOOL NAME

## OFFICIAL HIGH SCHOOL TRANSCRIPT

DISTINGUISHED DEGREE PLAN

| STUDENT INFORMATION | SCHOOL INFORMATION |
| --- | --- |
| **Student's Name** | **School Name** |
| **CommonApp ID# XXXXX** | **School Address** |
| **County, State** | **School City, State, Zip** |
| **DOB: Month, day, year** | **CONTACT: Name of Counselor** |
| **GUARDIANS: Parent's names** | **Counselor's phone number & email** |

**ACADEMIC SUMMARY**

**CUMULATIVE GPA:** 3.96 (UNWEIGHTED)

**CREDITS EARNED:** 23.5

**RANK:** NA

**EXPECTED GRAD. DATE:** MAY 2018

**DIPLOMA EARNED:** HIGH SCHOOL

**GRADING SCALE**

| Grade | Points |
| --- | --- |
| A | 4.0 |
| B+ | 3.5 |
| B | 3.0 |
| C+ | 2.5 |
| C | 2.0 |
| D+ | 1.5 |
| D | 1.0 |
| F | 0.0 |

**AWARDS & HONORS**

- ☑ INTEL SCIENCE FAIR – 1ST PLACE
- ☑ TEEN COURT ATTORNEY 9TH – 11TH
- ☑ MODEL UN 10TH-12TH
- ☑ HABITAT FOR HUMANITY 8TH- 12TH
- ☑ PHI THETA KAPPA – PROTEM LEADER
- ☑ JRROTC – CAPTAIN
- ☑ AP SCHOLAR

**ACT – 34** **SAT - 750/680 super scored**

**NOTARY & SIGNATURES**

*I do hereby self-certify and affirm that this is the official transcript and academic record of* Student's Name.

Signature: ______________________ Title: ______________________

**STATE OF** __________________ COUNTY OF ______________________

This instrument was acknowledged before me on __________ (Date) by ______________________ (Above Endorser)

______________________________
Signature - Notary Public

My Commission Expires: ________________

(Stamp)

**Student's Name: John Doe** **D.O.B. 10/31/00**

## OFFICIAL ACADEMIC RECORD

**FRESHMAN YEAR (9TH) 2014-15**

| Course Title | Level | CRs | Grd | Counts Toward |
|---|---|---|---|---|
| English 9 w/grammar | PAP | 1.0 | 92 | ENGL |
| Algebra II | | 1.0 | 98 | MATH |
| Equine Science | | 1.0 | 100 | SCIN |
| W. Geography (Score 3) | AP | 1.0 | 92 | SOCL |
| Latin III | Honors | 1.0 | 94 | LANG |
| Healthy Life Choices | | 0.5 | 98 | PE |
| Swing Dance | | 0.5 | 100 | PE |
| Window Dressing | | 0.5 | 100 | ARTS |
| Biblical Worldviews | Honors | 1.0 | 98 | ELEC |
| SAT Prep | | 0.5 | A | ELEC |

**Credits: 8.0 GPA: 4.0 Cum. GPA: 4.0**

**SOPHOMORE YEAR (10TH) 2015-16**

| Course Title | Level | CRs | Grd | Counts Toward |
|---|---|---|---|---|
| English 10* ENGL 1301 | Honors | 1.0 | 95 | ENGL |
| Algebra3* MATH 1314 | Honors | 1.0 | 99 | MATH |
| Marine Biology | | 1.0 | 92 | SCIN |
| W. History (Score 3) | AP | 1.0 | 92 | SOCL |
| Latin IV | CLEP | 1.0 | 94 | LANG |
| PE & Fitness | | 0.5 | 100 | PE |
| Computer Coding | PAP | 0.5 | 98 | COMP |
| Personal Finance | | 0.5 | 94 | ELEC |
| Bible Doctrines | | 0.5 | 100 | ELEC |
| ACT Prep | | 0.5 | 100 | ELEC |

**Credits: 7.5 GPA: IP Cum. GPA: 4.0**

**JUNIOR YEAR (11TH) 2016-17**

| Course Title | Level | CRs | Grd | Counts Toward |
|---|---|---|---|---|
| English 11* ENGL1302 | Honors | 1.0 | 92 | ENGL |
| Trig* MATH2324 | Honors | 1.0 | 97 | MATH |
| Physics* PHYS1405 | Honors | 1.0 | 98 | SCIN |
| US History* HIST1301 | Honors | 1.0 | 98 | SOCL |
| Spanish 1* SPAN1411 | Honors | 1.0 | 89 | LANG |
| Government (Score 4) | AP | 1.5 | 91 | SOCL |
| Nutrition | | 0.5 | 98 | PE |
| Band/Clarinet | | 0.5 | 92 | ARTS |
| Debate & Forensics | | 0.5 | 100 | ELEC |

**Credits: 8.0 GPA: 3.89 Cum. GPA: 3.96**

**SENIOR YEAR (12TH) 2017-18**

| Course Title | Level | CRs | Grd | Counts Toward |
|---|---|---|---|---|
| English 12 (score 5) | AP | 1.5 | IP | ENGL |
| PreCalc* MATH2344 | Honors | 1.0 | IP | MATH |
| A&P* BIOL 2401 | Honors | 1.0 | IP | SCIN |
| US History* HIST1302 | Honors | 1.0 | IP | SOCL |
| Spanish II* SPAN1412 | Honors | 1.0 | IP | LANG |
| Driver's Ed | | 0.5 | 100 | ELEC |
| Humanities* HUMA1315 | Honors | 1.0 | IP | ARTS |
| Photography | | 0.5 | 99 | ARTS |
| Work Study | 15hr/wk | 1.0 | IP | ELEC |

**Credits: 8.5 GPA: IP Cum. GPA: IP**

*Colleges Courses taken at Northlake College IP = Classes In Progress

My sample transcript is relatively self-explanatory but a few clarifications might help. For instance, a class can be designated 'AP' if the student took and passed the test that is associated with that class. DE classes are college level courses and deserve an "Honors" classification. Class names should follow a standard convention even if the content of that class is anything but standard. For example, the sample shows PE courses named Swing Dance and Healthy Life Choices. These still fill the spot on the degree plan reserved for PE. Driver's Education is allowed to be included on the transcript without taking up a space on the degree plan so feel free to include it. Take a look at the tenth grade science class. Science is science no matter what the class is actually titled. Marine Biology or Anatomy is just as appropriate in this spot as regular Biology would be.

After each semester in dual credit, the high school transcript will need updating. One way to add DE credits to the transcript is to just list the class as it would be named in high school, then add an asterisk out beside the course to signify that it was a class taken under the umbrella of dual credit. Now, add the DE class title after the asterisk using the same Common Course Numbering designation the colleges use. Ex: English 11* ENGL 1301. Then either in a legend or at the bottom of the page, include a notation for the asterisk just as seen on my sample transcript.

Next we need to convert the college credit to high school credit. For ENGL 1301, we do not record the 3.0 college credits but rather the 1.0 high school credit. Do not worry that we are somehow losing two credits by converting from 3 college credits to 1 high school credit. When DE students apply to universities, they will be required to submit an official transcript that arrives directly from the DE college. All three credits will be clearly documented on that transcript. A high school transcript should only show high school credits.

Since all college classes are a single semester long, in most cases, one semester of college will translate to a full year of high school. If History 1 & 2 are taken in DE, History 1 takes the place of 11th grade history while History 2 becomes 12th grade history. There is an obvious advantage to this. A student can get all the credit needed to graduate high school in half the time of her peers. The fact that she will also complete her first year or so of college while she is at it is just a neat little bonus. When unsure of what credit to assign a particular DE class, follow the LeeWay DDP. If you are a homeschooler and want to give more credit than is noted on the LDDP, then feel free to do so as long as the amount or level of work was notable.

When students apply to universities at the beginning of their senior year, they will be required to submit both their high school transcript, which will come from their school or parent, and their college transcript, which the student will need to order from their dual enrollment college. Any dual credit courses will be clearly noted on both transcripts. The grades should be identical even if the credits are not. In fact, you may choose to not give any credit on your high school transcript for some of your DE classes. Or you may choose to apply only part of your DE credits towards high school graduation and ignore the rest. Why on earth would you do this?

Well, colleges are a bureaucracy and just like most things in officialdom, the right hand does not always know what the left hand is doing. This results in things not always going as they should or as intended. Things have only gotten worse as the population has grown and universities grow ever bigger.

In the old days, if you took a class from an accredited public college and then transferred anywhere, that class would automatically transfer with you. The government set up the system that way and for decades the universities have honored the rules. In recent years, probably in response to the government getting so large that it can not police itself, colleges have begun to push the boundaries by treating transferred credits in willy-nilly ways that are in favor of the receiving college instead of the student. This is partly in response to marketing pressures from corporations (think private education firms, test makers, and test prep companies) who make money off of students having to retake classes or take specialized tests.

The net result is that at a tiny (but growing) number of select universities, a DE student can not use her DE classes for both high school AND graduation. She can still take DE classes while in high school but she can't NEED those classes in order to graduate. At a few colleges, a student who uses her DE credits towards high school graduation will not be given her DE credits as college credits in keeping with the letter and intent of the guidelines that govern the dual enrollment program. Eventually, someone will push back on these colleges and the practice will come to a halt or the rules will be changed but in the meantime, if you are headed to one of these rare schools, you should prepare your transcript accordingly.

A simple solution is to list the DE classes in a separate section of your transcript (often at the bottom or even a special 'honors' section), instead of showing them as regular high school classes. You would show the name of the DE class and the final grade in that class but you would not show any credit for the class. This means that class will not be used towards graduation. NOTE: You will still get college credit for the class via your college transcript but you will not get high school credit. For most kids, this is not a problem as they do not need their DE classes in order to graduate; but if you do need a DE class in order to graduate, then you must list it as previously noted and take your chances with the admitting university.

I suspect this is a topic that we will hear a lot more about in the future. The kathelee.com and leewayusa.com websites will certainly be dedicating one or more of my Live Chats w/Kathe Lee to this evolving topic as we always stay up to date with the latest college planning news, so check us out online!

However you choose to report your DE classes, they will end up on the transcript in one fashion or another. Once all classes, both regular and DE, are noted on the high school transcript, the GPA must be calculated for each year of high school and then accumulatively. Be aware that the overall high school GPA and the DE college GPA may not be identical. They may not even be on the same scale. Regardless of how a college calculates their GPA, you should follow the 4.0 scale for a high school transcript and use the grading legend that I have provided below. You may certainly use a 5.0 or 4.5 scale but this unweighted grading legend works best for most.

## Classic Grading Legend

| | | |
|---|---|---|
| *A* | *= 90-100* | *= 4.0* |
| *B+* | *= 85-89* | *= 3.5* |
| *B* | *= 80-84* | *= 3.0* |
| *C+* | *= 75-79* | *= 2.5* |
| *C* | *= 70-74* | *= 2.0* |

## NON CREDIT COURSES

When talking about credits and GPA there are some special types of classes that requires mentioning. It is often necessary for a DE student to take a remedial course, such as developmental math. These classes are usually considered non-credit. They are still represented on the college transcript but are not given credit. Instead, they may be denoted as pass/fail. Additionally, many DE programs allow students to take exploratory classes that may be part of their continuing education system. Such classes will not be part of the college GPA. However, these classes should always be added to the high school transcript. Since they are not considered core college or high school classes, these courses are usually assigned a high school credit of only 0.5 regardless of the difficulty or time requirements of the class and they often fall under the heading of "Electives".

Making a high school transcript and converting DE college courses into credits that are inline with a traditional high school schedule can be the trickiest part of custom schooling. As a parent or counselor in charge of customizing a student's high school to college plan, it is essential to be familiar with this conversion so as to properly represent a student's efforts on an official high school transcript. The transcript must always sync up with the degree plan. Public and private school students have some control over their transcript as well and should pay close attention to changes and additions made to this document. One should continually bear in mind that the high school transcript will be closely considered by colleges when deciding whether to admit a pupil or give any non-loan financial aid. That makes it one of your most valuable high school to college assets. Treat it accordingly.

# 19☞

# FRESHMAN STATUS

## When Applying To College

*Don't take anything at face value!*

This is perhaps the greatest lesson I have learned throughout my years as an academic advisor. There is often a very large gap between what is supposed to happen and what actually happens. Ask any college advisor in America if a student can obtain a bachelor's degree from an accredited university without ever taking a math class, and most, if not all, will tell you absolutely not. Yet, I have seen it done.

Ask any financial aid officer if a scholar can earn merit-based aid without ever taking a standardized test. They will reply with a firm, "No Way!" Nonetheless, I have dozens upon dozens of students who have done just that.

It is not that the advisors are wrong. They are, in fact, speaking the truth as they know it. They are doing exactly what anyone would do who had to answer generic questions from strangers all day. But if you dig a little deeper, you will find that there is often a big difference between what is supposed to happen and what actually happens. In other words...

*What people say and what people do*

*can be two very different things.*

*Never assume you know what will happen until*

*you have actually tried it. . .twice!*

The best example of this is perhaps the most common and blatantly false misconception about dual credit, *"If you take college classes in high school you have to be careful not to go over 29 hours or you will lose your freshman status."* False!

Freshman status is a big deal for university admissions since most of the top dollar merit-based scholarships and grants are reserved for freshman applicants. But the belief that freshman status is gone after 29 credits is patently wrong, if those credits are in dual enrollment! I have personally marshaled uncountable students into universities on freshman scholarships when those students had more than 29 college credit hours earned through the dual enrollment program. Yet, I must confess that I have heard versions of this exact sentiment from the mouths of college counselors, admission officers, and even a university dean. This fallacy needs to be corrected if dual enrollment is to reach its maximum potential and help students optimize high school.

While at a recent convention for admission specialists, I overheard this statement being made. As a guest lecturer on a related topic, I felt it prudent to correct the error. My input, while welcomed, was not easily digested. The discussion was at times intense as everyone had a strong opinion along with several anecdotal personal accounts to bolster their claims that anyone with more than 29 college hours was a transfer student. Fortunately, I had facts and years of documented evidence to support my position that no matter how many DE hours a student completes, she is still a freshman for admission purposes. This fact was debated for several uncomfortable minutes before the truth sank in. After all, I was standing in the middle of a room full of college admission experts telling them that a core tenet of their belief system was faulty.

Help came from an unlikely source when a few members of the group began to acknowledge that they were aware of students who had entered their respective colleges with more than 29 credits yet received considerable freshman aid. One officer even remembered admitting one of my LeeWay Academy students. That student received a full freshman scholarship!

This was news to many and absolutely appalling to some. The Director of Admissions from a well-regarded university told me later that she was genuinely shocked to learn the truth about how DE classes <u>should</u> be handled for college admission purposes. After my lecture and our lengthy private conversation, she confessed to being previously unclear on the matter and was horrified to realize how many families she had potentially misled over the years with flawed advice on the subject. She proffered an invitation to me to train her staff.

Fortunately, the system itself tends to process dual credit students with fairly good accuracy despite the individuals involved. Nevertheless, it is to the reader's benefit to understand how DE classes <u>should</u> be treated by the receiving university and be prepared to explain the rule to a potential college admissions officer if the occasion should arise.

The rule is stubbornly hard to wrap your head around, at least at first glance. So, I will explain it to you exactly the way I explained it to those professionals. First, I will state the rule. Then, I will give you an example. Lastly, I will share an almost comical case in point. Now, for the rule.

## THE RULE

All classes taken under the umbrella of dual enrollment are not counted as official college credits until a student is out of high school and enrolled in a college or university. Huh? That's right. Let me put it a different way.

*Dual credit student are high school students who just happen to be taking college level courses. They are NOT college students, at least not yet.*

Once they graduate high school, if they enroll in a college or university they will become official college students for the first time. At that point, any credits earned in DE will be added to the overall count for purposes of determining status as a freshman versus sophomore or even junior.

While still in high school, DE classes are treated as nothing more than high school credits. Yes, there is an official college transcript generated at the end of each semester, meaning that

DE students have both a high school and college transcript, but their college classes do not affect freshman status until the student becomes an official college student -- which will not happen until she graduates high school and is admitted to a junior college or university. This is the rule!

*Dual credit student are not college students. Therefore, they can not lose their freshman status until they become college students.*

## THE EXAMPLE

A LeeWay Academy student from Los Angeles completed 47 hours in DE before graduating high school as an AP Scholar with honors. Dual credit was ideal for her schedule as she was a regular cast member on a Disney Channel comedy show. Despite her 47 hours of college credit and no SAT score, she was accepted into Stanford University as a freshman with merit-based financial aid. That was one very happy client!

As required, her DE transcript was submitted to Stanford during the application process. Because she had completed 47 college credits, admissions waived all testing requirements and admitted her as they would any valid transfer student. She did not get freshman aid because she applied as a transfer student. However, her only goal was getting in to Stanford and transfer admission has a higher acceptance rate so she chose this route.

Despite being a transfer student on paper (based on the number of college credits on her dual enrollment transcript that she submitted to the university), when she started university classes in August she was designated a freshman. This required her to attend freshman orientation and move into the freshman dorms just like every other college freshman.

This happened because her DE hours had not yet been converted to college credits. This was ideal as it allowed her to have the full new-to-college experience that she wanted. No one had to tell Stanford to do this, the system just took care of it all by itself, which is usually what happens. And when it doesn't automatically happen, we petition. A petition is simple, easy, and almost never fails. But in this case, the system worked.

Our student took a full course load of 14 credits her first semester. When she completed her fall classes in December, her Stanford transcript showed not 14 credits but 61 credits (47+14). Her status was changed from freshman to junior over night. This was actually a big deal as it instantly qualified her to register for classes in the first round, which resulted in a special schedule of Tuesday-Thursday classes that allowed her to travel over the long weekend for work . . . exactly as I had strategized for her four years earlier! This is an excellent example of a great dual enrollment strategy in action.

## HUMOROUS CASE IN POINT

If you've taken some time to fully process the scenario above and still find the DE/Freshman thing confusing, let me relate an amusing little synopsis of a real conversation I had with the admissions officer at a top-tier university, regarding another client, Jamie P. Jamie was a girl with a problem.

This private schooled, fresh faced, learning-differenced 16 year old came to me at the end of tenth grade with a story of woe. She had been bullied mercilessly at her public middle school. The family had relocated twice but school had simply become unbearable for her. They were currently in a private high school where things had not improved, mostly due to Jamie's understandable anxiety. Her grades were slipping due to stress and her tests scores were a consistent problem. She was not only unlikely to get admitted to a top college and avoid debt by earning merit based scholarships, she was in danger emotionally.

Since Jamie was finished with tenth grade, I asked her if she would like to start college early and leave her high school nightmares behind her. She jumped at the chance.

Following my plan, she completed 72 hours of dual credit courses during her last two years of custom high school and graduated with the LeeWay Distinguished Degree Plan and a proven GPA of 4.0 -- quite a feat for even a top student, much less one with a diagnosed learning disorder and stress. Jamie actually had enough credits at the junior college to complete her Associate's Degree, but we deferred that option as it would have interfered with the financial aid plan we had created.

Jamie applied to thirteen notable universities and got accepted into eleven. She received full merit-based financial aid offers to six of them. Jamie now had the choice to attend any of these great colleges absolutely free.

Just as they should, each college had treated her dual credit classes as high school courses for admission purposes with the full intent of transferring the credits over to regular college credits once Jamie had graduated high school and begun her tenure as a true college student. No fuss, no muss. This was exactly what my office expected as we had seen this system work time and time again.

While eight out of thirteen colleges got it right the first time around, two took a bit of convincing. One top southern university, her number one pick, took things to a whole new level. Even now, I find this scenario mind boggling.

You may recall that Jamie had a learning difference that had haunted her throughout school. This caused her to be a poor tester. With a documented above average IQ, consistent work ethic, and great attitude, Jamie had always won the hearts of her teachers, hence her fantastic GPA and college references. Most colleges judge an applicant, almost exclusively, by their GPA and tests scores. Jamie's GPA was great but her test scores . . . well, her test scores did not exist because I did not have her take any tests. Why set her up for more failure? With her anxiety, processing disorder, and general negative attitude towards testing, ACT and SAT were a risk I was not willing to take. Her problems were fixable, but it would take time. By the time I met Jamie, we were out of time so instead of trying to fix her problem, we worked around it. We focused on her strengths and had her take impressive classes in dual enrollment but with teachers, were known to produce good outcomes.

Since Jamie was extremely focused, we also had her take full advantage of flex terms, which allowed her to complete the maximum number of DE classes; seventy-two credits. What we did not have her do was take an oversized standardized test like the SAT or ACT, or face a daunting AP exam. I would never set a student up for failure, and testing was a nemesis that Jamie was not prepared to face at that point.

By now you know that either an ACT or SAT is required for all freshman students to enter university. It is a basic requirement of the admissions package. Jamie had a great GPA and enough college credits through DE that we could have just had her apply as an honors transfer student. As such, she would have had automatic admission to several good schools without taking a single test. And given her grades, she would have qualified for an honors transfer scholarship and been instantly eligible for a good portion of her tuition and fees.

But while the honors transfer route is optimal for more kids than not, Jamie had an exceptional College Package. A perfect GPA, a boatload of honors credits thanks to DE, membership in Phi Theta Kappa, and lots of service. All she was missing was good tests scores. Otherwise, she was a top candidate for merit-based freshman aid. Freshman merit aid is always the ideal, since it is automatically renewable and tends to come in large denominations. Therefore we had Jamie apply as a freshman, albeit, a freshman without any standardized test scores. We felt this was the best financial route for our student.

Under any normal scenario, a freshman applicant without a standardized test score would be ceremoniously rejected. But because Jamie had 72 hours of college credits she clearly met the school's published guideline which decreed that test scores were only required of students with less than 29 college credits, aka freshman applicants. Jamie was a freshman applicant but she was also a transfer student!

As her high school counselor of record, I was the one who received the now infamous call from the school's admission officer. The purpose of her call was to tell us that Jamie had an amazing application and was exactly the kind of student that should come to their top ten ranked university. However, there was a glaring problem with her application. They were missing her official tests scores.

**ADMISSIONS:** *(completely professional) We are unable to process this application as it is incomplete. You will need to complete this application no later than November 1st if the student still wants to be considered for early decision.*

**ME:** (equally professional) Oh, I completely understand; yes we do want early admit. What exactly do we need to do to make that complete?

**ADMISSIONS:** *We still have not received her SAT or ACT scores. Can you have those sent over right away?*

**ME:** Oh, I'm afraid we don't have any test scores. She never took an SAT or ACT. Is that a problem?

**ADMISSIONS:** *(Sympathetic) I'm afraid that all freshmen applicants are required to submit either an ACT score with writing or an SAT score.*

**ME:** (Good natured) Oh, well that's good to know. But I guess I'm confused because I was reading on your website that only students with fewer than 29 college credits were required to submit test scores.

**ADMISSIONS:** *Yes, that is correct. Does this student have more than 29 college credits?*

**ME:** Yes, she has 72 college credits with a GPA of 4.0. She is a straight A honor's student. You should have her official college transcript on file. We sent it with her application.

**ADMISSIONS:** *(pause) Yes, I see it here. Okay, I see the problem now. You submitted the wrong application. You* *submitted a freshman application, but you should have used the transfer application. (pleased with herself)*

**ME:** Oh, why would we submit a transfer application for a freshman applicant?

***ADMISSIONS:*** *(rising irritation) Does she have college credits or not?*

**ME:** (matter-of-factly) Yes, as you can see on both her high school and college transcripts she has 72 college credits and a GPA of 4.0.

***ADMISSIONS:*** *Then she is clearly a transfer applicant.*

**ME:** But all her college hours were done under the umbrella of dual enrollment.

***ADMISSIONS:*** *Then she is clearly a freshman applicant.*

**ME:** Great, then we're all good?

***ADMISSIONS:*** *(confused) Yes. Well. (pause) No. (pause) Well, yes. Except that as a freshman applicant she will need an SAT or ACT on file.*

**ME:** Oh, but your website states that "an SAT or ACT is only required for applicants with fewer than 29 college credits" (figured they can't argue with their own published literature).

***ADMISSIONS:*** *(dazed and confused) Oh, yes. I see what you are saying. No. You are right. She does not need any test scores.*

**ME:** Great, then we're all good?

> ***ADMISSIONS:*** *(dazed, confused and speechless) Uh. Umm. Uhhhh. Can you hang on for just a minute?*
>
> **ME:** Sure!
>
> ***ADMISSIONS:*** *(long break) Hello. I'm ____________, the Director of Admissions. I understand you have some confusion about how to complete an application for our school. Perhaps I can clarify the process for you.*
>
> ***Repeat entire previous conversation up to the, *"Can you hang on a minute?"* followed by…
>
> ***ADMISSIONS:*** *(excited) Wow! I had no idea. What an amazing program. Every student should do it. Can you send me some information for my daughter. She just finished eleventh grade and I would love to …*

We all learned a lot from this conversation. Jamie learned that using resources wisely can pay off big time. She moved south to wear the famous blue & white in exchange for an 80% tuition scholarship plus a stipend for housing. She is doing great at her new alma mater and her parents are thrilled that she is starting her life free from college debt. She continues to work with a therapeutic tutor to develop effective test taking skills and a counselor to teach her coping skills to help address her anxiety. She has embraced all aspects of her major and expects to do study abroad next year.

The admissions officer learned that dual enrollment provides a purposeful loophole for students who use it wisely. I have since provided private advising for that adviser's daughter, who is doing great at a private and expensive liberal arts college in the east after completing 31 hours of free dual credit classes through a local bond-funded program. Mom continues to refer students to me for college planning and financial aid assistance.

And much to my chagrin, I learned that I say "Oh" way too much! Although I have made a valid attempt to pare down its usage, it continues to get a modest amount of overuse in my everyday conversations. Small steps, always small steps!

Hopefully what this amusing anecdote has taught you is that information is a resource that, when welded with expertise and patience, can yield amazing results! Dual Enrollment is one of the most useful resources you will find when trying to build a College Package that gets the attention of university admissions officers and financial aid personnel. But to use it well and with confidence, you will need to have a clear understanding of how it works and why. It is true that the rules are constantly changing, but I am confident that we are all capable of keeping up with such changes. It is clearly worth doing so.

# 20☞

# SPECIAL TESTS

## How & When To Use Them

We cannot have a conversation about getting into college and getting it paid for without discussing a few other specialized tests such as the College Level Examination Program (CLEP), Credit By Exam (CBE), and Advanced Placement (AP). These tests play a considerable role in many aspects of high school life especially in public, private, magnet, and charter schools.

*CLEP and Advanced Placement are each a single test that can give a student college credit.*

The upside to these tests is that a single comprehensive exam can give a student credit for either high school or college. The downsides range from the overkill of busywork inherent to Advanced Placement courses to the waste of CLEPs that go unused. Each of these tests can be valuable but only if used at the right time in the right way. Not surprisingly, they are at their most useful when used in conjunction with dual credit.

## College Level Exam (CLEP)

**College Level Examination Program -** Simply put, the CLEP test is the quickest solution for earning either high school or college credits. Do a bit of prep, sit for a single, relatively short test, get a 50-60 or better, and you are done. You will receive pass/fail recognition for up to 8 college credits for a single test. That is a pretty powerful tool! But things do not always go smoothly. For the right student in the right situation, CLEP is sheer perfection. Fast and cheap, two words both students and parents love to hear. What could go wrong?

CLEP may be fast and cheap, but as the old Spanish proverb goes, *"Lo barato sale caro!"* Simply translated, "The cheap comes out expensive!" CLEP is not always the best route. There are many reason for this. The first issue is that not all CLEP tests are accepted by all colleges. Most colleges accept some CLEP tests but very few accept them all. It is entirely possible to spend time and money on a specific CLEP that is not usable at the school you end up at.

*"Currently, 2900 colleges and universities grant credit for CLEP, and each institution sets its own CLEP policy."* [1]

That does not mean that CLEP should be avoided, it just means that it should be used as part of a larger, well-planned strategy. As an advisor, I use CLEP only after a student has been accepted to a particular college. It is only at this point that I can be certain which CLEP(s) to take, meaning the ones that the admitting college accepts.

Once a student has accepted enrollment at a university, then we go online and see exactly which CLEPs that university will recognize and how many CLEPs are allowed. Then we have the student do a bit of prep, often with a tutor, take a single CLEP test, and submit the scores to the target college for credit. When used this way, CLEP can get a student through college in a fraction of the time that it would take to sit through classes. It is also cheaper. Entire books have been written on the subject of how to use CLEP to get college paid for, some are better than others. The one thing to remember is that not all colleges accept all CLEPs, so choose wisely.

Once you decide to take a CLEP in lieu of a college class, you will need to prepare for it. CLEP tests are much shorter and easier than AP so the prep is very straightforward. Pick an official CLEP prep book for a given subject and review it for at least three weeks but no more than a semester. How much time is needed depends entirely on the student and his or her familiarity with the subject chosen. There are practice tests online that can give a quick taste of what to expect. That would be a great place to begin. For students who are less motivated, hire a tutor to review the CLEP material with the student.

Once prepared, pupils can sign up online and take the test at a nearby specialized testing center. Obtain a score of 60% or better on the test, and that subject can be checked off the to-do list. The score can be as low as fifty percentile for some schools but we aim for 60 just to be on the safe side.

Each test costs $80 with no fee waiver currently available, although it would be worthwhile for families on federal assistance to ask about a sliding scale rate. If a student takes a CLEP test while in high school and makes a 50 or better, that subject can be added to the high school transcript with a pass/fail designation. If you want an actual grade on the transcript, just find out what the max score is for the test taken then calculate a number grade for that "class".

It would be inaccurate to say that I never use CLEP for high school as I have had many clients whose situation clearly called for these relatively fast, small, easy tests. For students who are struggling emotionally, a CLEP can be a great way to help them feel successful and start to overcome testing hang-ups.

If a CLEP test is taken by a student in the dual enrollment program, we usually submit their CLEP scores to the DE college and let that college transcribe it into an official college credit. This assures that the CLEP is accepted by all future colleges. Nonetheless, when a student decides to submit CLEP scores to the DE college, it is prudent to confirm how a receiving university might treat them as well.

When there is no test anxiety, no behavioral concerns, and the student is a provably great tester, I tend to opt for AP instead of CLEP just because I do not have to worry about AP being accepted at every college. Again, I am talking about the AP test not AP classes. AP is seen as being a bigger accomplishment than CLEP, which can be useful when aiming for admission to top colleges such as Harvard, Columbia, Stanford and the like. CLEP, in short, is an excellent way to test out of classes once enrolled at a university or junior college following high school graduation. Just be sure the CLEP test taken, will be accepted.

## Credit By Exam (CBE)

**Credit By Examination -** For students in public, private, or charter schools, CBEs are the preferred option. Credit By Exam is a program used by public schools for placement when a student moves to a new school district or wants to jump ahead a year. Just like CLEP, CBEs are available in many subjects but tend to be more difficult and require more prep than CLEP. CBEs do not confer college credit like the AP and CLEP. But CBEs can waive classes or provide a pass/fail addition to the transcript. In most cases, CBEs are strictly for primary and secondary public or private schools.

Eligible students in K-8th can use CBEs to move ahead a single grade. High school students can use CBEs the same way or use them to get credit for a class that they have not or will not take. Each state's school board has different policies on how CBEs can be used, but the most common way to use CBEs is when a student has missed a semester or more of courses then wishes to return to public or private school. This is most often a homeschooler who decides to return to their previous public or private school after schooling at home for a period of time. Or it may be a student who has missed a lot of class time due to illness or family circumstances. CBEs are the preferred way to prove that a previously homeschooled or truant student is qualified to start 9th, 10th, 11th, or 12th grade at a state-sponsored school.

CBEs are harder than CLEPs because CLEP tests cover more universal concepts whereas CBEs cover material that is taught in a particular region in a given year. For example, the 10th grade English CBE in California will require a reading list of literature specific to the current year's state curriculum for all sophomores. This makes it a very difficult test to pass for students who were not in a state school that year. I avoid CBEs when possible, but sometimes it cannot be avoided such as when a homeschooler decides to re-enter public school. In such cases, CBEs are often mandatory with little recourse. Smart, well-rounded students will not have any trouble with CBEs and there is no real downside to not passing a CBE. Use them as needed.

## Advanced Placement (AP)

**Advanced Placement -** For good testers from any type of school, AP test are a great option, but only if used correctly. I would even argue that for the top few percent of students, the really great testers, AP is a more efficient route to college admissions and financial aid than dual enrollment. Unfortunately, most students are average testers at best and are not well served by the Advanced Placement program. Thankfully, those students have the options of dual credit.

AP is something of a household word among high school families, and the connotations are not generally positive. AP is known to most as a class in school but, in reality, AP is a test. The AP test was created for a very valid purpose. In every high school, there have always been students who did significantly better than others. It seemed like a great idea to find a way to confirm who those students were and promote them in an appropriate manner. Perhaps even allow them to skip a class or get early college credit just by proving themselves in some way. This is what the AP test was designed to do. Precocious students could take a comprehensive test in a single subject and if they did well enough they would not have to take the next level of that subject, even if the next level was college level. It was a great idea with a dark side that was soon to come. Without any prep, many schools had students who aced these special tests and were not required to take certain courses in high school because of their achievement. But as might be expected, not all schools fared equally. Some schools just seemed to have smarter kids. This did not go over well.

In very short order, AP courses were developed as a way for the "less successful" schools to prepare students for the test. It was predicted that with proper preparation, outcomes would improve. It worked. Initially, students who took AP classes did better than those who did not take AP classes. The logical next step was that more schools began offering more and more AP classes to more and more students. Thanks to excellent marketing, huge financial benefits were bestowed on high schools that enrolled large percentages of students into AP classes. Very quickly, AP standing became a way to label a high school as "exemplary", a status that brought public recognition and federal dollars. Private schools quickly got into the mix, as having a lot of students in AP classes allowed schools to charge higher tuition. The competition was on and has never slowed down. More students take AP classes than IB, CLEP, or DE!

Today, high schools shove as many students into AP courses as they can handle with poor regard for who is actually suitable for such classes. Ironically, schools do not let every student who is taking an AP class sit for the corresponding AP test. Turns out that students in AP classes today do not always do so well on the test. In fact, just the opposite. When students fail the test it makes the school look bad and threatens their rankings. An easy solution is to cherry pick who can and cannot take the test each year. This is exactly what many school districts have done. Some have even gotten caught. [3, 5] (Check out http://blog.prepscholar.com for a great take on the state of Advanced Placement.[4])

The problem is not the tests. The problem is the classes. AP classes are too much information administered too fast. [4] **The good news is that students do not need to take an AP class in order take an AP test**. Any student in any high school can sign up for and take an AP test each May. Additionally, any student who passes an AP test will get an AP credit regardless of whether or not an official AP course was completed. Of course, not just any student can sit down and pass (make a 3 out of a possible 5) on an AP test. This is exactly what makes Advanced Placement so valuable and so problematic.

*"According to a recent study by College Board, nearly 50% of high school students taking Advanced Placement (AP) courses do not pass the exams to qualify for college credit."* [2]

But I still like AP test. One reason is that colleges like to see "AP Scholar" on an applicant's resume. Any student that completes three AP tests with a score of 3 or better by the end of 11th grade will be classified as an AP Scholar for college application purposes. This distinction is noticed by admission officers and can play a role in offers to university honors programs as well as potential aid. Additionally, if a score of 4-5 is attained, then the student will get some degree of college credit in that subject. Some colleges even give AP credit for lower scores. The AP Scholar designation and college credits are reasons the

AP is not without merit. But we do not need the massive burden that many AP classes have become.

In my practice, over 80% of students earn the designation of AP Scholar but have never attended an AP class! How do we manage to pull this off when entire school districts spending oodles of money cannot? The process is surprisingly simple. It is all about honoring how the brain actually learns.

The brain likes information to be presented in relatively small blocks. Just a few weeks of attention on a single subject is about all most brains can tolerate. Anything more and it tunes out. The brain likes to interact with information in a tangible and meaningful way. That means it wants to apply what it has learned to test and correct any faulty concepts. This is exactly the opposite of what schools do when they lecture on a subject daily for 9 full months. Books and lectures are a lethal combination.

At LeeWay Academy, our students use one of two curriculums. Both are succinct, stepwise, and clear, just like the brain prefers. Our learners cover the material in a group of three with a teacher or tutor. They use my feedback teaching methodology and work with a teacher that can deliver the information in an engaging manner without burning the students out on mindless review and homework.

Homework at LeeWay is never book based. We apply what we have learned by making it application based, even if only as a mental exercise. For AP, we prep for no more than four months in the spring then take the test in May along with all the other high schoolers. The four month timeframe is critical as optimal recall will begin to deteriorate past this amount of time. Perhaps this is why students who spend a full school year in AP courses do so poorly on the test . ☹

When deciding which AP test to take each year, my advice is to guide the student in making the decision. There are over 30 AP subjects and some are easier than others. My preferred tests are World History, Human Geography, English Language and Composition, Art History, Psychology, or Economics. Ask the student which subject he feels strong in or which subject he would be most interested in studying right now. Students have varying strengths and interests. Go with their natural tendencies and engagement will follow. Engagement results in learning with retention which in turn facilitates good test scores. Older students can take harder AP tests but I always recommend avoiding AP Calculus and AP Physics until the senior year, and even then only if that subject is a true passion.

LeeWay is about tailor-made schooling. A student does not need to suffer through a subject to which he does not feel a connection. When it comes to testing, we must never forget that a happy brain is a smart brain. At LeeWay, we ask students to work with a peer and tutor, interact briefly but frequently for only a few months, then take a comprehensive test over the material that was discussed. It works! By letting students pick their own test each year, you give them both ownership and respect. In return, they give us their very best and usually a passing AP score as well. They also learn!

At LeeWay Academy, we have found two series of books that consistently work well for AP prep: *Five Steps to a 5* and *Crash Course AP*. Both series have books in all the main AP subjects. These books cover the same material but in different ways. I personally prefer *Crash Course* but certain types of brains will do better with *Five Steps.* Let the student look at both and decide which one feels right. You can't go wrong since both of these series covers everything one needs to know in order to do well on an AP test. This is the only AP curriculum we use.

A student can work at home with a parent or tutor, or a group of students can study together at a co-op or after class. The results are consistent either way. If documented good testers pick a subject they like, put in the time, use the recommended book, and get feedback instruction, then they will score a "3" or better and earn an AP designation by the time they apply to college. But never skip the steps noted here. And only take the AP tests that are noted for a particular grade level. A motivated student with solid testing skills can earn both credit for high school and college by way of a few AP tests. But taking math or science too early can lead to failure and a lot of frustration for the student. Pick carefully.

Universities have a system for converting an AP score into college credit. For example, if a student takes the AP English Language test and scores a 4, a college will likely give that student full credit for ENGL 101 and allow the student to move on to ENGL 102. At some colleges, a score of 5 would waive the student out of both levels of English and shorten the college curriculum by two courses. This is true for math, science, language, etc. Just be aware that some of the very top colleges are not as generous and require a 5 in exchange for college credits; other colleges give credit for just a 3.

The downside to the AP is that it is only offered each May. Students take the test at a local high school along with their peers regardless of where they actually attend school. An average student will only be able to earn one AP credit per year unless he wants to dedicate his entire spring semester to nothing but AP prep then sit for multiple comprehensive tests that will all be given within days of each other. We have had students do this successfully but it is not necessary. Three AP tests total is the ideal. Completing one in each of the first three years of high school will easily achieve the goal of AP Scholar.

Advanced Placement is not for everyone. Yet public, private, and charter schools make AP classes highly attractive by assigning them to the best teachers and populating them with well behaved, high achieving pupils. What parents would not want their child to have the best teacher and be surrounded by other good students? I am often forced to advise a student to take more AP courses than they need just because the alternatives are sub par in multiple regards.

*If a student is not likely to do well on the AP test, then it is generally advisable to avoid taking the actual AP course if at all possible. However, seniors may want to take a class without the associated test just to boost their GPA.*

Without a sufficient score on the test, the class is nothing but a lot of work. Yes, AP classes do affect the GPA in potentially positive ways. This is how school districts, backed by big business, lure students into classes that eat up time and energy but boost school budgets. The offer is this. *"Take the harder AP classes and we will give you a higher GPA."* Put another way. *"Don't take AP classes and you will not have a shot at a Top 10%*

*ranking."* This is a selling point that is not lost on many of my clients. But GPAs go both up and down. The onerous nature of most AP classes can quickly damage an otherwise healthy GPA. Even so, AP testing can be used very effectively for extremely industrious students who are self-directed and proven test takers.

Advanced Placement, like CLEP and CBE is a no-fault option. This is why we recommend everyone try an AP as early as possible to find out if this option should be part of their high school plan. If a tester's first AP score is a "1", then bypass the AP route and move on to dual enrollment exclusively. If the first test is a "2" then consider giving it another try the following year if the student is up for it. If the baseline score is a "3" or better then AP is the way to go.

Clearly, dual credit is not the only option for college planning, although it is usually the best. The right test taken at the right time can be a powerful part of a high school to college plan. In order to know which option is right for a given student, we must be very honest about that student's odds of not only getting into a good college but getting the money needed to attend, without taking on major debt.

# 21☞

# GETTING IT PAID FOR

## Financial Aid 101

My grandpa used to say, *"There's more than one way to skin a cat, Katie dear!"* Thankfully, I have never skinned a cat, but I will concede his point. There is also more than one way to get college paid for without taking out loans, taking on debt, or dipping into personal savings. The most obvious way is to follow my SECRET FORMULA. Build a great College Package, apply to schools a screening says will reward the package you have, and earn scholarships. Whether through National Merit, a combination of primary and secondary awards, or a string of smaller third party grants, good testers who follow my blue-print can get a college degree free of any major debt.

But not everyone is a good tester and regrettably, building a top-tier College Package is a task that few students bother to do. Mainly because they are too busy with classes and homework to do well at preparing for college admissions! While a quality College Screening can connect applicants to colleges that will love whatever package he ends up with, many unenlightened students will only apply to a handful of local favorites without really considering financial aid realities. This is a costly mistake that will soon be difficult to ignore.

One solution to this continuing problem is to make college financial planning an integral part of the high school curriculum. Another option is for high schools to provide professional College Screenings for juniors & seniors. In many cases, the real solution to the outrageous cost of college is for students to take a slightly different route from the one currently in vogue. Attending a junior college before heading off to an expensive university will minimize debt, give students time to mature before they are paying the big dollars for school, and allow students time to figure out what they really want to study. A reality is that most students go straight from high school to a university without a plan and without financial aid. They pay a hefty price.

*If a university degree is in your future, then so is a massive outlay of cash, or serious debt.*

Whether you are a student, parent, school administrator, teacher, or local school board member, you should never lose sight of the fact that college is expensive and in any given year a lot of students are competing for the same college dollars. What students do in high school, what they have in their College Package or on their high school resume, will determine how successful they are in the increasingly fierce competition to earn non-loan financial aid for college. The only way for a student to avoid debt is to earn scholarships, obtain grants, receive merit or need-based financial aid, or be blessed with a resource who can afford to pay outright to the tune of tens of thousands of dollars each year. Assuming grandma and grandpa are not inclined to fork over a significant chunk of their retirement dollars, the time for a Financial Aid Primer has come.

## Seven Ways To Get College Paid For

Need-Based Assistance

National Merit Scholarships

Merit-Based Scholarships

Institutional & Departmental Aid

Performance Dollars

Transfer Scholarships

The Military

There are twelve ways to get money for college that does not have to be paid back. Seven deserve a detailed discussion. **Need-Based dollars** are awarded to families with lower incomes. **National Merit Scholar** is such an honored status that some colleges give a full ride for this one achievement. **Merit-based scholarships** are all about the College Package as are **institutional and departmental aid**. **Performance dollars** is money for students with a skill that can be used by the college; think football star! And the **Honors transfer route** is a little known secret that should be the go-to for the majority of all high school graduates, while **the military** is only for an elite few who feel compelled to serve their country through the armed forces.

These seven routes to college financial aid can be combined in a myriad of ways to produce outstanding opportunities. Unfortunately, the typical student is only really aware of need, national merit, and primary merit aid. And even these three resources are woefully under-utilized. The big dollars for the average student are in secondary merit and transfer scholarships, which are overlooked by even advisors. If you want to optimize high school for college financial aid, then you absolutely must understand these seven resources and you must have a strategy that allows you to make optimal use of them.

*This is a good place to point out an exciting truth.*

*Just like students compete against each other to get into top*

*schools and earn top non-loan financial aid,*

*colleges compete against each other to*

*entice top students to their programs.*

College is a business and in business a key goal is sales. The other goal is to beat your competition. "*Families think their sons and daughters are awarded a merit scholarship because of the fact that they are wonderfully smart and talented," says Robert Massa, a vice president at Lafayette. "[T]he primary reason for awarding a non-need-based merit scholarship is to change a student's enrollment decision from another institution to our institution. That's why colleges do it."* [1]

Colleges want to sell themselves to top candidates, preferably ones who can pay full freight. So when an applicant has a great College Package, colleges will actually compete against one another for the privilege to educate that student. This is true for both academic scholarships and program dollars.

➊

## NEED-BASED AID

### (Governmental Assistance)

When a family has a proven income that falls below the congressional mandate, their children will potentially qualify for need-based aid. This aid comes from the state or federal government and is very limited. A few thousand in grants. A little less in work study. And some subsidized loans.

Need is determined by the juxtaposition of two things: Cost of Attendance (COA) and Expected Family Contribution (EFC). COA is the total cost of attending a college for one year. This includes tuition, fees, room and board, books, transportation, and personal miscellaneous. EFC is the amount a family is expected to pay each year before aid will be granted. EFC is determined by the free financial aid application known as FAFSA (CSS Profile is another option). One of these forms needs to be completed each year in order to be eligible for aid.

The thing to understand is that cost is relative to expense. At a state college few will have need; but at a school that costs $70,000 per year, even a relatively well-off family would have need. I had a family just yesterday with an AGI over $500,000 that qualified for need because they had triplets in private colleges all at the same time! COA directly affects EFC.

If true need can be shown, via FAFSA or a CSS Profile, then colleges will try to meet that need by channeling monies paid to them by various sources into your financial aid packet. One word of caution. **Colleges can only provide aid if they have it to give.** A recent client with a family adjusted gross income (AGI) of less than $24k/year failed to receive a penny in aid simply because the coffers at that college were empty by the time she applied in April. She received an official award but no money was dispersed. Her college simply did not have the cash to hand out. The early bird really does get the cash.

Many schools like Stanford and Harvard have promise plans that guarantee full tuition scholarships to students who are admitted and have a family income under an AGI threshold. [2] Most families with this level of income would never get need-based dollars at their state schools. Even if they managed to qualify for federal need-based aid, it would include thousands in loans per year of attendance. This is where DE helps. Every class taken for free or cheap in DE is equivalent to getting a scholarship for that course. Given the current debt levels for college students, that makes DE a huge bargain. There is a lot of documentation to show that college is expensive and most students take on debt whether they plan to or not.

*"A Fidelity Investments study released in May 2013 showed that 70% of the class of 2013 was graduating from college with college-related debt, averaging $35,200."* [3]

❷

# NATIONAL MERIT SCHOLARSHIPS

## (Money For Top PSAT Scores In 11th Grade)

All students will take a PSAT in high school. If they have been advised well, they will take it as a baseline in 9th or 10th so that they know where they stand in terms of potential eligibility for a National Merit Scholarship (NMS). NMS is the single best way to get college paid for but less than 1% of students will ever qualify. NMS is a designation given to 50,000 of the 1.6 million kids who take the PSAT in 11th grade. It is based on a score called the Selection Index. Score high enough in your state and you could be a finalist. Become a finalist and you could end up a winner. Finalist and winners can parley NMS into huge college scholarships via either corporate or institutional sponsors. Ivy League schools and most of the top 25 universities in the country no long offer scholarships just for NMS but hundreds of well-known universities and colleges still do. One test with one top score and a student could have it all.

The problem with NMS is three-fold. One, very few students can make the 200 plus selection index score needed to be a finalist. Two, even if you win you still have to strategize a way to optimize your win by applying to the right schools. And three, you will not know if you win till after you apply to colleges so you have to have a backup plan in place in case you don't make the cut. These are serious limitations but if your baseline PSAT shows you are in the range for NMS, then going after this one prize should be a high priority throughout high school. Just make sure to plan for other aid as well since you will need a backup to NMS while you wait to qualify.

❸

# MERIT-BASED AID

## (Money For Being A Great Tester)

You now know that top students can earn money for college based on their academic prowess. They can earn National Merit Scholarships in 11th grade via a top score on their PSAT along with an honors transcript. Students with great PSATs who don't win NMS are good candidates for primary merit aid. They simply use their PSAT prep to obtain excellent scores on their SAT & ACT. Anyone within striking distance of NMS is certainly a sure-thing for a great ACT score if managed correctly.

Many colleges have automatic dollar amounts of aid that they give a student in exchange for nothing more than a certain SAT or ACT score and the right classes on the high school transcript. For students with top test scores, a great transcript, a top GPA, and notable extracurriculars, there can be significant automatic merit-based aid. This is called a primary scholarship. They often have names like President's Award, Provost's Scholars Grant, or Founder's Scholarship. These awards are doled out in response to a completed admissions application and has equated to massive money for my clients. Primary aid is my first goal. It is often automatic and is easy to get. Simply give a college a package that matches their criteria, meet a specific deadline, and snip-snap you've got primary aid. No negotiations, no special applications. You give the college X and they pay you Y.

**This is what makes a College Screening so critical. What you choose to list. How you choose to list it. Even how you word it can directly affect whether or not you get primary aid and even how much it ends up being.**

Primary aid can be as much as a full ride but is usually no more than 50% of tuition and fees. In most cases, more money will be needed. Secondary aid is how we fill the gap. Secondary aid requires special applications which have firm deadlines. To win these big dollar awards, the applicant must have a full quiver of community service, competitions, and leadership. For this reason, it is always highly recommended that students put as much time and energy into extracurriculars as they put into academics. At many schools, the academic load is so egregious that community service, competitions, and leadership opportunities fall by the wayside. This is a costly mistake. Heed this advice from an admissions officer at a top university: Consistent Extracurriculars Matter.

*"A long-term commitment and deep involvement in a few extracurricular activities result in those activities becoming a regular part of daily planning — just like the course schedule — making it easier for the student to manage. We admissions officers are fans of students with deep involvement in a few activities. We are not fans of students who pad their list of activities in their junior and senior years to look more engaged."* [4]

**Without a doubt, the biggest money to be had by the average student is merit-based aid, be it primary or secondary. These are big dollars that never need to be repaid. Not going after these dollars is the single biggest mistake a college-bound senior can make.**

But you can't get this money if you have not done all the right things at exactly the right time (aka CrowFly). And you can't do all the right things at the right time if you are swamped by AP classes and your senior year commitments. It pays to plan ahead and make adjustments to the academic course load in order to free up time to earn scholarships.

By far the most important thing that a high schooler can do with their free time is service to others from 8th grade onward. I call this making a difference. The key is to start early and to be consistently involved throughout high school.

**Primary Aid** - When students apply to a college, their admissions application will qualify them for any federal, state, or institutional dollars related to need or merit. A separate application is not necessary. If an offer of admission is forthcoming, then the school will also send a notice about any primary aid the applicant qualifies for. This award may be related to need. If so, it will be funded through the federal or state government or even through the university.

In most cases, the award will be related to merit. If so, the funding is likely to come from the college's endowment system or associated organizations. Either way, the process is fairly automated. One simply needs to submit a great College Package via the application and apply while money is still available. Give them X and they will give you Y. (Some colleges have competitive primary aid but that is not the norm.)

Primary awards are large but not full rides except in a few cases like National Merit. If a student has a great Package but does not receive an award letter with his admission offer, find out why. There are things that can be done within a few weeks of notification that would correct the issue and allow a student to still qualify for money. With a great College Screening, almost anyone can get primary aid somewhere.

**Secondary Aid –** Since primary aid usually covers no more than 50% of tuition, it is important to do a bit of extra work and go for the other source of big college cash, secondary aid. These are scholarships that can come from sources within the college itself but just as often are part of a foundation that has some association to the university. Either way, secondary scholarships require a separate application and each application has a deadline. These deadlines often start in November of the senior year, which is why getting all college admission apps submitted no later than October 31st is so important.

Before you can apply for secondary scholarships, you have to know which scholarships to apply to! The best way to find secondary aid is to contact the financial aid department of any college that gave primary aid and simply ask. For my students, we tell them to call the financial aid office and ask for "*a list of any merit based freshman scholarships specific to my major that require a separate application*". The college may email a list or refer the student to a link on their website. These list are often large, poorly managed, and difficult to screen though. A new and welcomed trend is colleges offering a single application that screens for much of the secondary scholarships offered at their school. ApplyTexas and CommonApp have gotten involved and even offer such applications on their website alongside the admissions app.

This is a great use of technology. Secondary scholarships are often linked to a given major or interest and have rather narrow eligibility requirements. In most cases, there is only one secondary scholarship at each college that matches a given student. These new centralized scholarship applications can dramatically reduce the time needed to search for and apply for secondary scholarships. Sadly, few schools have yet to develop this tool. In the meantime, students will need to continue getting help looking for secondary scholarships and filling out individual applications by their recommended deadlines.

Either way, every merit student should complete at least one secondary app, and preferably more, for each college they have applied to, and do it in a timely fashion. Secondary aid tends to come in very large dollar amounts and is readily available. It is easier to get than third-party scholarships but always requires a separate application with early deadlines. Apps start in November and are really all over by March 1st of the senior year, so plan accordingly.

**Tertiary Aid –** Even a cursory look at scholarship planning websites will expose the billion dollar network of tertiary aid. This is all those third-party dollars that reportedly go unclaimed every year. I can't say how true that statement is but there are lots of additional scholarships available for students with special interests and talents. The problem with 3rd party aid is that it is hard to screen for, often demands a lengthy and detailed application, and the awards are usually very small by comparison to primary & secondary aid. I only advise students to go after tertiary aid when all else fails.

Good online screeners like www.scholarships.com or www.fastweb.net are free and effective when used correctly.

These sites are essentially giant search engines. What one gets out of them is completely dependent upon what one puts in. When using these sites, it is critical to minimize what you put in. Enter too much information about yourself and you will get a list too large to screen through. I like to change just one parameter at a time, then see what pops up. I view by deadline first, then number of awards, and finally by the amount of each award. It is time consuming and offers minimal payoff, but it may be the only option if primary and secondary aid is overlooked.

Financial aid not only seems complex, it is complex. Even the people who manage the system do not understand it well and very few use it optimally. My single best advice is to not wait until you need money to start planning. By the start of 8th grade, students needs to be building an ideal College Package that any university will be happy to reward with an offer of admission and aid. To do this will require that the student have the time to develop a serious portfolio of community service, leadership, and competition, as well as a solid GPA and at least one notable test score. The extracurriculars package, along with great test scores and proven college readiness though dual credit, will give any student a shot at great financial aid which should never include loans if at all possible!

❹

## INSTITUTIONAL & DEPARTMENTAL AID

### (Money From Your Major)

Sometimes a great student does not win the PSAT, SAT, or ACT lottery. If this happens, there are still options for merit-based aid. This student should spend the time or money for a professional College Screening. Screenings match a student's

College Package, career goals, and personality profile to colleges that are known to reward packages like the one the student already has. This can earn a student big dollars from the college itself or even from a specific department. Departmental aid is mostly reserved for already admitted students who have proven themselves to be tops in their department. But for those in the know, there are some excellent departmental opportunities specifically for freshman applicants.

For example, some universities are working very hard to increase the number of females in their engineering programs. To draw in applicants, the engineering departments are shelling out big bucks in the form of scholarships and grants. This is money that never has to be paid back. For above average applicants of the female persuasion, with notable math skills and an interest in the sciences, applying to one of these colleges could result in an offer of thousands of dollars per year in departmental aid. A comparable college without such a directive may give no scholarship at all to the exact same applicant.

For students interested in STEM careers, DE can play a vital role in proving math and science aptitude at the college level and getting a student ready to jump into the higher level college math that will be required for an engineering major.

Departmental dollars play a role once a student is already enrolled at a college. Top students in each department are eligible for liberal amounts of departmental aid. This money is paid out on a first-come and as-needed basis. It only goes to students who are tops in the major and have a good working relationship with their respective departmental heads. Plus, the student has to actively request these dollars. This makes it critical that top students take the time to interact regularly with their department staff and services. This money will not usually help with freshman debt, but keep it in mind for future years.

❺

## PERFORMANCE DOLLARS

### (Activity-Based Scholarships)

A student can earn money for college by participating in a competitive sport, dance, music, art, debate, robotics, speed math, League of Legends, forensics, chess, or a slew of other competitive pastimes while in college. Sports is a well-known example of performance dollars.

Collegiate sports is big business and every sport is big somewhere. No matter what someone is good at, there will be endowed dollars for it somewhere. Even at small, private liberal arts colleges, there are a wide variety of performance -related scholarships available for both men and women. From equestrian at Wesleyan to science fair at Duke to 3-D sculpting at the University of Texas, if a student has a competitive skill to offer, there is some school that will pay for it. And pay big!

If a student realistically falls into this category, the trick is to get the right college to pay some notice. If a student's awesomeness goes unrecognized by the people who matter, then money is not likely to be in the offering. The way to get noticed is through interviews, auditions, active scouting, and shameless self promotion. The best way to get scouted is to be great at something, then toot your own horn about it. Personal websites and uploaded resumes are excellent tools. Interviews and auditions are available upon request but the process needs to start early, certainly no later than winter break of the senior year. And finally, being realistic about your skill is critical. Don't undersell but avoid overselling as well. By the same measure, getting in touch with the right colleges can mean getting everything versus getting nothing.

While DE does not necessarily interfere with getting program dollars, it may not directly help. Building a portfolio, finding a college that rewards your particular skill, and meeting interview or audition deadlines is the key priority here. DE should be secondary to getting noticed in your skill if program dollars is your optimal route to college aid.

❻

## HONORS TRANSFER ROUTE

### (Transfer Aid)

When it come to getting a college degree and getting it paid for, there is truly something for everyone. When a student with a great attitude and strong work ethic fails to impress a college with his freshman College Package, there is still a way to earn a fabulous scholarship. The Honors Transfer Route (HTR) to college requires students to complete 31-60 college credits. This can be done in DE or in junior college (JC) after high school. Keep the college GPA at or higher. Meet strict admission deadlines. And gain automatic admission plus a scholarship of varying amounts. HTR is good at all state colleges and many private schools. The amount of money awarded is based on GPA and community service recorded.

Even more money will be awarded if the student manages to get admitted to Phi Theta Kappa while in DE or JC. The Honors Transfer Route allows a hard working student to get college paid for without being a great test taker or planning ahead or even building a great College Package. Dual Enrollment is obviously a cornerstone to this route as the more credits a student completes in DE the less he will have to pay for at junior college or university after high school. And don't forget the fact that transfer students never have to take the SAT or ACT!

NOTE: There is a long-semester rule that prevents students from "transferring" from dual credit straight to a university. So plan accordingly.

❼

## THE MILITARY

### (ROTC, Service Academies, G.I. Bill)

Most people are somewhat familiar with the G.I. Bill and the fact that a student who commits to a prescribed amount of time in service to one of the branches of the U.S. military can obtain a heavily discounted or free college education. This is an extremely simplistic description of a complex mechanism. There are at least three primary ways to get dollars for college via the military. I can only recommend the first two.

☞ Qualified applicants can attend an ROTC college and enlist in the ROTC program. This will add a major load to the student's daily schedule. Students must remain active in the ROTC program throughout their time at college. After graduation there will be a contractual agreement with a branch of the U.S. Military that must be fulfilled. If all goes well, graduates will leave college with a diploma and an officer's rank and pay. A great option for some.

- ☞ For anyone who can meet the extremely selective entrance requirements to one of the military service academies, a completely free, top-of-the-line education awaits. This route is superior to the others but very few make the grade. The admissions process is equivalent to MIT or Yale.

- ☞ Capable high school graduates can enlist in the military, go through basic training, serve their time, then apply for reimbursement for their college expenses after they leave the service or even while they continue to serve. Almost anyone can qualify for this route but many students have trouble collecting on the promise of free college. If it is important then get it in writing before you sign up.

The military route is a highly personal decision that should be discussed extensively with family and advisers before embarking on what will be much more than just a college degree. While I completely support the young men and women who serve our country so valiantly, I do not believe that anyone should ever feel forced to do so because of financial need. DE can give students an alternate path.

## SUMMARIZING FINANCIAL AID

By far, the majority of scholarships are merit-based. Since few students will be National Merit Scholars or star athletes, creating a merit-worthy high school resume is goal number one for college-bound pupils who do not want to take on debt. If this is you, be careful not to over expend time and money on test prep in the belief that one big test score will pave the road to college gold. That test score will need a great GPA and a solid dose of focused extracurriculars in order to pay off optimally. Shifting time from test prep to extracurriculars is almost always a winning strategy unless a top test score is assured.

Even with great tests scores, few students will earn a true full-ride from any one form of aid. For students who are not going to be candidates for National Merit, dual enrollment is a winning resource. Top students should use dual credit for key classes like math and science. This will boost the applicant's College Package in a very tangible way while eliminating the redundancy of taking these already difficult classes in high school and then again at a university.

More often than not, dual enrollment classes should also be used to replace Advanced Placement courses. Taking classes in DE instead of AP allows time for test prep, college visits and professional screenings, admission and scholarship applications, and those oft overlooked, but increasingly valuable, extracurriculars. Ironically, this will also protect the GPA since DE is more likely to produce top grades than AP classes. And not inconsequentially, dual credit classes are cheap college. If getting money for college is a number one goal, then dual credit is a number one resource.

# Do We Need College?

*"College is increasingly expensive and stressful.*
*As students try to compete with greater numbers of*
*their peers to get into reputable schools, they face*
*mental health problems at alarming rates,*
*graduates face crushing debt,*
*and the job market for college grads is bleak.*
*Why should any of us want to endure college?"* [1]

~ Psychology Today, Sept 2014

# 22☞

# A FINAL THOUGHT

## Why Go To College?

There is a mounting debate over the value of a college degree, with many experts suggesting that some students would be better off pursuing an alternative route to a career. Despite such counterintuitive comments, most parents and employers are still of the opinion that a college degree is the mark of a successful person. In much of the world, having a college degree is something to brag about and something that families are willing to pay more and more money to obtain. I am certainly not opposed to getting a college degree. I have one myself as does my husband and each of my children. (See there, I'm bragging already.)

The problem is a handful of nagging little statistics that make the decision of whether or not to go to college a lot less black and white. Some are more powerful than others.

- ☞ 70% of Americans will study at a 4-year college, but less than 2/3 will graduate. [2, 3]
- ☞ 30% of college and university students drop out after their first year. [2, 3]
- ☞ Being unable to balance school, jobs and family is one of the top reasons for dropping out. [2, 3]

Of course, it is all relative. Where one starts off in life is often a good indicator of where he or she will end up.

- ☞ 40% of college dropouts have parents with nothing beyond a high school diploma. [2, 3]
- ☞ 60% of college dropouts had no help from parents in paying for tuition. [2, 3]
- ☞ 50% of college dropouts have incomes lower than $35,000. [2, 3]

Obviously, there must be some upside to getting a college degree or why would everyone be trying to do it?

- ☞ A high school graduate earns 84% less than a typical graduate from a four-year college. [2, 3]

☞ Those without a college degree are twice as likely to be unemployed as those with one. [2, 3]

☞ A college degree is worth $365,000 for the average American man after you subtract all the direct and indirect costs over a lifetime. A college degree is worth $185,000 for the average American woman! [2, 3]

Facts can be scary because they are – well – facts! Should you push your student towards college or not? Will they be better off for it? Will they make more money over their lifetime? Will they be happier adults? What should we believe when the facts seem to negate each other? There are no RIGHT answers to these questions. Even with clear 20/20 hindsight, I am still unsure if college was right for my own children, or even myself. That is a very hard admission for someone who specializes in college admissions!

**I often say to my clients that I do not always know what does work, but I absolutely know what does not work.** I refer to these "won't work facts" as statistical realities. Such realities can be very useful when making decisions that have no obvious right answer. A great example of this has to do with the statistical reality of how people choose to live their life.

There are some very real stereotypes, for lack of a better word. Who we are in elementary and high school is often identical to who we are in college, on the job, or even in life. Who we are in school is NOT a determinant of our future selves, but there is a very close correlation that I call statistical realities. These correlations leave us with some apparent truths that are worth being aware of. So, for what it is worth, here is the truth as I see it after thousands of students and more years than I care to admit. Do with it what you will.

If you are a novice to being the parent of an emerging adult then you may not be aware of it, but from a career perspective there are a finite set of categories that people eventually fall into in terms of how they earn their living. Not everyone will achieve or maintain the same quality of life.

As much as I dislike labels and feel they are an oversimplification at best and at worst an insult, they are useful in allowing us to talk about consistencies. Knowing these statistical likelihoods allows us, as parents and educators, to plan appropriately and increase the odds that our students end up on a path that is most likely to work **for them**. Knowing the possibilities helps us put them on paths where they can succeed. Success is not the same for everyone. Success is not always a college degree or a house in the Hamptons. Success is doing what you are good at AND making a living at it. Success is looking back on your life and being happy with it. Success is what ever makes the individual feel that life is worth living.

*Lots of people make six figures, including plumbers, business managers, attorneys, high school principals, military officers, technicians, landlords, tutors, and people in thousands of other professions. The common denominator is that they've figured out what they're good at that other people are willing to pay them to do.*

# SIX CATEGORIES OF (L)Earners

For purposes of college planning, I use a self-devised system to categorize students in terms of attitude, intellect, personality, and potential. These are not tiers or levels, as one is not better or worse than another.

These categories are simple classifications that seem to fit the population in general. A student may fit in one or more categories. They are certainly not pigeonholed and are free to cross into another group at any time (and often do). Which group a student falls into while in high school has turned out to be a consistently sound determinant for which route he or she should take to college or career, and which majors or careers are most achievable for them.

This system has been of great help to me in planning high school, dual enrollment, college and careers for more students than I could possibly put a number to. The results have been consistently exceptional so I am confident in making this system available to the public. A discussion of these categories among students, parents, teachers, and educational staff is both prudent and helpful. Be careful not to elevate one group over another. They are not hierarchical. <u>They are absolutely equal!</u>

I recommend reading through each category with a particular student in mind. As you read, ask yourself is the student in question more like this category or less like this category. Use a scale of 1-5, with one being least similar and five being most similar to the description given in that category. All students will fit somewhere, possibly in more than one category.

That is normal. But each person will clearly fit into one category better than all the rest. A four or five in a given category makes it a safe bet that the student would benefit from the considerations and path to college or career that is summarized at the bottom of that section.

I would caution to avoid over analysis. It is very easy to impart personal beliefs and opinions where none are warranted. **There is no shame or honor in belonging to one category over another.** Society is happily made up of persons from all six of these categories. And while it is true that people in certain categories have seemingly easier lives than those in other categories, it would be woefully inaccurate to say that one group is better than any other. The whole point is to recognize that there are innate differences among students from a very early age, and that if we honor these differences as we strategize for success, we are likely to have better outcomes.

❶

## THE SKILLED

By far the most common category is the skilled worker. As a student he tends to be extremely typical. He takes on minimum leadership roles in school and rarely competes except within a team. This student will likely graduate high school and even go off to a university. He will complete a semester or two before starting to feel overwhelmed by the wrong major or a particular set of circumstances. At least half will eventually finish a degree but the long term outcomes look the same with or without a diploma. He will take jobs in every industry from low level employee to manager. His future will look bright but his path will be often uncertain and at times rather bumpy. In the end, if his health and the economy holds up, he will be able to support a family and eventually enjoy retirement. Anyone can fall into this group even if they start out solidly in one of the other five categories. It has little to do with intellect or ability and everything to do with core personality.

> *DE is very important for this group since with even a little bit of college, say while in high school, a student in this category can get further up the ladder than his non-college peers. It doesn't matter which ladder he climbs but life is always a bit easier at the top. For this student, you will want to start DE early and use it to the max. Consider certification programs as well. This student may drop out eventually, but with support and patience this student will often return and complete his degree at some point. And if he does not, then he has a sound foundation of higher learning to parley into later job advancement. This student will always be happy doing anything as long as they feel valued by family and friends.*

## THE AUTONOM

As a student, this one may struggle despite being constantly told how smart she is if she would only apply herself. Grades are inconsistent, being very high in many classes and very low in others. She does well in what she deems important. Any low grades are usually due to poor attitude rather than intellect or learning differences. She chafes at authority but tries very hard to please during the elementary years. This student leaves home earlier than most, sometimes even before graduation. (Although boys in this category will often fall into the Slacker category.) She cuts her own path through life and is often the source of parental frustration. She rarely asks for help and when she does she fails to follow through on it. This is not a good child gone bad. This is an intelligent, strong-willed person whose belief system is not in sync with a dominant parent or primary authority figure, or maybe even out of sync with her cultural upbringing. Patience and acceptance is key. She longs to find her place in life.

> *DE can be an early intervention for this student although it may not be clear yet that she is going to need any intercession. Focus on engaging subjects and caring teachers. Go slow and protect the GPA as this student feels empowered by successes of her own making. Sometimes DE is the only college this student will ever do so start early and make it all about the student. Let her follow her passion and she may surpass even your wildest dreams. But she will not likely follow your path so make sure she knows her options, then follow her lead.*

❸

## THE SLACKER

This group is growing by leaps and bounds, especially among males. As a student he is very bright and appears to be a highly-promising student in the elementary grades. Even throughout high school, he makes easy As and can really impress when he wants to. In high school, grades are either excellent or failing, a pattern that continues into college. This learner needs to feel there is a value to his actions. Without a meaningful reward, this pupil will quickly lose momentum. This group is different from the autonom only in that he lacks any drive to get out and fight the injustice he see in the world. It just builds up inside!

He mostly does as told when young but quickly falls out of sync with his parents' goals once he reaches the last two years of high school. This pupil always goes to college, usually graduates, and may even get multiple college degrees as he finds going to college easier than getting out in the real world. But the opposite extreme is common as well. Arguably the result of indulgent parenting, this student simply finds the comforts of home more enticing than the responsibilities of a spouse or career. Emotional imbalances in adulthood are not uncommon.

> *DE can be used for these students to help them explore career options and find something that stokes their passions. Pushing them towards a major is a major mistake. This student will accept the push then shut down and do nothing when he discovers he has been pushed to do something that is not of his own making. He needs ownership and control This is in contrast to the autonom who does not shut down when pushed, but simply heads in an opposing direction or goes along willingly but is secretly living out an alternative. The Slacker may also go along at first until he's had enough and simply quits.*

❹

## THE ENTREPRENEUR

You know this one. This is the kid that has a lemonade stand at 7 and a lawn enterprise at 14. Academically, they are a mixed bag, especially in the early years. Hardworking and motivated, these students work for reward. They have solid IQs and lots of ideas about everything. These students thrive in a hands-on environment but are usually stuck in high performance AP style classes because they seem so capable of buckling down and doing hard work when required. Burnout is common. The higher the bar, the harder they will work even if it means eventually coming unglued to reach that bar.

When younger, they do so well in standard classrooms that they never get the one-on-one, hands-on experiences that their brain is wired for. If allowed, these students will have a small business up and running before they leave high school. Social, self-motivated and purposeful, these students feel held back by the constraints of a college degree but willingly start college usually majoring in Business Administration, Management, Entrepreneurship, and such. Double majors are common. Drop out rates are not uncommon because these students are ready to implement ideas, not spend time on formal degrees that don't seem directly connected to their interest. But most finish since a degree is a bragging right that matters to them. This group is competitive. Whether or not they stay and finish college depends on their home life and overall personality. Fortunately, many end up successful either way. A percentage of these students will suffer from "Golden Boy Syndrome" and crash in college. Drugs and alcohol are a real threat and life long battles with minor addictions and dalliances are often kept somewhat hidden by all members of the family.

> *These student belong in business but not in business school. They would be better off looking for alternative majors that allow them to backdoor into a business degree. Good options are available at every college. Integrated Marketing & Communications or Interdisciplinary Studies comes to mind. Such alternatives have to be suggested with conviction as these students have to really believe it is okay to do something different, which they will often interpret as "less than". By using*

*DE to focus on specialized courses of interest, this student will thrive. This student needs to slow down without feeling guilty. Their pressure comes from within. The sooner they are freed to just be themselves, the better their overall achievement in both college and career. They also need to avoid the wrong friends as they are highly susceptible to influence.*

❺

## THE LABORER

Anyone can end up in this category but as a student they can be easy to spot early on. They start out strong then tend to struggle by the 3-4th grade. Clear issues may be seen in math, reading, and/or time management from an early age. Often saddled with labels such as ADHD or dyslexia, a learning differenced student does not automatically end up in this category, but differenced kids are much more likely to end up here than in any other. There is substantial evidence that with proper, consistent, and early intervention, pupils with learning differences will go to the top of any field that they are passionate about. With these students, it's all about keeping them interested and focused. They can be taught self discipline but real learning is not actually happening, which is revealed by standardized testing. This group should avoid AP & IB classes due to heavy lecture component, which produces no real mastery.

They thrive when given hands-on learning and personal empowerment. They also need constant positive reward. Without proper guidance, this group often ends up unskilled due to dropping out of school. They shy away from college since they have come to believe they are not good students. When they do go to college, they never finish. (Although, they continually wish they had and occasionally attain a college degree much later in life.) This student may have a very high IQ but streets smarts are even more impressive.

As adults, many of these kids work in family businesses or the service sector and live from one paycheck to another. Time and resource management is a constant issue. No one is divinely destined for this category, but if they end up in it, there is no reason that they should feel ashamed. The planet is truly run off the backs of such people. Without an educated service sector, the infrastructure of our world would come tumbling down around our heads. When students ends up in this category, family and society should extol their value, make them feel worthwhile. We need this category. Let's embrace it! The better they feel, the more they achieve.

*DE is a Godsend for these students, who usually struggle in high school and rarely make it through college. By achieving early college success in DE, this student can eventually migrate to the realm of the skilled through vocational degrees or transfer classes. Start early, take as many classes as possible, and aim for success above all else. This group is the most diverse and most difficult to help. They need highly customized schooling throughout their life and their social network will play a huge role in their adult behaviors.*

*These students can become increasingly frustrating to their parents and mentors towards the end of high school yet this is when they need our acceptance and support the most. The laborer is often the most earnest and well intended student but just does not fit into the mold of modern education. Patience, loose guidance, and unconditional acceptance is advised.*

❻

## THE PROFESSIONAL

This student is difficult to pigeonhole while in elementary or even high school as anyone can end up in this category. But there is a personality that strongly lends itself to this group. As a student, this one seems to always do everything "right". This student goes to the right school, gets the right degree, snags the right job in his or her field, marries by 30, has 2.5 children, goes on cruises, and contributes regular Facebook posts about his mid-life crisis. They rarely make it "big-time" financially but they are regularly in the top 25% of wage earners. They are either all the way up or all the way down, but usually up.

This group comes from all walks of life, but the apple does not fall far from the tree. Professionals tend to have parents who are equally successful, at least by outside appearances.

*The LeeWay DDP was designed for this student. Follow the program exactly as written, meet all the deadlines, and this child will not disappoint. Be aware that all humans are emotionally fragile to varying degrees. If pushed too hard to over achieve, this child will often break and slip from this category to one that makes them feel inferior. This student will be all in until they are all out!*

## A FINAL WORD

No matter where your student seems to fit in this pecking order of learners and earners, knowing what to look for can help you determine how to use both high school and the dual credit system in an optimal way for your specific student. The sooner you recognize their leanings and limitations the more accurately you can customize their educational path or seek interventions to potentially alter their course.

If you are worried about limiting your student or making them feel bad by pointing out which category they seem headed towards, trust me, students are keenly aware of their own vulnerabilities. They are eager to understand what makes them unique, they just want the experience to be a positive one. Discussing a perceived weakness becomes easier for our children when we focus our comments equally on their strengths. Never harp on a problem. Address it. Work on it. And focus on what is going right. To do otherwise promotes negative thinking which is always counterproductive. I never look at someone's differences as inadequacies. I simple honor that this is who the student is. In doing so I am able to accept them fully. Isn't that ultimately what we all need, to just be accepted for who we are?

It would be great if we adults could simply waive a magic wand and our children or charges could suddenly see their potential the way that we see it. Alas, no such sleight of hand exist. However, as parents and educators we do have tremendous power. The power to knock them down or build them up is certainly in our grasp but the greatest power we have is the power to accept them for the person that they are. This is not easy at times. I have found that if I listen to someone -- really listen, that I can start to see them in a more positive light.

We also have the power to inform them of all their options, not just the ones we want them to gravitate towards. We sometimes have the power to remove any unduly harsh stressors such as an objectionable educational environment. As the adult in their lives, we can not let fear of being seen as different keep us from taking such steps when they are clearly needed. We can also partner with them to gather information and make choices. Teens tend to listen to whoever makes them feel empowered. The earlier a student is empowered, the happier he or she will be, and the better the outcome. When we empower our students, we are not giving away our power or abdicating our duties. We are passing our hard-earned knowledge on to the next generation. This seems a logical progression. After all, they are our future!

KL

# Works Cited

## Preface: Getting Educated


1. http://www.higheredinfo.org/dbrowser/?year=2010&level=nation&mode=data&state=0&submeasure=119
2. http://www.nationsreportcard.gov/reading_math_g12_2013/#/
3. http://nces.ed.gov/programs/coe/indicator_cgg.asp
4. https://www.cchrint.org/2013/04/23/more-teens-abusing-adderall-ritalin/
5. http://youth.gov/youth-topics/youth-mental-health/prevalance-mental-health-disorders-among-youth
6. http://www.huffingtonpost.com/2012/08/23/annual-survey-finds-17-pe_n_1824966.html
7. https://www.dosomething.org/us/facts/11-facts-about-high-school-dropout-rates
8. http://www.highereducation.org/reports/college_readiness/gap.shtml
9. http://collegedebt.com/


## Chapter 3: LeeWay A Customized Solution


1. http://nces.ed.gov/nationsreportcard/subject/publications/main2013/pdf/2014451.pdf
2. http://www.howyouthlearn.org/research_teenagebrain.html#sthash.rJr7tCPG.dpuf


## Chapter 4: Prepare to Be Amazed


1. NCHEMS National Information Center for Higher Education Policymaking and Analysis http://www.higheredinfo.org/
2. Higher Ed Data Stories http://highereddatastories.blogspot.com/2015/07/what-happens-to-100-9th-grade-students.html

## Chapter 5: Taking College Classes in High School


1 http://www.prnewswire.com/news-releases/research-shows-dual-enrollment-programs-have-promise-for-all-students-98351989.html

2 http://www.cbsnews.com/news/50-state-universities-with-best-worst-grad-rates/

3 The Postsecondary Achievement of Participants in Dual Enrollment: An Analysis of Student Outcomes in Two States By: Melinda Mechur Karp, Juan Carlos Calcagno, Katherine L. Hughes, Dong Wook Jeong & Thomas Bailey

4 http://www.air.org/project/evaluation-early-college-high-school-initiative


## Chapter 6: Is Dual Enrollment The Right Choice?


1 http://www.nationalmerit.org/nmsp.php and 2013 National Assessment of Education Progress (NAEP)

2 http://www.nationsreportcard.gov/reading_math_g12_2013/#/

3 http://www.americaspromise.org/high-school-graduation-facts-ending-dropout-crisis

4 http://www.nsf.gov/nsb/sei/edTool/data/highschool-06.html


## Chapter 10: The Ideal Schedule


1 https://www.cde.state.co.us/choice/homeschool_law Title 22, Colorado Revised Statutes: Education Article 33: School Attendance Law of 1963 Section 104.5, as amended

2 http://www.isbe.net/homeschool/

3 https://projects.propublica.org/graphics/homeschool


## Chapter 12: Planning Wisely Step-by-Step


1 http://www.whatkidscando.org/specialcollections/voices_middle_grades/voices_judgeus.html

2 http://www.totalregistration.net/AP-Exam-Registration-Service/2014-AP-Exam-Score-Distributions.php

## Chapter 13: The LeeWay Distinguished Degree Plan

1 http://www.washingtontimes.com/news/2014/jun/1/fedewa-american-schools-are-failing/?page=all

2 http://www.higheredinfo.org/

3 http://www.higheredinfo.org/dbrowser/index.php?submeasure=119&year=2010&level=nation&mode=data&state=0

## Chapter 14: A Special Word About Math

1 http://www.usnews.com/news/blogs/stem-education/2012/01/18/american-students-are-taking-harder-math-science-courses

2 http://www.edweek.org/ew/articles/2009/08/19/01act.h29.html

3 https://www.nms.org/AboutNMSI/TheSTEMCrisis/STEM EducationStatistics.aspx

4 http://www.wsj.com/articles/number-of-college-students-pursuing-science-engineering-stagnates-1422334862

5 http://www.usnews.com/education/blogs/high-school-notes/2012/08/22/high-school-students-not-prepared-for-college-career

6 http://www.collegeatlas.org/college-dropout.html

## Chapter 15: Managing Science and Foreign Language

1 http://www.bloombergview.com/articles/2013-07-17/why-american-students-don-t-major-in-science

2 http://tea.texas.gov/Texas_Schools/General_Information/Finding_a_School_for_your_Child/Home_Schooling/

3 http://www.desmoinesregister.com/story/news/education/2015/02/22/college-foreign-language-requirements/23689343/

## Chapter 16: Solving Problems: LeeWay Recovery Plan

1 http://www.brainhealth.utdallas.edu/research/research_topic/strategic-memory-advanced-reasoning-training-smart

## Chapter 17: Getting Into College

1 http://www.collegedata.com/cs/content/content_payarticle_tmpl.jhtml?articleId=10064

## Chapter 20: Special Tests

1 https://clep.collegeboard.org/overview/collegecredit

2 http://www.foxbusiness.com/features/2012/04/25/why-50-students-fail-ap-exams-and-how-to-change-that.html

3 https://www.propublica.org/article/americas-most-outrageous-teacher-cheating-scandals

4 http://blog.prepscholar.com/the-5-worst-problems-with-college-board-ap-program

5 http://teach.com/education-policy/dartmouth-college-stops-accepting-ap-credit

## Chapter 21: Getting It Paid For

1 http://www.npr.org/sections/money/2012/05/02/151759177/how-colleges-fight-for-top-students

2 http://news.stanford.edu/news/2015/february/tuition-trustees-aid-021015.html

3 http://kwhs.wharton.upenn.edu/2014/07/dual-enrollment-scholarships-creative-ways-cut-college-tuition-bill/

4 http://thechoice.blogs.nytimes.com/2013/05/13/selecting-high-school-courses/?_r=0

## Chapter 22: A Final Thought

1 http://www.apa.org/monitor/2014/09/cover-pressure.aspx

2 http://www.collegeatlas.org/college-dropout.html

**This document cites statistics provided by the National Institute of Mental Health. www.nimh.nih.gov**